SHORT COURSE SERIES

WORLD TRADE PRESS®

Professional Books for International Trade

## THE SHORT COURSE IN INTERNATIONAL TRADE SERIES

*A Short Course in International Business Culture*

*A Short Course in International Business Ethics*

*A Short Course in International Business Plans*

*A Short Course in International Contracts*

*A Short Course in International Economics*

*A Short Course in International Intellectual Property Rights*

*A Short Course in International Joint Ventures*

*A Short Course in International Marketing*

*A Short Course in International Marketing Blunders*

*A Short Course in International Negotiating*

*A Short Course in International Payments*

*A Short Course in International Trade Documentation*

A SHORT COURSE IN

# *International Business Ethics*

3rd Edition

Combining Ethics and Profits
in Global Business

Charles Mitchell

Editor:
Dr. Jeffrey-Edmund Curry
(AUDENCIA Nantes Ecole de Management)

Published in arrangement with World Trade Press by

**ATLANTIC**
PUBLISHERS & DISTRIBUTORS (P) LTD

7/22, Ansari Road, Darya Ganj, New Delhi-110 002
Tel: 40775252, 23273880, 23275880, 23280451; Fax: +91-11-23285873
E-mail: orders@atlanticbooks.com; Web: www.atlanticbooks.com

**World Trade Press**
800 Lindberg Lane, Suite 190
Petaluma, California 94952 USA
Tel: +1 (707) 778-1124
Fax: +1 (707) 778-1329
USA Order Line: +1 (800) 833-8586
E-mail: sales@worldtradepress.com
www.WorldTradePress.com
www.WorldTradeREF.com (international trade and logistics)
www.BestCountryReports.com (business travel, communications and culture)
www.GiantMapArt.com (Giant maps for building lobbies, conference rooms and education)

**A Short Course in International Business Ethics, 3rd Edition**
By Charles Mitchell
Short Course Series Concept: Edward G. Hinkelman
Cover Design: Ronald A. Blodgett
Text Design: Seventeenth Street Studios, Oakland, California, USA
Desktop Publishing: Brian Duffy



ISBN 978-81-269-1244-5
**First Indian Reprint 2009**

This edition is for sale in Indian sub-continent only.



**Library of Congress Cataloging-in-Publication Data**
Mitchell, Charles, 1953–
A short course in international business ethics: combing ethics and
profits in global business / Charles Mitchell -- 3rd ed.
p. cm. – (The short course in international trade series)
Includes bibliographic references.
1. Business ethics. 2. International trade--Moral and ethical aspects.
3. International business enterprises--Moral and ethical aspects.
4. Business ethics--Case studies.
I. Title: International business ethics. II. Title. III. Series.
HF5387.M58 2009
174'.4--dc21

2009042253

Printed in India at Chaman Enterprises, 1603, Pataudi House,
Darya Ganj, New Delhi-110 002

## TABLE OF CONTENTS

CHAPTER 1

# Why Ethics Matter

*THE MORE ONE KNOWS ETHICS, THE MORE IT IS USED AND THE MORE USEFUL IT BECOMES.* – PLATO

DEBATES ABOUT INTERNATIONAL BUSINESS ETHICS are as old as international business itself. In past decades, business ethics was predominately a subject taught at business schools and debated by academics. It had little impact in the international business world, where the prevailing attitude was that anything goes and everyone is paid to cut a deal. Many governments (including France, Japan and Germany), recognizing the reality of doing business in certain parts of the world, actually allowed businesses until fairly recently to write off overseas bribe payments as expenses on their corporate income tax.

## Ethical Challenges Everywhere

Every executive, regardless of his or her geographic location, every corporate board, regardless of where it sits, has at some point faced a decision that challenges their ethical standards. The course of action taken often does not quite pass muster with basic ethical standards. In other words, it "smells."

A European manufacturing company trying to break into the Asian market is asked to "donate" to a charitable foundation run by the brother of a high government official. A German drug company offers government health officials from developing countries lavish entertainment as an inducement to buy its drugs. A local government hoping to have its city become a venue for the Olympics arranges for the local university to provide entrance for offspring of selection committee members. A US Internet company sells information gleaned about its customers' online habits without their consent or even their knowledge.

In each case, the company's managers can reasonably argue that they are pursuing the interests of shareholders in a lawful manner. A decade ago, not breaking the law may have been enough. Today, however, the global business playing field is changing. The pressure to act ethically, to act as a good corporate citizen of the world, is growing in both developed and developing nations.

For example: One-third of UK consumers claim to be seriously concerned about ethical issues when shopping—although only half of that number put their principles into action and buy (or boycott) products because of the manufacturer's reputation. The MORI research firm, commissioned by Britain's Co-operative Bank, found one-in-four consumers claim to have investigated a company's social responsibility at least once: one-in-two shoppers say they have bought a product and recommended a supplier because of its socially responsible reputation. The report shows a heightened awareness of ethical issues among the UK public and a boom in the market for ethically-oriented products and services. The ethical consumer market, which encompasses a whole range of products from stock investments to green beans, is worth an estimated 8 billion pounds per year. And it is growing annually.

## Ethics: Good for Profits?

According to the survey conducted by the UK-based Prince of Wales Business Leadership Forum and Environics International Ltd., an Australian consulting firm, 40 percent of 25,000 respondents in 23 countries had thought in the past year about punishing a specific company perceived as not being "socially responsible"; half of their respondents—one-in-five consumers worldwide—have avoided the product of a company or spoken out to others against a company perceived as shirking its "corporate citizenship" role. Meanwhile, consumers were just as likely to "reward" a company perceived as socially responsible by purchasing their products.

Business leaders and CEOs read these numbers and realize the bar has been raised. Corporations of all sizes, especially multinationals, are more attuned to the bottom-line value of being a good corporate citizen and playing by the rules. Individual business people are seeking to do "what is right" (though this is often prodded by corporate ethics standards and local laws) rather than maintaining an attitude of "anything to close the deal."

All these factors, along with the growth of large multinational companies, have transformed the concept of business ethics from an academic discipline into an emerging operating force. Along with corporate ethics, corruption and bribery in international business have surfaced as important issues in an interdependent world economy. No longer seen purely as a morality play, the increasingly accepted view of corruption and bribery is that they hinder competition, distort trade and harm consumers and taxpayers while undermining public support for government. As a result, more and more corporations see business ethics as a bottom-line issue—not an optional one of morality. The acceptance of ethics as contributing to corporate operating profits or losses means they are receiving unprecedented attention.

It is for this reason that "behaving ethically and responsibly" may be the wave of the future, if only because the right thing to do can also be the profitable thing to do. Consider:

- A two-year study by The Performance Group, a consortium of seven international companies—Volvo, Unilever, Monsanto, Imperial Chemical Industries, Deutsche Bank, Electrolux and Gerling—concluded that improving environmental compliance and developing environmentally friendly products can enhance company earnings per share, increase profitability and also be important in wining contracts or investment approval in emerging markets.
- A study by the US journal *BUSINESS AND SOCIETY REVIEW*, showed that 300 large corporations found that companies which made a public commitment to rely on their ethics codes outperformed companies that did not do so by two to three times, as measured by market value added.
- A study by DePaul University found that companies with a defined corporate commitment to ethical principles do better financially (based on annual sales/ revenues) than companies that don't.

The challenge—and part of the problem—is that business has been globalized faster than the development of a universally recognized framework for a code of ethics and conduct. Technology has raised ethical issues that only a few years ago simply did not exist. Ethical debates now rage on issues from genetically modified food and animals to human cloning to privacy on the Internet. Globalization also brings companies into more frequent contact with other countries and cultures that (sometime to their surprise) do business by different rules. This raises a pivotal question: "Whose ethics are we talking about?"

Corporations are only beginning to learn that while expanding into profitable new markets, they must also begin to take into account the social agendas and cultures of these new markets. While no global standard of ethics and conduct yet exists—there are several suggested standards being promoted from the Paris-based International Chamber of Commerce (ICC), the United Nations and the US Department of Commerce—the world is seeing a convergence of sorts in what corporations and consumers from all cultures deem important. For example, although values and cultures differ, there is universal acceptance of the notion that a good corporate reputation is a competitive advantage in global business. How that reputation is built is another matter.

## History: Why Business Has Ethical Problems

We are living in an era when "The Captains of Industry" have become somewhat deified, gracing the covers of news and business magazines and appearing as larger than life icons meant to inspire us lesser mortals to success. Considering historical attitudes towards the ethics of business people, this amounts to a major comeback for the profession of business. (There are many business analysts who will argue that this celebrity status has actually proven to be a major distraction to many CEOs who are more concerned about their personal image than their company's bottom-line and long term performance.)

Of course it wasn't always this way—and it still isn't in some societies. (The popular attitude towards today's oligarchical new capitalists in Russia—one of outright contempt and loathing—is one example.) In fact, since the dawn of recorded history, the businessperson, the merchant and the trader have been on the bottom rung of the social ladder. Doing business and being good were considered mutually exclusive.

Karl Marx, a failed stockbroker turned economist, wrote that greed is inherent in humankind—he meant it as a negative, of course. He seems to have been on to something. If there is one constant in history, it is the fight against people's seemingly innate urge to take advantage of others. Beginning with the Code of Hammurabi in the 18th century B.C., society has tried to play a role in introducing some basic ethics for business. Hammurabi was the chief of Babylon which is considered by many to be the world's first metropolis, complete with a form of organized commerce.

The code regulates in remarkably clear terms the rules of society—and business. It would not be a stretch to call it the first corporate code of ethics. It behooved the merchant-trader to follow the rules—or else. Bad business practices were harshly punished with a biblical eye-for-an-eye mentality. For example, if a man built a house badly and it collapsed, killing the owner, the builder was to be killed in retaliation. If the owner's son was killed, then the builder's son was slain. This is an early indication of the problems of defining ethical behavior.

### THE ANCIENT GREEKS

The ancient Greeks continued the trend of imbuing businesspeople with less than honest motives and intent. Hermes, the Greek god of Commerce and the Market, was the official patron of traders and merchants. However, he was also considered the official patron of thieves. His distinguishing qualities were cunning, ingenuity, knowledge and creativity—all valued qualities in the world of business—and criminal activity. He was the fastest of the gods (Hermes became the Roman god Mercury), and one of his main tasks was leading the souls of the dead to the Underworld. He spun lies and illusions (too bad there was no truth in advertising laws back then) that turned those who came into contact with him into some of the earliest victims of fraud. The ancient Greek priests, eager to maintain their own power, lumped together the virtues of successful business people and successful con men. It has been a stigma that has proven very hard to shake.

### THE WORLD'S GREAT RELIGIONS

Since their inception, the world's great religions have been preaching the need for ethics in business. Holy books are strewn with warnings about wealth accumulation without accompanying social responsibility. All seem to be suspect of successful business practitioners, equating business success and making gobs of money with, in some cases, eternal damnation.

For example, the Bible's Book of Exodus (23: 6-8), warning against "greasing the wheels" with cash, states: "Thou shall take no bribe, for a bribe blinds the officials and subverts the cause of those who are in the right."

And Ecclesiastes (5:12) warns against too much business success: "Sweet is the sleep of the laborer whether he eats little or much; but the overabundance of the rich will not let the rich sleep."

The Islamic holy book, the Koran (Surah CIV) singles out the unethical businessperson for a one-way trip to Hades. "Woe to every slanderer, defamer who amasses wealth and considers it a provision against mishap. He thinks that his wealth will make him immortal. Nay, he shall most certainly be hurled into the crushing disaster."

And the Jewish Talmud is a must read for any businessperson with plans for a post-retirement stint in heaven. The Talmud discusses what types of questions people are asked by God after their deaths. The very first question, says the Talmud, is *NASATA V'NETATA BE'EMUNAH*—"did you conduct your business affairs with honesty and integrity?"

## Business Bashing in Great Literature

William Shakespeare made *THE MERCHANT OF VENICE'S* Shylock a despicable character (as well as an enduring symbol of that less-than-respectable profession of loan sharking). It is Shylock who greedily demands "a pound of flesh" in payment for a debt. It wasn't a slip for Mr. Shakespeare—he generally held merchants and those in commerce in low esteem, often portraying them as plotting, conniving and generally unethical lowlifes. It wasn't personal but rather a reflection of the prevailing attitudes of Shakespeare's society.

Charles Dickens chronicled the horrors of sweatshops, child labor, debtors' prisons and the practices of swindlers and Scrooge-like characters in such epics as *A TALE OF TWO CITIES* and *THE CHRISTMAS CAROL*.

And the noted 18th century French Philosopher Honoré de Balzac reflected the mood of his times (and in many cases modern times) with his often repeated quote "Behind every great fortune... is a crime."

In cultures as diverse as Japan and England, merchants and traders or any engaged in commerce were looked down upon by nobility but tolerated nonetheless as necessary evils. Indeed, the English class system of recent centuries judged individuals not on their wealth but rather on how they came about their money. The retail trade was the lowest of the low. Those with "new money," that is money made in commerce rather than through family inheritance, had little clout or respect (though one has to question the attitude of a society in which a penniless "Lord" brought low by gambling and excess might engender more respect than a hard-working, successful merchant).

This disdain and distrust of commerce had real effects on the relative development of some nations. China, for example, a country were the merchant class occupied the bottom of the social scale, remained a feudal state for centuries, partly because of its dim view of businesspeople.

## Moving Towards Acceptance

The status of those with commercial ambitions improved somewhat during the European Renaissance. Merchants were no longer excluded from political power and, in fact, aspiring to wealth through commerce was considered a socially acceptable vocation in many parts of Europe. It was partly this newfound respectability that opened the door to the industrial revolution and the accumulation of mega-wealth by individuals engaged in commerce.

Despite some grudging admiration, or at least acceptance, of wealth accumulation, industrialists in the United States had managed by the mid-19th century to undo all the newfound goodwill. They were, often deservedly, referred to as "Robber Barons," ruthlessly running their railroads and steel mills and manipulating financial markets with little regard for employees, consumers or the public good. Monopoly tactics, predatory pricing and near slave labor conditions were basic practices of big business. There was a reason for the stereotyping of the successful capitalist as a fat, over-dressed, cigar smoking white male with a hardened heart of coal and no sense of social responsibility. It is no wonder that out of this dismal period of business behavior sprang the beginnings of trade unionism and the search for a kinder, gentler way of doing business. The hangover from this era of business irresponsibility—at least in the United States—can still be felt.

## The Ford Pinto and the Global Ethics Boom

The 20th century's two world wars took some of the heat off big business but the mentality in the United States that "what is good for General Motors is good for the country" was short lived. The ethical consciousness of the US population was reawakened in 1965 when Ralph Nader brought the rather slip-shod ethics of big car manufacturers to the public's attention with his book, *UNSAFE AT ANY SPEED*. Still, not until the 1970's did business ethics became a major issue for the American consumer (and later the world), thanks to Ford Motor Company's infamous Pinto—a subcompact car that had a tendency to explode when involved in a rear-end collision.

Before Lee Iacocca became famous for rescuing Chrysler from bankruptcy, he was president of Ford. Eager to follow up on his success with the Mustang, and facing increased competition in the small car arena from foreign upstarts like Volkswagen, Iacocca and Ford engineers conceived the Pinto.

The mission statement for the car was simple and uncompromising: "The Pinto was not to weigh an ounce over 2,000 pounds and not cost a cent over US$2,000." It was rushed through production without regard to serious design flaws that would eventually land Ford in court.

It came to light that having relied on a "cost-benefit analysis" of strengthening the fuel tank design against rear end impact, Ford had estimated that its unsafe fuel tanks would cause 180 burn deaths, 180 serious burn injuries, and 2,100 burned vehicles each year. It calculated that it would have to pay US$200,000 per death, US$67,000 per injury and US$700 per vehicle for a total of US$49.5 million. However, the cost estimates for saving these lives and injuries ran even higher. Alterations would cost US$11 per car or truck, which added up to US$137 million per year. Essentially, Ford's executives reckoned that it would be cheaper to pay lawsuit damages rather than recall the vehicles.

Jurors were naturally outraged over Ford's low-value attitude toward human life and awarded the victims huge settlements. However, the final insult came once Ford ordered a recall. The costs of alterations were just over one dollar per car, not the US$11 it had used as the basis for its "cost-benefit analysis" defense.

Many ethics experts believe the Pinto settlement and the outrage caused by Ford's attitude fuelled current-day skepticism about the ethics of American business. The ethics genie was out of the bottle and waiting to spread worldwide. It also showed that big corporations were vulnerable to pressure groups and PR (public relations) disasters.

## Global Business, Global Disasters

Just 50 years ago, catastrophe meant natural disasters such as hurricanes, volcanoes, famines, and earthquakes. Now with the explosion of technology and the globalization of commerce, the damage caused by ethical lapses in business can lead to catastrophe on the scale of traditional natural disasters. Perhaps more importantly, the scope of these human-made catastrophes can easily spread across international borders.

Apart from fundamental challenges to national sovereignty, cultural tradition and human rights, globalization has unleashed a broad range of complex and unprecedented ethical challenges in areas as diverse as foreign investment, education, medicine, poverty, environmental sustainability, immigration, marketing, intellectual property, the Internet and sports. The intensity of competition, the scale of commercial activity and the speed of communication have given a frightening momentum and sinister urgency to the concept of the survival of the fittest.

The wealth-driven 1980s were a time when many modern companies and governments first confronted the moral dilemmas presented by globalization. The US-based Union Carbide Corporation was confronted with the nightmare of the Bhopal chemical plant accident in India. The Soviet government was faced with a cross-border disaster when the Chernobyl nuclear power plant in Ukraine exploded, sending a radioactive cloud drifting over Western Europe as far as Scotland.

But it was the Bhopal incident that first posed serious questions about ethical standards for multinational corporations. Just after midnight on December 3, 1984, a pesticide plant in Bhopal accidentally released 40 metric tons of methyl isocyanine into the atmosphere. The incident was a catastrophe with an estimated 8,000 deaths, 100,000 injuries and significant damage to livestock and crops. The long-term health effects from the incident were difficult to evaluate; the International Medical Commission on Bhopal estimated that, even a decade later, upwards of 50,000 people remained partially or totally disabled.

The incident had serious implications for US-based multinational corporations, both at home and abroad: the US-based Union Carbide Corporation was the parent company to the Bhopal plant operator Union Carbide India Ltd. (UCIL). Questions that would be addressed in the ensuing trial included:

- Should Union Carbide be held responsible for the design of, maintenance for, and training on equipment at the Bhopal plant?
- Should Union Carbide be responsible for informing the local government and community of the hazards associated with the plant?

The Bhopal incident is considered a watershed for awakening multinational corporations to the demand for greater accountability outside of their home country. This incident is cited as a factor in the development of industry standards such as Responsible Care under the Chemical Manufacturers Association, and the development and implementation of US environmental legislation and regulations, including the US Chemical Safety and Hazard Investigation Board.

The Chernobyl nuclear accident in April 1986 was kept secret by Moscow for almost a month and caused an international furor. It underscored the potential international implications governments face if they choose to act in an unethical manner. Moscow's initial silence on the affair was an amazingly unethical act despite the tendency of communist governments to control information flow.

## A Journalistic Watershed

The 1990s brought a media feeding frenzy surrounding corporate missteps, especially in the environmental area. The Exxon Valdez oil spill in Alaska again called into question the corporate ethics of a large American company. Also the Dutch company Shell Oil suffered two blows to its reputation in 1995.

The first blow came from its attempted disposal of the Brent Spar oil rig in the North Sea and the second came over the company's failure to oppose the Nigerian government's execution of Ken Saro-Wiwa, a human-rights activist in a part of Nigeria where Shell had extensive operations. Since then, Shell has rewritten its business principles, created an elaborate mechanism to implement them and worked harder to improve its relations with non-governmental organizations (NGOs). NGOs have been a major thorn in the side of multinational corporations because of their demands for greater corporate responsibility on a global scale.

What makes Shell's response an important event in the realm of international business ethics is that the firm's actions were not the result of anyone holding a legal or financial gun to its head. Shell was not compelled to do anything. Neither incident did lasting damage to the company's share price or sales—although the Brent Spar incident resulted in a brief dip in Shell's market share in Germany following a consumer boycott. The epiphany was that being a responsible corporate citizen made good sense and in the long run was a better business practice than lurching from crisis to crisis.

One reason Shell officials have given for acting in a pre-emptive manner: Shell employees around the globe were uncomfortable with the company's involvement in these high profile incidents and with the company itself. Senior management concluded that people are happier working for organizations they regard as ethical—and in a tight job market that proved to be a powerful incentive to act.

## What Business Ethics Are and Are Not

Sociologist Raymond Baumhart once posed the following question to a gathering of business professionals: "What does ethics mean to you?"

Among their replies:

- "Ethics has to do with what my feelings tell me is right or wrong."
- "Ethics has to do with my religious beliefs."
- "Being ethical is doing what the law requires."
- "Ethics consists of the standards of behavior our society accepts."
- "I don't know what the word means."

The answers are insightful and provide clear reminders of what applied ethics are not.

Philosophers have been debating the concept of ethics since before the time of Socrates, more than 2,500 years ago. Many would say there has been little progress—and even less agreement on exactly what ethics are. In its simplest form, the concept involves learning what is right—or wrong—and then doing the right thing. The real problem lies in coming to an agreement on just what "the right thing is" at any particular time.

Many academics will say there is always a right thing to do based on accepted moral principles. Others will argue that "the right thing" is really based on a combination of specific situations, national cultures and personal morals. Ultimately what is right depends on what the individual thinks is right. (For a further discussion of the principle of relativism in ethics see Chapter Two: Are Ethics Culturally Based?)

The real business world is made up of multiple shades of gray. A business manager is not perplexed by black and white choices such as "should I steal from the company" or "should I lie to the public." The really hard ethical choices are inevitably more complicated.

A factory manager who spent more than a decade working in developing countries in Africa and Asia says not a day went by without having to make "judgement calls" on what was "the right thing to do" in dealing with employees, government officials and the company headquarters back home. He was armed with company guidelines and legal statutes, but the guidelines only addressed vague generalities and the laws were always filled with loopholes you could drive a bulldozer through.

His basic attitude to these questions: "I often used to think back to the ethics courses I was forced to take in graduate school. Most of them seemed to discuss theory and laid out situations that were obvious. Now I have to make decisions on the fly. Decision that affect real people. My instincts tell me what is the right thing to do. They pass my personal smell test but you know I could never give you an exact accounting of how or why I arrived at some of those decisions. I know they were right but I can't always tell you why. And you know, someone else might have made the opposite decision—and they too could be right. There are often many, many roads to choose and all of them can be argued ethically."

## Business Ethics as a Social Contract

Business ethics are based on broad principles of integrity and fairness that tend to focus on shareholder and stakeholder issues such as product quality, customer satisfaction, employee wages and benefits as well as local community and environmental responsibilities issues that a company can actually influence. According to scholars it means going well beyond simple legal compliance.

Business ethics defines how a company integrates its core values—such as honesty, trust, respect and fairness—into its policies, practices and decision-making. Business ethics, of course, also involves a company's compliance with legal standards and adherence to internal rules and regulations. As recently as a decade ago, business ethics consisted primarily of compliance-based, legally-driven codes and training that outlined in detail what employees could or could not do in regard to areas such as conflict of interest or improper use of company assets.

Today, a growing number of companies are attempting to design values-based, globally consistent programs that give employees a level of ethical understanding that allows them to make appropriate decisions, even when faced with new challenges. At the same time, the scope of business ethics has expanded to encompass a company's actions with regard not only to how it treats its employees and obeys the law but to the nature and quality of the relationships it wishes to have with stakeholders including shareholders, customers, business partners, suppliers, the community, the environment, indigenous peoples and even future generations.

## The Concept of Corporate Citizenship

All of this angst over ethics codes and corporate social responsibility is currently being played out against a backdrop of debate over how far companies can and should go in meeting social expectations—or if they even consider it at all. The million-dollar question that is yet to be answered is: Isn't the business of business really just business? Thirty years ago Milton Friedman, doyen of market economics who among other things advocated private ownership of roads, argued that "there is one and only one social responsibility of business—to use its resources and engage in activities designed to increase its profits."

Such a statement might seem to be a mere fact for someone like Mr. Friedman but these words send chills down the spines of anti-globalization activists such as French premier and union leader José Bove.

The view of the minority Friedmanites is quite simple. If society wants companies to put social agendas ahead of the pursuit of shareholder value, then governments should regulate business accordingly, however, society must be willing to accept the economic fallout.

NOTE: The British government did just that in 2000 with the creation of a new ministerial post for corporate social responsibility. The move received a mixed response from business, which warned it should not be used as an excuse for imposing extra legislative burdens on companies.

The more common view today is that societies can and do have the right to expect business to function at certain levels of ethical standards. After all, common sense and marketplace rules dictate that it's not a simple either/or question—ethics or business. No company can thrive, or even survive, if it does not carry out sound business practices and make a profit. But on the other hand, people are reluctant to do business with a company that cheats its customers and suppliers, ruins the environment and fails to build trust with its employees and investors.

People in every country throughout the world make an agreement with business to carry out the necessary work to provide goods and services to society—and often make concessions to business to do so. In return, society has the right to expect that productive organizations will enhance the general interests of consumers and employees. With large mergers and the development of new markets around the world, major corporations now wield more economic and political power than the governments under which they operate. In response, public pressure has increased for businesses to take on more social responsibility and operate according to higher ethical standards. Firms in developed nations now promote—and are often required by law to observe—nondiscriminatory policies for the hiring, treatment and compensation of all employees. Some companies are also now more aware of the economic and social benefits of being active in local communities through sponsoring events and encouraging employees to serve on civic committees.

Businesses will continue to adjust their operations by balancing the competing goals of earning profits and responding to public pressures for them to become beneficial social institutions. Even those who think companies have wider responsibilities can't agree on the most efficient method to achieve them. Ulrich Steger, who teaches Environmental Management at the International Institute for Management Development in Lausanne, Switzerland, says that companies should aim for "responsible shareholder-value optimization." That is, a company's number one priority is to optimize shareholders' long-term interests; but, within that constraint, it should seek to meet whatever social or environmental goals the public expects of them.

## Sustainable Development: The Latest Trend

The concept of sustainable development has as many definitions as some global companies have regional offices or product brands. The concept, which came into vogue in the 1980s, has been until recently dominated by environmental issues. Today, it is being interpreted by business to mean much more than tree-hugging or saving rainforests. It is about people, profits, ethics and a better economic and social future for all.

The United Nations defines sustainable development as "providing for the needs of the present generation while not compromising the ability of future generations to meet theirs." In fact, many thought this definition was too negative and too limiting. It seemed to encourage maintaining a sort of status quo, without calling for improving the lot of the world's population. It seemed to call for a world with "less" rather than a world with "more." New technologies and new products, all potentially profitable to businesses, could also improve life on earth—and not just for the rich.

In the 1990s, under pressure from consumers, governments and non-governmental organizations, global businesses began to move away from the narrowly focused path of environmental awareness to the more broad based notion of sustainable development. However, the UN definition just didn't fit the bill. Today, sustainable development is more about environmental protection, social equity and economic growth. The more acceptable definition these days is more positive: "sustainable development is about ensuring a better quality of life for everyone, now and for generations to come."

Indeed, the notion of improving the quality of life has been a breakthrough concept of sustainable development. Businesses have started to see how their technologies and innovations could make a real difference in solving environmental and social problems as well as in addressing frustrations in the lives of consumers by making life better, healthier and just downright easier.

Today, it is accepted that achieving a truly sustainable future must go beyond simply addressing the clash between human activity and the environment. Economic and social balances must be achieved.

Business, more so than government, now seems to be the sector most capable of achieving these noble goals for some very good reasons:

- Business has the resources and global reach to achieve these aims.
- Globalization has made business the key player in many global issues.
- Business can react faster than government.
- Business has a vested interest in achieving success—after all no business can thrive on a dead planet.
- Consumers and investors are increasingly screening companies for better performance and commitment in the area of sustainable development.
- Consumers voluntarily use a firm's goods and services while governments compel behavior by law.

## Great Expectations

According to research done by the British-based Prince of Wales Business Leadership Forum and Environics International Ltd. in Australia, global consumers will expect corporations in the 21st century to:

- Demonstrate a commitment to society's values by actively contributing to social and environmental goals, as well as economic ones.
- Insulate society from negative impacts of the companies' operations, products, and services.
- Share the benefits of company activities with key stakeholders as well as with shareholders.
- Demonstrate that their company can "do well by doing good."

CHAPTER 2

# Are Ethics Culturally Based?

*TO KNOW GOOD IS TO DO GOOD, AND SINCE DOING GOOD IS MORE RATIONAL AND USEFUL THAN DOING BAD, TO DO BAD IS TO DO SO LARGELY OUT OF IGNORANCE. –* SOCRATES

PHILOSOPHERS AND ACADEMICS have spent lifetimes arguing whether there are truly "absolute ethical values"—universally valid moral principles that apply to everyone all the time. While such a debate about the existence of a one-size-fits-all morality, known as "Moral Objectivism," may provide great fodder for dinner party conversation, it bears little relevance for the global road warriors doing battle on the international business front.

The reality is that people from different cultures do business differently—and have varying sets of values, moral guidelines and ethical principles to guide them through the maze of life. What might be the "right" way to act in one culture may be considered the "wrong" way in another. Understanding the cultural context and ethical mindset of a potential foreign business partner or competitor can help in developing sound strategies for negotiations and deal making. What once seemed mysterious behavior may become more predictable—and ultimately be used to your advantage. At the very least, you will not be caught unawares by certain behaviors and attitudes.

## Contracts: Different Cultures, Different Ethical Views

Take, for example, the concept of a business contract. Not everyone views the meaning of a written contract in the same way. While Americans and Germans generally insist on intricate multi-page contracts that are meticulously followed to the letter of the law, other cultures—especially those where personal relationships are highly valued and contract law is rare, such as Russia, Nigeria or China—view contracts as more of a statement of intention rather than a formal binding obligation with real penalties—at least as it applies to locals. While an American or a German would view the breaking of a written contract as ethically unacceptable (not to mention as a clarion call for the lawyers to mop up the mess), a Russian or a Nigerian would lose little sleep over it—not because they have no conscience but rather because the societal view of a contract attaches no great ethical stigma to breaking it (of course, it helps that foreign firms have little legal recourse).

WARNING: There are worse things than lawsuits. Societies with little contract law also sometimes have their own "extra-legal" and usually violent means of enforcing contracts. The enforcers rarely engage in philosophical discussions.

How much ethical value is attached to contracts also hinges on which party is buying and which is selling in a given transaction. Buyers and investors usually determine the structure of the contract. The economic predominance of buyers generally offsets cultural concerns. Is it cultural imperialism to insist on contract adherence or just modern business practice? Buyers and sellers will usually have differing opinions on this matter.

## CONTRACTS AND CULTURES AROUND THE WORLD

A few examples of how different cultures approach the concept of the business contract from an ethics perspective:

- GERMANY Contracts are even more detailed than in the United States. Once signed they are strictly adhered to by Germans—and they expect the same from you.
- EGYPT Contracts are regarded as guidelines for business relationships rather than specific performance requirements. The content may be renegotiated, revised and appended many times to reflect changing circumstances—usually on the Egyptian side. To ignore provisions of a signed contract does not carry any great moral stigma within society or law.
- UNITED STATES Signing on the dotted line, as the Americans will joke, is the first step to a court appearance. Americans would sue their mother (in fact some actually have) if they thought she had reneged on a signed deal. To renege on a written contract reveals complete ethical and moral bankruptcy. Only crooks and cheats fail to live up to contracts. Needless to say, lawyers play an important role in the drawing up of contracts—a characteristic that is offensive to many cultures that interpret the presence of attorneys as a sign of moral and ethical mistrust. Of course, it depends who is buying and who is selling.
- JAPAN Contracts are guidelines and any problems are arbitrated rather than litigated. Every contract will include a *JIJI HENKO* clause that permits complete renegotiation if circumstances change. This is tied to the importance of giving and saving face in Japanese culture, that is, allowing plenty of wiggle room for both sides to prevent embarrassment. In fact a "gentleman's agreement"—an informal verbal commitment from a Japanese executive—often means more than a formal written contract. To violate such an agreement would represent a greater ethical breech for the Japanese businessman (a grave loss of face) than walking away from a formal contract.
- SOUTH AFRICA This is not a litigious society. Business contracts are not overly complicated; but sometimes they are left intentionally vague to give the local party some wiggle room should things not work out. The South African legal system, which is fair and mostly uncorrupted (at least for now), usually favors the local side over the foreign side in cases of corporate and business law. South Africans will make a good faith effort to meet contract deadlines but don't feel they should be punished if their non-performance is unintentional.
- RUSSIA It is important to remember that even if you have a signed contract with a Russian firm, it may not be worth much. Russians have a different view of contracts than Westerners and see contracts more as a statement of intention than a formal, morally binding obligation with penalties. Russian business law, while

improving, is still not sophisticated enough to deal with suits stemming from broken contracts. Russian business ethics are still very much in a developmental stage. In Russia, "extra-legal" processes are more the norm than legal regulations.

- MEXICO Contracts are more a matter of personal honor than a company commitment. Lawyers are useless in trying to gain compliance, which rests more on a signer's personal ethics rather than some over-arching principle of business ethics. Thus, if the person who has signed a contract should change jobs, drop dead or emigrate, you may be left holding a relatively worthless piece of paper. In such a case, re-negotiation would be expected.

## Understand A Culture and You Understand Its Business Ethics

If there truly are no absolute moral or ethical values (or at least no scholar has yet to find them), where can an individual look for guidance as to what type of behavior a business colleague will consider to be right or wrong? The answer: in a society's culture.

So what is culture anyway? It may seem obvious but culture is what makes the Chinese Chinese, the French French and the South Africans South African. The noted Dutch writer and academic Geert Hofstede refers to culture as "the software of the mind"—the social programming that runs the way we think, act and perceive right and wrong as well as how we perceive ourselves and others. The implication is that culture is not innate.

There is no gene that forces Americans to treasure individualism and brashness or Germans to value rigid order. It is learned behavior and hence can be changed. Just alter the internal programming and you too can think like a Yank or a Brit or a Kuwaiti. While this is certainly a useful and encouraging metaphor for anyone dealing in global business affairs, it is more difficult to implement than it sounds. It takes study, a keen sense of observation and above all a willingness to learn and relinquish the notion that "my native culture is superior." When is the last time you heard a foreign colleague admit that their way of doing things is inferior to yours? It doesn't happen. When dealing in a multi-cultural environment the "adapt or die" philosophy is a good one to remember, if only for the sake of appearances.

NOTE: To understand another culture is not the same as condoning all of its procedures.

A more formal definition is that culture is a set of learned core values, beliefs, standards, knowledge, morals, laws and behaviors shared by individuals and societies that determines how an individual or a group acts, feels and views itself and others. A society's culture is passed from generation to generation and aspects such as language, religion, customs and laws are interrelated. A society's view of authority, morals and ethics will manifest itself in how an individual does business, negotiates a contract, deals with a crisis or cultivates a potential business relationship.

## Three Basic Cultural Components

Viewing a national culture from the outside can be intimidating. But breaking down each national culture into its components and understanding how each component is related to the whole can help unwrap the enigma and provide some logic and motivation behind behavior and ethics. The three most crucial cultural components that relate to business transactions and the ethics that govern these transactions are:

### LANGUAGE

Remember, language is more than just spoken and written words. Non-verbal communications, such as gestures, body language and facial expressions all convey a message. When two people do not speak a common language and are forced to use an interpreter, non-verbal communication is the only direct contact, the only method available for individuals to take a direct read of each other. By failing to understand the context of non-verbal communication you run the risk of not only failing to read your colleague across the table but of actually sending what may be the entirely wrong signal to them.

### RELIGION

The dominant religious philosophy within a culture has a greater impact on an individual's approach to business ethics than most people expect—even if that individual is not a devout follower of a religion. In the Arab world, for instance, conversations are sprinkled with the phrase *INSHALLALA*—"if God wills." The deference to a higher power, a lack of control over many matters here on earth and the general what-will-be-will-be attitude that the phrase epitomizes carries over into everything from airline schedules to the pace of business negotiations.

### VALUES AND ATTITUDES

Obviously cultural values have an enormous impact on the way business is conducted. The most basic value differences to be considered are whether a culture emphasizes individualism, like the US, or collective mentality, like Japan, and whether societies are task driven, like Great Britain, or relationship driven like France.

## Defining and Classifying National Cultures

How people and cultures define themselves has a great impact on how they conduct their business practices. Consider the case of Japan where group goals and needs are almost always placed ahead of those of the individual. In Japan, the classic American hero—the self-made man or woman who blissfully and boastfully looks out for "number one"—is considered to be ethically deficient and hardly an ideal. In Japan the individual gives way to the group. Decisions are made on a consensus basis and group harmony is the status quo. Hofstede has developed a useful framework that illustrates the four major issues that define and classify national cultures. Each issue ultimately has a very real effect on how people process information and interact, whether in personal circumstances or with business colleagues.

## INDIVIDUALISM VS. COLLECTIVISM

Does a society cherish rugged individualism, the independent thinker, the person who values personal success over group success? Or does it demand that individuals subordinate their needs to those of the group?

Societies that rely on a collectivist mindset value conformity and control the behavior of the individual through external sanction—shame or expulsion from the group. The expressions, "the nail that sticks up is pounded down," which is associated with Japanese society, and, "the highest blade of grass is always the first to be cut," which governed the attitude of the "have-nots" in the former Soviet Union, are valid reflections of a collectivist societal attitude. Both express society's intolerance of the individualistic approach and the placement of personal success over group success. Today, in Japan, to change jobs for career advancement is still considered by many to be unethical while in the United States it is considered an important road to success. While group pressure controls behavior in collectivist societies, control in individualist-oriented cultures depends on self-generated sanction, namely guilt.

The practical implications of the contrast between group and individual are clear for business. While decision-making in an individualist culture may be more rapid, the implementation of a change in policy, such as a new manufacturing process or a new company ethics code, will be perceptibly slower than in a collectivist culture. The reason: in a society that values individualism, workers will question the new method and probably not sign on until he or she figures out how it will directly impact them—as individuals. It may take longer to come to a decision through consensus in a collectivist environment but once the group makes the decision, implementation is more rapid.

There are other subtle examples of how the individualist vs. collectivist mindset plays out in national business cultures. Take the example of attitudes toward executive compensation. The ratio of annual compensation for executives compared to line employees in the manufacturing sectors of highly individualistic cultures, such as the United States and South Africa, is far more disproportionate than in highly collectivist societies like Japan. In the United States executive pay is 28 times that of the average manufacturing worker and in South Africa it is 24 times. In Japan the top executive earns only about 10 times the average worker's pay. American executives measure their success through pay and perks while Japanese executives measure it through the overall health of their company and contentment of employees. To take monetary advantage of one's position would be shameful and unethical for the Japanese. This ancient social contract is the basis of most Japanese business organizations.

| EXAMPLES OF INDIVIDUALIST CULTURES | EXAMPLES OF COLLECTIVIST CULTURES |
|---|---|
| Australia | China |
| Canada | France |
| South Africa | Japan |
| United Kingdom | Russia |
| United States | Saudi Arabia |

### POWER-DISTANCE

The cultural dimension explains how individuals within a society view power and, in turn, their role in decision-making. In cultures with a low power-distance profile, individual employees will seek a role in decision-making and question decisions or orders in which they had no input. By contrast, in high power-distance societies employees seek no decision-making role. They accept that the boss is right, quite simply because the boss is the boss and is supposed to give orders. Employees in high power-distance cultures need direction and discipline and they look to management to provide it. A company's ethics code passed down to workers from senior management in a high-power distance culture, like China, is more apt to go unquestioned.

In low power-distance cultures, workers tend to be more individualistic in nature and may try and rationalize the code to suit a particular situation (this is known as Ethical Situationalism in academic circles). It would be a mistake for senior management to decree an ethics code by fiat in such a culture. Workers will be offended that they were not consulted since they expect management to seek their input.

| HIGH POWER-DISTANCE CULTURES | LOW POWER-DISTANCE CULTURES |
|---|---|
| Egypt | Australia |
| Italy | Israel |
| Japan | Sweden |
| Russia | United States |

### UNCERTAINTY AVOIDANCE

Societies that have a low measure of uncertainty avoidance generally value achievement over security, exhibit a less structured and more free flowing style of management and have fewer workplace rules than societies with a high measure of uncertainty avoidance. As expected, countries that exhibit low measures of this dimension experience high rates of employment turnover and job mobility.

This dimension (the United States is obviously a low uncertainty avoidance country) helps explain why a US executive might do little preparation in advance of a key meeting, preferring to wing it, relying on wit, charm and the ability to think on his or her feet to carry the day. It also explains why a German executive will make painstaking preparations—down to a full dress rehearsal—for a similar meeting.

| HIGH UNCERTAINTY AVOIDANCE CULTURES | LOW UNCERTAINTY AVOIDANCE CULTURES |
|---|---|
| Germany | Mexico |
| Japan | Singapore |
| Russia | South Africa |
| Switzerland | United States |

NOTE: The Germans so hate the idea of uncertainty that there is actually a set of laws (known as notstandsgesetz) which come into force when all other national laws break down.

## MASCULINITY—FEMININITY

This dimension speaks to both societal values and attitudes. Societies with so-called masculine values appreciate aggressiveness and assertiveness while respecting the goal of material acquisition. Feminine cultures value inter-personal relationships, putting quality of life before material acquisition and applauding concern for other individuals and the less fortunate.

The pace of business tends to be more pedestrian in cultures with a majority of feminine traits. Business hinges more on personal relationships—friends doing business with friends—than with pure efficiency and written contracts. Business people from feminine cultures are often more reserved and less time-driven than those from masculine cultures where achievement—closing the deal, next quarter's financial results—is more important than building a long-term business relationship. In masculine cultures big is good and boasting about it is even better

Few societies have all masculine or all feminine traits. This concept maybe seen as a continuum with a mix of traits between the two poles. Governments can be a solid indicator of where a society lies on the masculine/feminine spectrum. A government that taxes high (Sweden, for example) and then freely spends on social welfare programs represents a highly feminine society by demonstrating strong concern for others.

Masculine societies can certainly demonstrate feminine traits and in some cases move fairly freely along the continuum. South Africa is an excellent example. A country where material wealth is a highly sought after goal, where assertiveness is part of the business culture and where achievement is respected, will have a government that has shown great concern for the have-nots, the victims of the old policy of racial segregation known as apartheid.

| MOSTLY MASCULINE CULTURES | MOSTLY FEMININE CULTURES |
|---|---|
| Australia | France |
| Brazil | Greece |
| South Africa | Japan |
| United States | Sweden |

One would expect that countries exhibiting mostly feminine traits would be leading the trend towards creating and adopting complex ethical codes for businesses. That is simply not the case; but the answer serves more to re-affirm the traits of masculine vs. feminine cultures than contradict them. The United States—one of the most masculine cultures—is generally recognized as the global leader in fostering formal ethics codes in the world of business. While on the surface this appears a contradiction (we can be reasonably assured that it does not reflect an overall landmark societal shift to a more touchy-feely feminine culture), the US lead in formalized ethical codes is made necessary because of its masculine traits rather than in spite of them. In the United States at least, it may be necessary to legislate to force more noble behavior rather than to rely on a natural inclination to "do good for the sake of doing good."

The recognition that a good reputation and good behavior is viewed by customers as a strong positive that eventually leads to a better company bottom line has as much to do with the relatively recent concern with business ethics than any thought of purely doing good for good's sake.

## Other Cultural Traits

Culture also influences how individuals within a society process information, set priorities, manage time and interact with other individuals. To an individual from a monochronic society (where each task is handled individually according to a schedule), time is used for ordering one's life, for setting priorities, for making a step-by-step list to do things in sequence and for dealing with one individual at a time. Americans—and most northern European societies—are monochronic. When faced with crowds, they form orderly lines to accomplish their task, whether it is to pay a bill or to get into a sports stadium.

To an individual from a polychronic society (many tasks at once, no schedule), a sequential approach to tasks is seen as unnecessarily constraining. (You would be hard pressed to find a Chinese executive that keeps a prioritized "to do" list—one of the most basic features of Western time management courses.) Time is used to accomplish diverse goals simultaneously and to interact with as many individuals as possible—even at the same time.

---

NOTE: Polychronism tends to be a hallmark of a "developing" economy and foreigners are requested to accept the commercial inefficiency of not working according to a schedule. As economies modernize the importance of time begins to take hold. The ethics of "produce on time, get paid on time" are very compelling.

---

### HIGH CONTEXT VS. LOW CONTEXT

People from different cultures process and disseminate information differently. Low context cultures are much more precise in their communication, providing mountains of detail and groping for the correct word or phrase to summarize an event. They assume a relatively low level of shared knowledge with the individual they are communicating with, and thus, feel a strong need to explain all in great detail. Low context cultures—such as the United States, Britain and the Scandinavian countries—focus more on what is being said rather than by whom it is being said. Body language, hand and facial gestures are secondary, if not entirely ignored, in place of the message itself. Business may be conducted successfully by letter, telephone, fax or e-mail in such cultures. It is not necessary to meet face-to-face with a colleague to get things done.

High context cultures are the exact opposite. Communication tends to be imprecise and as much attention is paid to the person delivering the message as to the message itself. In high context cultures—such as Latin America, Southern and Latin Europe, Central and East Asia, the Middle East and Africa—personal encounters are essential before business can begin. People in high context cultures need as much ancillary information as possible. They pay more attention to physical surroundings and how a business colleague is dressed or coiffured—the general ambiance of the negotiations—than individuals from low context countries. Body language, facial gestures and voice inflection are important methods of communication. The physical venue for a meeting or a business meal is just as important as the substance being discussed.

### RELATIONSHIP VS. TASK DRIVEN CULTURES

This classification deals more with the business culture within a society but it does have application to societies as a whole. Cultures, especially in business dealings, are either relationship driven (which Hofstede's theory would classify as a feminine culture) or task driven (the masculine side of Hofstede's theory). Knowing which side of the fence your potential business partner sits on, will allow you to prioritize your presentation while predicting the time frame for closing a potential deal.

Task driven cultures are usually low context cultures, while relationship driven cultures are high context ones. When making a presentation to an individual from a task-driven culture, their main concern will be the price, quality and guarantees associated with a product or service. A sale can be closed on the first meeting. When making a presentation to people from a relationship-driven culture, your deal may be "dead on arrival" unless you have established a personal relationship. The product could be the greatest thing since Velcro, but until you sell yourself, they won't want to hear about what you have to sell.

Perhaps the easiest way to remember this idea is through a truism: In the Middle East—a relationship-driven, high context culture—business partners are friends who do a deal. In Europe, business partners do a deal—they may or may not be friends.

## The Way the Real World Views Ethics: It's Mostly Relative

It should now be easy to see why the business ethics of your partner in America, your supplier in China, or your customer in Poland, may vary because they have their root in the culture of their home society. This idea, formally known in academic circles as "cultural relativism" states that the "right way to act"—what is "good behavior"—is nothing more than behavior that is socially approved by the majority within a culture. As the Greek philosopher Protagoras (480-411 BC), perhaps the earliest proponent of "cultural relativism" advised: "Man is the measure of all things." Such a view would hold that gender discrimination is neither good nor bad objectively; but it is good if the society disapproves of it (think Saudi Arabia, Iran or Afghanistan here) and bad if the society thinks it is (think the United States and all its legislation against it). Another clear example: in China abortion is a government-approved method of birth control while in Ireland it is strictly forbidden by government edict.

At the heart of cultural relativism is the view that there are no absolute moral values and that different societies simply disagree about morality. It holds that one should not view another country's behavior as wrong, but rather just different. Of course, the real world rarely follows academic theory to the letter—and if one were to take "cultural relativism" to its logical conclusion, the theory would border on the ridiculous.

For example, if the real world were truly viewed solely through the prism of "cultural relativism" it would be impossible to legitimately criticize what goes on morally and ethically in other cultures and times. The most obvious examples would be the Roman's persecution of the Christians, the treatment of Jews and other minorities by Nazi-era Germany, the international slave trade, South

Africa's apartheid policy, the genocide in Rwanda or Japan's harsh occupation of China and Korea during World War II. While these incidents and policies may have met with the approval of the perpetrating societies—and thus fall under approved behavior under the "cultural relativism" doctrine—there is virtually no society today that would find all of them without fault.

In reality the application of ethics and morality depends on the cultural setting and moral principles as cultural products. However, just because we find them in place doesn't mean they must be accepted as morally correct. Still for all its faults, "cultural relativism" does help to explain why certain societies hold different views on what constitutes proper norms of behavior.

One British manufacturing executive recalls a debate he had with an Iranian colleague about the treatment of women. He remembers telling his Persian friend just how abhorrent he found the idea that certain jobs were off limits to females and that women could not be seen in public with a male companion who was not her husband.

"I really let him have it," says the Brit. "I mean this blatant discrimination just seemed wrong to me. But as we talked more I began to realize that how the Iranians treated women stemmed more from a difference in factual beliefs than an evil intent. The religious Persians believe that women truly do hold a different place in society and need to be treated accordingly. Many women I spoke to agreed to such a view and in fact, saw the different treatment as a sign of respect rather than discrimination.

"Indeed my colleague said he felt we were morally bankrupt in Britain because we forced women out into the working world and ignored their special status. What appeared to be a difference in moral beliefs concerning respect toward women actually turned out to be more a difference in factual beliefs about the role of women. It was a real eye-opener."

In the real world and virtually all cultures, there is a basic set of core moral principles that are followed to one degree or another. For example, all societies concur that it is wrong to kill innocent people, to cheat or to steal. These basic core beliefs are necessary for societies to function. Where they disagree is upon defining "innocent," "cheating" and "stealing." Most ascribe to the notion that it is wrong to lie—but the Japanese, for example, will lie to avoid offending you and may promise action on a deal they have already rejected. In this case, the ethical principle of allowing you to save face overrides the one about telling the absolute truth. It is fair to argue that the Japanese don't really condone lying. The concept of saving face is more about etiquette than it is about moral principles or ethics. Ethics, as they are practiced in the global business world, is truly a gray area.

## Beware the Subjectivist

We all practice a bit of subjectivism in business. After all, "what constitutes the best deal" depends on a multitude of factors—not all of which can be quantifiably measured. "I trust her more," or "they seem like a reliable bunch" or "we just got along better" are all valid, if highly subjective reasons, in choosing one competitive bid over another. But when it comes to ethics, it is best to beware of the "subjectivist" who holds that it is the decision of the individual, not the society, that determines which moral principles are valid.

While theorists and scholars mention "subjectivism" as a valid theory on ethical views, its practice causes problems if a firm is simply a reflection of the boss' "feelings." Feelings are important, but are not by themselves an adequate basis for morality.

## Situationalism: An Even Grayer Area

The theory known as "situationalism" holds that ethical principles can and should be flexible—that is, in some cases the morality of an action depends on the situation and not the application of law. Actions that are normally impermissible are permitted. Situationalism is the opposite of Absolutism—a theory that has little credence in the real world. For example, if a firm is in dire need of cash flow, is it permissible to go to the black market to keep the firm running and people employed until legal business opportunities arise? A Situationalist would say, sure, it's OK based on the circumstances. An Absolutist would say, illegal activity is wrong no matter what. Situational ethics recognizes that a person should be ready in any situation to compromise ethical principles in the interest of a greater good.

To a situationalist, nothing is always right or always wrong and sometimes it is acceptable, even good, to lie. Have no doubt, the notion of situational ethics thrives in the business world. It is what keeps managers and employees up at night.

One German drug company official relates how he became an ethical situationalist while working in a developing country in Africa. It seems his company was prepared to sell a potentially life-saving drug to the Health Ministry at a steep discount—a drug that could save the lives of tens of thousands of individuals. However, an official of the country's customs and excise department was refusing to grant an import license to the company unless a bribe changed hands. Bribing was against his company's published ethics code.

"I took it upon myself to try and view the big picture here. This drug could save thousands of people and all that was holding it up was a demand for a few thousand dollars—not one percent of the total cost of the deal. I struggled but it just seemed that under the circumstances, paying a few thousand dollars to save all those people seemed the right thing to do. It really was the lesser of two evils."

## Is It All Simply About Style Rather Than Principles?

In the global business world, just as there are many ways to be devious, so too are there many ways to be ethical. There is clearly no one single theory of ethics that can be considered the best or the most correct for all cultures. While there certainly are a few social norms that most cultures embrace, it often comes down to nothing more than a matter of style—for both societies and individuals.

Admitting that different cultures have different ethical views and principles does not mean that the theory of relativism or subjectivism is correct, or that ethics can be reduced to a matter of personal taste. Rather, it simply admits that differences exist in the application and view of moral principles—and it would be smart for any business person dealing on the world stage to be aware of it.

After all, the most successful global wheeler-and-dealers are the ones that understand, appreciate and yes, take advantage of, cultural differences. They are the ones who manage to transcend their own cultural blindfolds and see the big picture through the eyes of the other person.

## Some Common Myths About Business Ethics

- Business ethics is more about religion than good profitable business management.
- Business ethics is a discipline best led by philosophers, academics and theologians.
- Our employees are ethical so we don't need an ethics policy.
- Our organization complies with the law, so we're ethical.
- Personal character doesn't matter as long as job performance is not affected.
- Ethical behavior in the workplace can't be taught.

CHAPTER 3

# The Costs to Individuals, Companies and Society

*IT IS LESS SHAMEFUL FOR A KING TO BE OVERCOME BY FORCE OF ARMS THAN BY BRIBERY.*

– GAIUS SALLUSTIUS CRISPUS (C. 86-35/34 B.C.)

BECAUSE IT IS EVERYWHERE, everyone has a word for it. The Russians call it *NA LEVA*. Arabs and many Africans call it *BAKSHEESH* and the Chinese refer to *HONGBAO*. It is *KITU KIDOGO* in Kenya, and *UNA MORDIDA* in Mexico. The Germans call it *SCHIMENGELD* and the Italians *BUSTARELLA*. The Americans sometimes call it grease, the British just call it plain bribery or perhaps more politely "a transaction expense." No matter what you call it, the plague of bribery and corruption perpetuated by the givers and takers in the business world has a much greater impact on the lives of hundreds of millions of people than you would think. Payoffs to facilitate a deal, accelerate a bureaucracy or overcome competition are one of the world's dirty little secrets.

As ancient as it is ubiquitous, official corruption has been casually accepted as an inescapable fact of life as far back as the time of the Pharaohs. Today, unethical business practices, especially corruption and bribery, represent real costs in terms of time, money and social well-being, not only to corporations and governments but also to individuals.

For decades, international organizations such as the World Bank and the International Monetary Fund (IMF) refused to get involved, claiming it was mostly an internal affair of the countries that received their loans. Today, however, with the increase in international investment, the World Bank and the IMF, along with the United Nations, are convinced that corruption erects a barrier to prosperity.

Just how widespread is the rot? A late 1990s World Bank survey of 3,600 firms in 69 countries showed 40 percent of businesses paying bribes. The figure in industrial countries was 15 percent and in the former Soviet Union it climbed to 60 percent.

## An American Restaurateur in Moscow

"When I look back, I guess I really never had a chance to make it," mourns an American businessman who attempted to open a restaurant in Moscow in the mid 1990s shortly after the fall of communism.

"Before I even rented a property or bought a piece of equipment I had spent almost US$150,000 to bribe city officials, pay for protection and hire the niece of a local mafia don as an assistant manager. Not a day went by when I didn't

## Bribery and Corruption Around the World

| Country | Term | Meaning |
|---|---|---|
| **Argentina** | *DIEGO* | a bribe, a ten percent bribe (also simply 10 pesos) |
| **Arabia** | *BAKSHEESH* | bribe money, payment for something, not legal |
| **Brazil** | *MOLHAR A MÃO* | to grease the palm |
| **China** | *HONGBAO* | "red packet" or red envelope filled with money that can be a bribe or simply a "good luck" gift given to children |
| **France** | *UN POT-DU-VIN* | a pot of wine |
| **Georgia** | *SAKMIS CHATSKHOBA* | fixing the deal |
| | *PADARKA* | a "gift" derived from the Russian slang for bribe. |
| **Germany** | *BESTECHUNG (EN)* | bribe (to bribe) - verb |
| | *SCHMIERGELD* | bribe, pay-off, payola |
| | *SCHMIERGELDER* | bribe money |
| | *NEBENEINNAHME*(n) | kickback (very current and popular term) |
| **India** | | |
| Punjab | *VODI DANA, GHOOS* | black money |
| Hindi | *RISHWAT* | under the table |
| Hurdu | *RISHWAT* | bribe money |
| **Iran** | *BAJ DODAN* | to give payment, a bribe |
| **Iraq** | *BAKSHEESH* | bribe money, payment for something, not legal |
| **Italy** | *BUSTARELLA* | bribe |
| | *CORRUZIONE* | corrupt money |
| **Japan** | *HANAGUSURI* | bribe/hush money |
| | *KOUHAKU* | yellow and white/gold and silver/bribery/corruption |
| | *INMOTSU* | a present/a bribe |
| | *TSUKAIMONO* | present/gift/bribe/usable article |
| | *JUTAKUSHUUWAIZAI* | (the crime of) bribery |
| | *SHUUWAI* | accepting bribes/corruption/graftþ |
| | *SHUUWAIZAI* | (the crime of) bribery Pronounced shoo-oo-wy-zy |
| | *ZOUSHUUWAI* | bribery/corruption |
| **Kenya** | *KITU KIDOGO* | something small |
| | *CHAI* (or) tea | asking for a bribe, as in "give me some tea" |
| | *MAJI YA WAZEE* | "water for elders" and "money for beer" |
| **Korea** | *NE MUL* | a bribe |
| | *NE MUL JUDA* | to grease palms, to give a bribe |
| | *NE MUL PATTA* | to have your palms greased, to take a bribe |
| **Malaysia** | *RASUAH* | to take a bribe |
| **Mexico** | *UNA MORDIDA* | a bite, as in take a bite of something |
| **Saudi Arabia** | *BAKHSHEESH* | bribe money, payment for something, not legal |
| **South Africa** | *MA LINI E BRIBE* | how much? Common term in South Africa. |
| Xhosa | *KHAWENZE* | "before we can even talk, let's have it" Xhosa dialect. |
| Zulu | *UYA HLI NZA* | "you have to slaughter first" Zulu dialect |
| Afrikaans | *OM KWOP* | "bribe" derived from old German. |
| **Russia** | *VZIATKA* | bribe money |
| | *NA LEVA* | bribe |
| **Sweden** | *MUTA* | to butter someone up (not necessarily always with money) |
| **U.K.** | back-hander | the most current slang |
| **United States** | grease palms | to bribe, to make things happen |
| | kickback | money illegally paid to a buyer for agreeing to a sale |
| **Vietnam** | *AN HOI LO* | to take a bribe, to have itchy fingers |

have to pay someone something to do what really was their normal job. I had to bribe the bakery driver to deliver bread on time. I just got used to it," he says.

The American could not have picked a worst time to try to build a business in Moscow. The number of organized criminal groups that had come to the attention of the authorities increased from 785 in 1990 to 8,000 by late 1995. In 1996, there were approximately 29,700 premeditated murders or attempted murders in Russia compared with 15,600 in 1990: an increase of more than 90 percent. Most of them are thought to be related to organized crime. By 2008, it was estimated that close to 70 percent of Russia's private companies had *mafiya* connections.

"In the end I lasted less than 18 months. I just couldn't make any money because of all the payouts. It's a shame and I just don't know how anyone really manages to run an honest business. It's the people that lose. They either pay ridiculously high prices because the corruption costs are passed on to them or they go without services because it is too expensive for an honest man to operate a business. Before I went through this I would never have believed just how pervasive corruption is there."

## Corruption: The Hidden Tax

Corruption damages a country's development in several ways. It reduces growth, scares away foreign investment and channels investment, loans and aid funds into "white elephant" projects, which offer high returns to the corrupt decision-makers but little or no benefit to the people.

According to research conducted by the World Bank, widespread corruption can cause the growth rate of a country to be 0.5 to 1.0 percentage points lower than that of a similar country with little corruption. A study based on the Transparency International Corruption Perceptions Index (TI is a Berlin-based group formed by former World Bank officials to campaign against corruption) shows that a rise in corruption levels from that of Singapore (considered very low) to that of Mexico's (considered very high) is equivalent to raising the marginal tax rate by over 20 percent. As a single percentage point increase in the marginal tax rate is calculated as reducing incoming foreign investment by about five percent, in the example given, corruption has cost the country and continues to cost the country virtually all of the foreign direct investment it might otherwise have expected to receive.

Globalization has meant that national economies and corporations have developed greater interdependence, and businesses are recognizing that corruption in one region can affect the entire global market.

Also, the world's largest multinationals have come to realize perhaps the hardest truth of all: unethical cross-border businesses are not only the perpetrators of corruption, they are its victims as well.

## Not Just A Developing World Problem

Corruption and unethical government behavior is not just a problem in the developing world. Witness the corruption charges in France and Japan or the battles for campaign finance reform in the United States. Hans-Ludwig Zachert, former head of the German Federal Bureau of Criminal Investigation, has stated: "No matter how much government apologists may maintain otherwise, corruption in the public service is not just a matter of a few black sheep but an alarmingly everyday occurrence in Germany." According to Zachert, the cases uncovered number in the thousands. Corruption inflated Italy's outstanding government debt by 15%, or about US$200 billion. As a result of Italy's recent crackdowns on corruption, bids for public works projects are coming in at 40 percent below cost estimates.

Swiss authorities reckon that Russians have stashed away US$40 billion in bank accounts in their country. Nearly half of that money is believed to have been criminally acquired.

The amount of money hidden by the British in tax havens totals between £200 and £400 billion. It is estimated that about a third of the wealth of the world's wealthiest individuals is held offshore, out of reach of tax authorities.

One Hong Kong-based British businessman with several projects in China says bribery of Chinese officials has moved from the obvious (envelopes stuffed with cash) to more subtle methods following a crackdown on corruption by the Chinese Communist Party. (The Communist Party, fearing dissent because of such blatant corruption among officials, expelled more than 120,000 party members from its ranks for corruption. At least 37,000 were prosecuted for criminal acts. Several high ranking officials have been imprisoned. But this was the "tip of the iceberg" if ever there was one.)

## What Is Bribery?

Bribery is the offering, promising or giving of something in order to influence a public official in the execution of his/her official duties. Bribes can take the form of money, other pecuniary advantages, such as a membership in an exclusive club, a promise of a scholarship for a child, or non-pecuniary advantages, such as favorable publicity. Every bribery transaction involves a supply side (the briber) and a demand side (the public official).

## The Price Individuals Pay

The amount of bribes paid in international business are conservatively estimated at US$80 billion a year—roughly the amount that the UN believes is needed to eradicate global poverty.

A list of specific cases of unethical behavior by governments and companies would fill this book alone. For example, consider the plundering of health insurance funds in Argentina, the chaotic privatization and resultant plundering of national assets in Russia or the blatant squandering of government funds in Kenya. In the wake of these scandals, and the role that corruption played in the financial crises in South East Asia in the 1990s, awareness has grown about the social, political and economic costs of corruption. It is a cost that no country can afford.

Unethical behavior by governments and the companies that deal with those governments, erodes public confidence in political institutions and leads to contempt for the rule of law, says the Organization for Economic Cooperation and Development (OECD). It distorts the allocation of resources, inflates spending on public procurement and undermines competition in the marketplace. It has a devastating effect on investment, growth and development. Furthermore, corruption exacts an inordinately high price on the poor by denying them access to vital basic services.

It is certainly true that poor people suffer most from corruption. In developing countries and most of the so-called transition economies of the former Soviet Union and eastern Europe, people often have to bribe teachers and doctors to get services which are supposed to be free. Local police and judges frequently want their palms greased. Foreign-donated medicines and other items of aid disappear into private hands.

Bribes were found to take 7 percent of the revenue of firms in Albania and Latvia and 15 percent in Georgia. Some 14 percent of Georgian households admitted to paying bribes and 11 percent in Latvia. Not surprisingly, the survey, which covered between 350 and 450 enterprises, also showed that businesses would be willing to pay additional taxes if corruption were eliminated.

The losses can be even higher. In Uganda, according to the World Bank, public spending on primary education trebled in 1991-93, but oddly, enrollment rates did not rise. A survey of 250 schools showed that over 70 percent of capital funding was misappropriated. Most non-governmental organizations working in the Third World downplay these scandals for fear of discrediting aid in general or making reform look too difficult.

---

NOTE: Many businesspeople consider bribery to be simply an informal tax system. In fact, the percentage paid out in bribes in some developing countries is roughly equivalent to the taxation and licensing fees found in the developed world.

---

## We're Mad as Hell

After decades of ambivalence, it appears that as we enter the 21st century the general public—the real victims of unethical behavior—have had enough. Corruption and unethical behavior are issues that now bring the crowds out to the streets.

In the 1990s, in Mexico, the Philippines, Italy, Brazil, Pakistan and Zaire, national governments fell partly due to public outrage against corruption in government. Captain Valentine Strasser's justification for the overthrow of Sierra Leone's government early in the 1990s was his allegation that members of government were engaged in the plundering of state resources to enrich themselves and, corruption had contributed to a falling standard of living. Similarly, in Mali, the coup of March 1991 was attributed to the people's outrage at the high-level of corruption and embezzlement that had come to characterize President Moussa Traore's government

Crucially, corruption can lower the quality of public goods and services and even threaten safety. The collapse of buildings and thousands of deaths in South Korea, Armenia and Turkey during recent earthquakes were partially blamed on substandard construction performed under corrupt contract agreements. Simply put, corruption decreases national budget resources. It also reduces the amount of public spending on health and social security.

Ultimately, corruption hits the poor the hardest, whether in the UK or Africa or Asia. From the scandal in Britain of Westminster council leader Dame Shirley Porter selling public housing for votes (at a loss of 27 million pounds to the council) to pilfered aid resources in India (where only 15 percent of aid money got through to its intended beneficiaries), corruption makes the poor poorer.

Bribes can also raise the cost of projects. When these projects are paid for with money borrowed internationally, bribery adds to a country's external debt. Ordinary people end up paying this back through cuts in spending on health, education and public services. Often, they also have to pay by shouldering long-term burdens of projects that do not benefit them and which they never requested.

The Yactreta Dam on the Rio Parana River between Argentina and Paraguay is a classic example of the way a project's costs spiral out of control with no real accountability. When work began by Italian and French contractors, the cost was put at US$1.5 billion. Twenty years later, it was still not finished and the bill stood at US$10 billion. Much of the money was siphoned off into the bank accounts of Argentinean and Paraguayan officials.

## The Cost to Companies

Bribery and corruption also create an environment of uncertainty in the operations of firms. According to Daniel Kaufmann of the World Bank, the probability of losing one's investment to corruption within five years is as high as 80 percent in some countries.

Corruption remains a major obstacle to trade. The US Department of Commerce estimates that, between May 1, 2001 and April 30, 2002, the competition for 60 overseas contracts worth US$35 billion may have been affected by bribery of foreign officials. Of these 60 contracts, US firms are believed to have lost nine contracts worth US$6 billion—due to their refusal to participate in bribery and corruption. In 1999, the US Department of Commerce reported that, in the preceding five years, bribery was believed to have been a factor in 294 commercial contracts worth US$145 billion. In 1996, the magazine World Business reported that the bribes paid by German companies alone were over US$3 billion.

The US Securities and Exchange Commission (SEC) to the Senate Banking Committee revealed, for instance, that Exxon's total bribes had amounted to US$78 million from 1963 to 1972. Lockheed Corporation had made secret payments totaling millions of dollars to help procure and maintain business overseas. (This all took place before the Foreign Corrupt Practices Act was passed in 1977, making such overseas bribery illegal for U.S. companies.)

Not just companies are involved. According to a French secret service report, the official export credit agency of France paid around US$2 billion in bribes to foreign purchasers of "defense equipment" in 1994.

## Society's Price

Even the global corruption watchdog Transparency International is reluctant to put an exact price on global corruption and unethical behavior. Most participants are not very keen to open their books. Most of the evidence is anecdotal—but it can be alarming.

Because of the secrecy with which they operate, so-called "offshore financial centers" (many are quite landlocked) have become excellent places to launder the proceeds of crime and corruption. They have been implicated in almost all money-laundering schemes. In 1996, the IMF estimated that US$500 billion—between 2 to 5 percent of global GDP—is laundered offshore every year. By 2008 it was in the US$ trillions and the banking systems of Switzerland, the Caymans and Luxembourg among others were feeling the heat from international authorities.

## Cost Is Not Only Financial

Corruption has many other serious damaging effects. Even if there were no economic effect at all, it would still be a critical problem, says Transparency International. Corruption is sometimes defended as a way of "getting business done" by "circumventing bureaucratic red tape."

In some parts of the world corruption and bribery are contributing to the rapid depletion of natural resources. In the Philippines, for instance, the number of logging concessions have been comparatively few, about 480 during the past 20 years; but it is estimated that they have amassed US$42 billion in profits, due to very low concession fees and taxes. The system enriched a few families while the livelihood of millions of others has been adversely affected by the loss of forest cover and the displacement of local communities, not to mention the public revenue foregone by squandering public assets. The impact on the environment has been disastrous: almost 90 percent of the Philippines' primary forest has been lost, leading to heavy ecological imbalances such as erosion and changes in local climate.

Similarly, it is estimated by the NGO Global Witness that the equivalent of US$50 in bribes is paid for every cubic meter of timber felled in Cambodia. In 1997, between 2.5 million and 4.5 million cubic meters of timber was felled, representing US$125 million to US$225 million in bribes alone. To this figure can be added the potential value to the state of the economic rent of the timber itself, between US$184 million and US$337 million. At the lower estimate, this represents a lost revenue of US$309 million derived from finite state resources, over 73 percent of the national annual budget of US$419 million. Official forestry revenue contributed US$12.4 million to the budget during the same period.

## A Counter Argument: Greasing the Wheels

This "grease-the-wheels" school argues that corruption sometimes provides the only way for businesses to skirt heavy-handed regulations, confiscatory taxation and/or an inept legal system. By allowing businesses to maneuver around a grasping state, the proponents of this argument claim, corruption may be neither inconsistent with nor antagonistic to the goal of development.

More than that, the grease-the wheels faction says, corruption may even foster growth. Bribery may be good since bribes act as incentives to low-paid and inadequately monitored officials to speed up the processing of paperwork. In an inefficient legal framework, payoffs to avoid numerous regulations and taxes may also lower costs for those who pay them. No small matter, either of these. One Belarusian businessman who was attempting to open a furniture manufacturing company said he required no less than 70 officials to sign off on the venture, a process that took him more than seven months.

Bribes, the argument continues, may also clear the market for scarce goods and services which governments often provide below market prices or for free. (In China, for example, the 1989 market price of coal was eight times the subsidized price.) Under competitive bidding for a government procurement contract, the biggest bribe will win—and the lowest-cost firm will be in the position to afford the highest bribe.

To those who grease the palms of state bureaucrats, such arguments ring the right bell—but they don't ring true. Bribes are often associated with the lowest quality goods or services, and are frequently paid to permit the most unqualified people to offer services or secure a benefit. And bribes aimed at winning major contracts and concessions (or at gaining title to privatized companies) are generally the preserve of high level officials and their cronies, who are usually insulated from prosecution.

Small wonder that high level officials from emerging economies rate public sector corruption as the leading obstacle to economic development in their countries. And they seem to have it right: a study of 39 countries by the World Bank shows that when high levels of corruption are accompanied by low reliability of bribes, investment rates may be reduced by half. More "reliable" corruption—some certainty that bribed bureaucrats keep their corrupt bargains—may be less costly, but it still hits investment hard. Relatively corrupt countries are likely to enjoy significantly lower investment rates, if for no other reason that investing in them is estimated to impose an additional 20 percent "corruption" tax.

---

NOTE: Transparency International has a useful guideline: "Five percent of US$200,000 will be interesting to a senior official below the top rank; 5% of US$2 million is in the top official's area; 5% of US$20 million is real money for a minister and his key staff; 5% of US$200 million justifies the serious attention of the head of state."

---

## Corruption Does Have Its Positive Points

Talk about silver linings. It may be expensive but corruption can teach countries and governments some valuable lessons.

1. Allows (even good) rules to be more responsive to individual circumstances; increases flexibility.
2. Provides exemptions to regulations, taxes, possibly in an efficient manner.
3. Allows bad rules to be circumvented.

4. Provides incentives for officials to work hard.
5. Could lower administrative and other costs; for example, a bribe might be socially less costly than the same size fine.
6. Corruption can provide information about the quality of laws and promote efficient reforms.
7. May increase some access to government for some socially marginalized groups.

## Common Defenses for Bribery of Public Officials

- It has always existed.
- Refusal to bribe is a Western "hang-up."
- Bribery is a parallel distribution system. Everyone does it.
- It is the traditional way of doing business in this culture.
- I have no choice. If I don't do it I will lose my job.
- The amount in question is small.
- It is the same as a tax.
- The payment is a deductible business expense (in some countries).
- The payment is a transaction cost.
- If our company does not do it, the competition will.
- The competition has fewer scruples and their products and services are inferior.
- A bribe in this country is no different from a tip in the home country.
- Payment of a bribe will enable the company to grow and, in so doing, create jobs in our home country.

Source: Henry-Claude de Bettignies, Professor, INSEAD & Stanford
The Conference Board's Working Group on Global Business Ethics Principles

CHAPTER 4

# Does Virtue Pay?

*SHARPNESS DOES NOT EARN ONE MONEY, AND HONESTY WILL NOT LOSE MONEY.* – CHINESE PROVERB

THERE IS, OF COURSE, NO CLEAR-CUT ANSWER to this question. In business as in life, virtue is sometimes its own reward. Perhaps one of the unfortunate global realities of business ethics is that the bad do not always do badly and the good don't always do well.

However, there is research that supports what appears to a clear trend. Simply put: being ethical in business provides no guarantee of superior profits or stock performance, but it certainly doesn't hurt the bottom line.

Finding a solid, clearly-defined direct link between ethical behavior and increased profits or shareholder value is the Holy Grail of academic research on the subject. There is research that shows companies' stock prices decline after reports of corporate unethical or illegal behavior. Companies that make a clear commitment to ethics in their annual reports have a higher share value than competitors that do not. On a micro scale there is research that shows that sales teams in the United States who exhibited more ethical behavior than competitors perform better. (But this was not the case in several Asian countries that were studied.)

While all this evidence may sound great on the surface, none of these studies really address, metaphorically speaking, what came first: the chicken or the egg? That is, do more prosperous companies with greater resources brought on by their business success become more socially responsible; or are these companies more prosperous because they are socially responsible? Or more succinctly: is virtue a rich person's prerogative?

## Having No Ethics Policy Can Be Costly

There are three broad categories that explain the reasons corporations are motivated to act in an ethical manner. Two of them have to do with making money.

### MORALITY

As part of the social contract between business and society, business has certain obligations to improve people's lives and the environment in exchange for the privilege to operate. Corporations act to fulfill this contract because, quite simply, it is the right thing to do.

COMPLIANCE

With more socially aware consumers, increasing government regulations on a global scale, and better enforcement, acting ethically avoids potential fines and even greater government interference and regulation that could prove costly.

OPPORTUNITY

Good ethical practices encourage greater customer loyalty.

## Good Ethics = Good Public Relations

Companies with strong ethics programs have found that these efforts can reduce potential costly fines, decrease vulnerability, improve reputation, provide access to capital, favorably influence their bottom line, positively affect their employees' commitment to work and enhance customer loyalty. Good ethics practices can help a company:

- STRENGTHEN FINANCIAL PERFORMANCE: Until there is an answer to the "chicken/egg" problem, there is a strong belief among businesses today that good ethical practices have a positive impact on a company's bottom line.
- IMPROVE CUSTOMER LOYALTY, SALES, BRAND IMAGE AND REPUTATION: In a global economy, brand image and reputation are among a company's most valuable assets. Customers seem to prefer brands and companies considered to have good ethical reputations. A strong reputation for ethical practices and integrity helps build customer loyalty and trust; and in times of crisis or ethical slips, can help soften the blow by winning increased understanding and empathy (and in some cases forgiveness) from the public. The flip side of the coin is, of course, a poor reputation for integrity undercuts a company brand and is difficult to rebuild. A survey by the *WALL STREET JOURNAL INTERNATIONAL EDITION*, the Japanese newspaper *NIHON KEIZAI SHIMBUN* and the advertising firm Bozell Worldwide found that when compared against nine "extremely important" general corporate citizenship categories, "ethics and values" ranked highest among consumers in the United States and Europe and third in Japan.
- STRENGTHEN EMPLOYEE COMMITMENT AND MOTIVATION: A corporate commitment to strong values and ethical goals helps employees find meaning in their work and strengthens their loyalty to an organization. A lack of commitment to ethical values can have the opposite effect, leading to staff turnover and the loss of skilled and valued workers—a danger in a tight labor market. An employee survey carried out in 1999 by Walker Information and the Hudson Institute found that only 9 percent of employees who thought their senior management was unethical were inclined to stay with their companies while 55 percent who believed their leaders were ethical wanted to stay. Employees responded so strongly to Germany's Hugo Boss AG's partnership with the Guggenheim, that several unions stipulated in employment contracts that Hugo Boss continue the sponsorship.

## Ethics = Cost Control

- MINIMIZE RISK Companies perceived to behave unethically toward shareholders, employees, the community or other stakeholders are more likely to find themselves the target of activist pressure, boycotts or even "denial of service" attacks on their Internet operations.
- AVOID FINES, COURT-IMPOSED REMEDIES AND CRIMINAL CHARGES Companies and their employees are required to comply with national, international and local laws governing their operations. Failure to comply with these standards can be costly in terms of time, resources, brand image and employee and customer loyalty. In addition, the development of strong ethics initiatives can greatly reduce the chance of fines resulting from wrongful, fraudulent, discriminatory or illegal activities. For example, the European Commission, which has the power to impose fines of up to 10 percent of a company's worldwide revenues, fined Volkswagen more than US$90 million in 1998 for violating competition rules.
- REDUCE OPERATING COSTS Practicing social responsibility and good ethics, especially dealing with the environment and workplace issues, can reduce costs by cutting waste and improving productivity and resource allocation. For example, Dow Chemical Co. and the National Resources Defense Council (NRDC) partnered on a three-year project to reduce production of 26 toxic chemicals at one of Dow's plants. Dow's US$3.1 million investment is saving the company US$5.4 million a year and, for some of Dow's businesses, has improved product quality or increased production capacity.
- AVOID LOSS OF BUSINESS Because of increased media attention and consumer action, it is no longer good enough for a large corporation to consider only its own ethical practices. It now needs to ensure that its suppliers conduct their affairs in an ethical manner as well. Vendors who are unwilling or unable to meet these requirements run the real risk of losing business. Royal Dutch/Shell once cancelled 69 contracts with companies that failed to adhere to its ethical, health and safety and environmental policies. The Japanese government suspended Credit Suisse's business license in Japan for "misleading and inappropriate" financial accounting practices involving US$4 billion in transactions.
- ENJOY GREATER ACCESS TO CAPITAL A company considered socially responsible can benefit both from its enhanced reputation with the public, as well as its reputation within the business community, increasing its ability to attract capital and trading partners. The Social Investment Forum reported that more than US$2 trillion in assets were managed in portfolios that are regularly screened for ethical, environmental and other socially responsible practices. This represents more than 12 percent of the US$16.3 trillion in funds under professional management in the United States.

## Where to Begin?

If your company has never thought seriously about where it stands on ethical and corporate social responsibility issues, these six steps can serve as a guideline to begin the process. While it's important to behave ethically, it is just as important to get the message out to the public if your firm wishes to benefit from "doing good."

1. Define what your company stands for and what values it brings to the marketplace. Is the public aware of these values? Do they have a favorable reaction to them?
2. Examine your company's internal and external relationships. Do they make sense and reflect your company values? The public and the media often proclaim guilt by association. Seek out new relationships with companies that meet your ethical standards.
3. Understand what the public expects of a company today. Are you prepared to meet these expectations?
4. Review the positioning, assets, liabilities and promises of your brands, products, public positions and community initiatives. Conduct a competitive analysis.
5. Compare your public profile with your private actions. Do they contradict each other?
6. Don't be bashful about getting the word out through the media, to your employees and the community.

## Cause-Related Marketing: Another Way Virtue Can Pay

There appears to be one sure-fire way to make virtue pay—cause-related marketing (CM). All things being equal, a sizeable niche of consumers around the world (well, almost every place around the world) would rather do business with a company that stands for something beyond profits.

Cause marketing is marketing that connects a business' product to a particular cause or set of values in the hope that consumers who hold those values will be more likely to purchase the product as a way of supporting that cause. The point is to attract consumers wanting to make a difference in society through their purchasing.

This is not corporate philanthropy in the traditional sense. Companies have long made contributions to a host of nonprofit organizations; but such donations often go unnoticed by all but the beneficiaries. True CM involves a high-profile partnership between a company and cause. It ties donations to sales or, in some cases, to corporate profits.

Companies around the world no longer want to simply write checks to charities. They want to get involved—and the reasons are not always altruistic. Corporations used to give to charities because they were philanthropically driven or were looking for a tax deduction. Now, when they give, they want something more in return. When properly executed, CM sells products, enhances image and motivates employees.

NOTE: The Body Shop company made a point of advertising its stance against product testing on animals as both a symbol of quality and as a means to attract customers sympathetic to the animal rights movement. Ethical behavior or good PR? Both, actually.

## Why Bother With Cause-Related Marketing?

Too many products and companies selling everything from computers to toothpaste to cosmetics are on the market, similar in quality, price and service. In the global quest to differentiate themselves in the sea of faceless product choices, companies have turned to cause-related marketing to make them unique in the eyes of consumers.

If surveys are to be trusted, the potential of CM to alter consumer behavior is enormous. Cone Communications, a consulting firm that specializes in developing cause-related marketing campaigns, produces a report called the Cone Roper Benchmark Survey. Among its findings:

- 78 percent of adults said they would be more likely to buy a product associated with a cause they care about.
- 66 percent of adults said they would be likely to switch brands and 62 percent would likely switch retailers to support a cause they care about.
- 54 percent of adults said they would pay more for a product that supported a cause they care about. Thirty percent would pay five percent more and 24 percent would pay 10 percent more.
- About one in five people, 58 million consumers, recalled buying products with a cause overlay in the past year; food sold in the supermarket was most often mentioned (50 percent).

The numbers from similar surveys in the United Kingdom are just as eye opening:

- 89 percent of consumers are more likely to buy a product that benefits a cause.
- 86 percent said they have a more positive image of a company that is making a difference in the world.
- 83 percent agree that companies should be involved in their community.

## Walking a Fine Line

Of course, exporting a successful marketing campaign from one country to another or one culture to another without doing your homework is asking for disaster. Cause-related marketing has its own set of land mines to avoid. Make too much noise about your promotion of a cause-related marketing campaign and consumers will accuse you of using the charity for selfish, profit-driven reasons. But if you remain overly humble, the campaign is likely to be flop because no one will hear about it. Choose a cause that has its own ethical problems and the net result is negative.

Even though CM has only recently become a phenomenon, consumers in some countries are already suspicious of its overuse. This suspicion can negate any benefit for the sponsoring company, and may in fact lead to a negative association in the consumer's mind.

WARNING: Causes, like fads, come and go. Choose with care.

## Some Good Old Fashioned Norwegian Skepticism

A study by Peggy Simcic Broenn, Assistant Professor at the Norwegian School of Management in Sandvika, Norway, found that, compared to Americans and British, Norwegians were considerably less enthusiastic about CM.

For example, 46 percent of Norwegians would choose brands that stand for a cause and 35 percent would be more likely to switch to another brand if they knew the brand supported a non-profit organization. However, they are less likely to pay a premium price for a brand that they know supports a non-profit organization than American or British consumers.

## A Comparison of Attitudes

| ATTITUDES TOWARD CM | USA | UK | NORWAY |
|---|---|---|---|
| Awareness of companies supporting causes | 79% | 68% | 7.5% |
| Likely to switch to brands that claim to help a cause | 76% | 86% | 35.5% |
| Likely to pay more for a brand that supports a cause | 54% | 45% | 29.2% |
| More likely to buy a product that supports a cause | 78% | N/A | 46.3% |

## Marketing Your Ethics

VISA U.S.A. Inc. kicked off a high-profile cause-related marketing campaign known as "Read Me a Story." Visa agreed to donate to the Reading Is Fundamental charity, one of America's best-known charities (with the aim of wiping out illiteracy). Reading Is Fundamental received US$1.1 million from Visa and Visa card sales jumped by 20 percent during the "Read Me a Story" campaign. Research revealed a significant increase in card use among consumers who were aware of the campaign. But the research also found that, while people consider children's literacy a meaningful cause, Visa needed to deliver a stronger, more focused message regarding its involvement with Reading Is Fundamental.

Accordingly, Visa doubled its advertising budget for "Read Me a Story" to US$20 million the next year. Visa ended up spending far more on the marketing campaign than it gave to the charity.

Purists say cause-related marketing may actually end up doing a disservice to charitable organizations and desensitizing consumers to their own selfishness. Consumers can both indulge themselves and do good at the same time while buying into the notion that by consumption, they help more people. The philanthropy of some consumers may simply end there ("I gave at the office" mentality). Companies may reap reputational benefits far out of proportion to their donations to charity. Meanwhile, companies that give generously through traditional channels that get little publicity will see scant return on their investment in CR.

## Creating a Winning CM Campaign For Your Company

A successful CM program should:

1. Promote sales and/or build traffic to their business.
2. Appeal to employees, offer them a way to be involved and, if possible, to control elements of the project.
3. Be easy to operate and manage by the nonprofit, therefore, requiring little time from corporate staff.
4. Be easy to explain and defend to shareholders.
5. Be newsworthy and appealing to the media.
6. Be compatible with your corporate giving guidelines.
7. Be low risk.
8. Encourage the cause's members and adherents to participate.
9. Allow for corporate review at predetermined checkpoints.
10. Be related to your line of business, if possible.
11. Appeal to customers' altruism.
12. Be simple, distinctive and easy to grasp.
13. Appeal to as wide an audience as possible.
14. Promote your marketing message.
15. Strengthen your image as a good public citizen.

## Strategies for a Profitable Set of Ethics

Part of making virtue pay is to strategically manage your reputation to pre-empt challenges from activist groups, shareholders and the media. This is especially true for companies involved in environmentally sensitive industries. Managing Environmental Issues: A Casebook by Alfred Marcus and James Post, details a set of best practices by companies who practice SEM—or strategic environmental management—a proactive strategy to pre-empt attacks from several quarters.

### STRATEGY AND ORGANIZATION

- Cut back on environmentally unsafe operations.
- Carry out research and development on environmentally safe activities.
- Develop and expand environmental cleanup services.
- Purchase environmentally safe businesses.
- Change structure, compensation and other systems.

### PUBLIC AFFAIRS

- Try to avoid losses caused by appearing insensitive to environmental issues.
- Attempt to gain environmental legitimacy and credibility.
- Collaborate with environmentalists.

### LEGAL

- Try to prevent confrontation with pollution control agencies.

- Comply early.
- Take advantage of innovative compliance programs.
- Rely on self-regulation rather than government requirements.

#### OPERATIONS

- Promote new manufacturing technologies.
- Encourage technological advances that reduce pollution from products and manufacturing processes.
- Modify production equipment and change manufacturing operations.
- Eliminate manufacturing wastes.
- Find alternative uses for waste.
- Recycle wastes.

#### MARKETING

- Tell the truth, the whole truth and nothing but the truth about your products' environmentally friendly features; avoid being attacked for unsubstantiated claims.
- Create consumer desire for environmentally friendly products as well as researching the market.

#### ACCOUNTING

- Demonstrate that anti-pollution programs pay.
- Show all effects of pollution reduction programs.

#### FINANCE

- Gain the respect of the environmentally concerned investment community.
- Recognize true liability.
- Recognize business opportunities.

## Global is as Local Does

Conducting a successful campaign of corporate citizenship on a global level requires a company to run programs on both a global and local scale. Companies must decide how best to meet their responsibilities to different sets of stakeholders in different regions. Typical strategic factors include giving as much flexibility as possible to local management within a clear global corporate strategy. Since social needs are usually greatest in developing countries where the resources are least, the trick is to balance central themes and local application. A sophisticated global corporate citizen is likely to have most or all of the following elements:

- A limited number of typically small projects at site or plant level which respond to local needs and are unrelated to any global themes.
- Many projects at local, national or regional level which fit broad global themes, but with differing local focuses and varying means of implementation.
- A few flagship projects which operate at national or regional levels, clearly and consistently branded, and following very similar implementation models.
- One or two global strategic alliances with NGOs or quasi-governmental bodies, such as the UN and sister agencies.

CHAPTER 5

# Codifying Business Ethics

*IS IT LESS DISHONEST TO DO WHAT IS WRONG, BECAUSE IT IS NOT EXPRESSLY PROHIBITED BY WRITTEN LAW?*
– THOMAS JEFFERSON

LARGE GLOBAL FIRMS OPERATE across borders and wield immense power and influence on the societies that court and play host to them. There is one school of thought that claims today's international corporations have usurped the power of governments and multinational organizations and are now the entities that have the most power to affect change on a global scale.

While it is true that the expansion of cross-border business has handed enormous power to these corporations, it is just as true that "big business" is often mistrusted and its motives questioned. The unfortunate fact is that not all companies play by all the rules all of the time.

With the development of borderless business and trade, and the explosive growth of global e-commerce on the Internet, multinational corporations are finding themselves doing business in different cultures with often dramatically different sets of laws and customs. Sometimes the challenges are as simple as producing an accurate and nuanced translation of a business document or arranging a conference call at a convenient time for cross-cultural team members located halfway around the globe. Other times the clash of cultures can lead to a major and costly crisis—especially when it comes to the practice of business ethics.

Operating so far from home—and away from a friendly comfortable culture—multinational corporations are beginning to appreciate the importance of the rule of law in the far flung countries in which they operate as well as the institutions that support the law. Without the basic rule of law, the global economic system risks outright collapse. The need for assurances that customers, suppliers, business partners and governments will act ethically and consistently has never been greater. Many corporations and governments are just now beginning to realize that good ethical conduct is in their own best interest

## Reality Bites: Hard Choices

So if the reality is that each country and each region has its own business ethics, history and standards, how can a multinational corporation effectively cope with a myriad of often conflicting customs and ethics?

For some companies, working and adapting to a different culture may mean they are required to make ethical compromises to do business in that culture. This may, in turn, lead them to do business in a way that is not only different from how they do business at home—it may actually be contradictory, if not downright illegal.

The great theoretical question that looms is: Can a multinational corporation risk making a profit in a country where customs and culture require it to make ethical compromises that may have a negative impact on its business operations in other countries or back home? Such negative impacts can range from greater risk of a tarnished reputation in some countries, to customer boycotts, to poor employee morale. In these days of cross-ownership and global expansion, it is not unheard of for divisions in the same company, but located in different world regions, to clash over ethical behavior. Consider the potential damage to reputation and employee morale in the case of a foreign subsidiary of a large corporation operating successfully using tactics not permitted within the firm's own domestic operations.

Perhaps the most common ethical conflict global manufacturing and retailing companies face is over the issue of child labor. In countries like Bangladesh, Pakistan and Honduras, not only does local custom allow for children, some as young as eight-years-old, to be employed, but the law permits it—and sometimes sets work quotas for the kids. While the parents and the children may be willing to provide the labor (maybe even demand the opportunity), it is risky for the foreign firms if news gets back to their domestic market. Here, a company must choose between impoverishing a family or keeping a child from his/her education. Not an easy choice.

## Is a Global Code Necessary?

Should national cultures or company codes control a firm's ethical decisions? Of course, some companies opt out for the less stringent of the two, defending their actions with the plea that "when in Rome do as the Romans do." Or in the PC (politically correct) spirit, their detractors retort that "We would never presume to impose our ethical standards on another culture. We are not ethical or cultural imperialists."

While this last argument hoists the anti-globalization movement on its own petard, it does not solve the problem of deciding which set of ethics to apply: local? foreign? or global?

There is no escaping the fact that not all cultures consider corruption to be an illegitimate and illegal behavior. Though no government in the world openly allows a politician or public official to claim to be empowered by law to commit corrupt acts, accept bribes or squander limited resources, it is declared often enough "sotto voce." The logic goes that since corruption is necessarily accompanied by secrecy, the more transparent international business becomes—the faster it moves towards a global standard of transparency—the better the chance there is of defeating corruption and bribery. Markets will work more efficiently for everyone's benefit, except, of course, for those people who have been taking bribes in the past.

Today, the consensus is growing among both developed and developing countries that business success comes to companies and countries that provide for a rule of law. This means good business ethics, good corporate governance and effective commercial dispute resolution, all of which are found in the world's most successful economies.

In many countries, society does not reward socially responsible behavior by businesses. If a company can get away with cutting corners, handing out bribes or ripping off the government or the consumer, it will be done. For global business to reach its full potential of benefiting societies, it must operate in societies that respect the law and appreciate and reward (or at least not punish) ethical behavior.

It is impossible for a company to ignore the overall moral climate of a country or culture. If the society suffers from moral confusion, lack of respect for the law, lack of trust and cynicism, what hope does a multinational corporation have of being successful? Therefore, business ethics not only needs to address the business of doing business, but also must be useful in helping to maintain a moral society.

---

NOTE: Demand for more uniform and organized business practices, based primarily on EU and North American models, is leading to a global standard for such practices as corporate ethics, corporate governance and corporate accounting. This does not always go down well with the developing economies of Asia or Africa. Morality can be both a tool and a cudgel.

---

### MORE TRENDS FAVORING AN INTERNATIONAL CODE

There are some basic macro trends that favor the development of an international ethics code:

- Corporations are realizing that in order to be successful they must address the needs and concerns of all stakeholders—customers, shareholders, employees, suppliers, host governments and host countries. Indeed, this growing recognition of stakeholders' interests means that corporations are no longer merely economic entities devoted to maximizing profit at any cost.
- Growing North American and European participation in world markets and the harmonization of their laws concerning bribery and corruption.
- The realization in developing markets, especially Asia, Africa and Latin America, is that Western-style business ethics is an important first step for achieving integration in the global economic community. Good ethical practices will also play an important role in their own domestic economic development as well as their access to global capital.
- The dangers of litigation and media scandal that make corporate and individual success dependent on business conduct as well as financial performance.
- The developing ethos of business professionalism. Ethics is fast becoming a management skill, not an occasional option.

## Not Everyone is on the Same Page Yet

Despite all the talk about the importance of corporate ethics, several studies have shown—at least outside of the United States—surprisingly few corporations have a written code of conduct and ethics. In Australia, for example, 71 percent of companies do not have a written code and in Japan the figure was 70 percent. In Germany, France and Britain the figure is still under 60 percent (though still low compared to the United States, it is a big improvement from less than 20 percent in 1984). However, even those large multinational corporations that have written codes rarely take the time and the care to ensure that it is coherent across cultures. Ethics, for many, remains a "policy book" issue like "diversity" and "employee empowerment"—fashionable in title but absent in daily practice.

WARNING: The biggest problem in setting up even a localized code of ethics is the inability to forecast a ROI (return on investment). In most cases, companies have to settle for a process of not losing money through lawsuits or disgruntled customers rather than making additional profits. Ethical behavior is often more cost control through risk management than a revenue center.

## Basic Principles of International Business Ethics

A codified set of International Business Ethics has become the Holy Grail of commerce. It is highly sought after, but not yet attained. Most proponents of international business ethics agree that an international code of ethical practice, and not a code based on each individual culture's unique norms and practices, will be an important tool for multi-nationals in the 21st century. The International Business Ethics Institute provides multinational corporations with these three basic principles to get started.

- INTEGRATION Business ethics must permeate all aspects of organizational culture and be reflected in key management systems. Companies start by integrating ethics into goal setting and hiring practices. When promoting workers to higher levels within the company, ethical principles must guide incentive programs.
- IMPLEMENTATION Ethical conduct is not just an idea, but requires the implementation of a plan of change in specific areas of work in the company. Some examples are efforts to modify personnel appraisal processes, promotion of improved environmental practices and referrals to specialists when needed.
- INTERNATIONALIZATION Increased internationalization is necessary to all successful business in the 21st century. Internationalization is achieved through the formation of international partnerships, trading blocs and implementation of GATT and other free trade agreements. Clarification of an organization's own definition of integrity that transcends national borders is necessary. A resulting program is not culturally defined and requires little or no modification when applied in global contexts.

## Sample Codes To Live By—Or At Least Conduct Business By

The summaries of international codes that follow all have one thing in common. While they appeal to the social consciousness of a corporation, they also appeal to the corporation's bottom line. All the codes emphasize the business case for ethical behavior and not the philosophical. This appeal to protecting a firm's profit centers and the potential for ROI is the only realistic means to gain widespread compliance.

All the codes clearly move well beyond the business of business and implicitly recognize the power of large multinational corporations to affect societal change as well. They impose a large burden on companies, but stress the idea of sustainable development—that the payoff of a stable and successful society is a stable and successful business.

## CODE 1: THE CAUX ROUND TABLE

(full text at http://www.cauxroundtable.org/)

In a world that is experiencing profound transformations, the Caux Round Table of business leaders from Europe, Japan and the United States is committed to energizing the role of business and industry as a vital force for innovative global change. The Round Table was founded two decades ago by Frederik Philips, former President of Philips Electronics, and Olivier Giscard d'Estaing, vice-chairman of the European Institute of Business Administration (INSEAD), as a means of reducing escalating trade tensions. It is concerned with the development of constructive economic and social relationships between the participants' countries and with promoting their joint responsibilities toward the rest of the world.

At the urging of Ryuzaburo Kaku, chairman of Canon Inc., the Round Table has focused attention on the importance of global corporate responsibility in reducing social and economic threats to world peace and stability. The Round Table recognizes that shared leadership is indispensable to a revitalized and more harmonious world. It emphasizes the development of continuing friendship, understanding and cooperation, based on a common respect for the highest moral values and on responsible action by individuals in their own spheres of influence.

In many ways the Caux Round Table guidelines may be the most international and universally applicable set of ethics yet produced.

### ■ SUMMARY

The Caux Round Table believes that the world business community should play an important role in improving economic and social conditions (sustainable development). As a statement of aspirations, this document aims to express a world standard against which business behavior can be measured. It seeks to begin a process that identifies shared values and reconciles differing values, thereby developing a shared perspective on business behavior acceptable to and honored by all.

These principles are rooted in two basic ethical ideals: *KYOSEI* and human dignity. The Japanese concept of *KYOSEI* means living and working together for the common good while enabling cooperation and mutual prosperity to coexist with healthy and fair competition. "Human dignity" refers to the sacredness or value of each person as an end, not simply as a means to the fulfillment of others' purposes.

The General Principles in Section 2 seek to clarify the spirit of *KYOSEI* and "human dignity," while the specific Stakeholder Principles in Section 3 are concerned with their practical application.

Business behavior can affect relationships among nations and the prosperity and well-being of us all. Business is often the first contact between nations and, by the way in which it causes social and economic changes, has a significant impact on the level of fear or confidence felt by people worldwide. Members of the Caux Round Table place their first emphasis on putting one's own house in order and on seeking to establish what is right rather than who is right.

## CODE 2: SOCIAL ACCOUNTABILITY 8000 (SA8000)

(full text at http://www.cepaa.org)

According to *THE FINANCIAL TIMES*, SA8000 provides what other global initiatives and ethics codes have lacked: a common framework for ethical sourcing for companies of any size, type and anywhere in the world. Also, performance against the code can be measured and compared.

The certification standard, Social Accountability 8000, has been developed under the auspices of the Council on Economic Priorities Accreditation Agency (CEPAA) to promote socially responsible production in facilities worldwide. The newly founded CEPAA developed SA8000 in accordance with 12 International Labor Organization conventions and United Nations human rights treaties. The SA8000 standard represents a consensus of recommendations from the international business community, non-governmental organization, and labor organizations. The objective of this group was to develop the first auditable international standard for socially responsible trade.

CEPAA accredits independent auditing firms to monitor conformity to the SA8000 Standard, applying the same criteria used for the well-established ISO 9000 and ISO 14000 quality and environmental management system standards. To qualify for certification, organizations must meet verifiable standards for child labor, forced labor, health and safety, freedom of association, discrimination, disciplinary practices, working hours, compensation and management systems.

### ■ SUMMARY

Increased productivity, improved efficiency, reduced waste and enhanced profitability allow companies to operate consistently, achieve a competitive edge, satisfy customers' needs, encourage investment and attain national and international recognition and reputation. Organizations who implement SA 8000 are registered by an independent third party that will prove to their customers and other interested parties that they are socially responsible.

SA8000 is also designed to improve business competitiveness by:

- Increasing customer recognition and loyalty.
- Promoting a globally-recognized standard of business behavior.
- Increasing the ability of businesses to trade internationally.
- Removing the need for a business to undergo multiple audits and monitoring.

If your company meets the standard, you will earn a certificate attesting to its social accountability policies, management and operations. Auditors will visit factories and assess corporate practices on a wide range of issues: child labor, health and safety, freedom of association and the right to collective bargaining, discrimination, disciplinary practices, working hours and compensation. Auditors will also evaluate the state of your management systems to ensure ongoing conformity in each of these areas.

The goal is continuous improvement, not exclusion. If you do not initially meet the standards, your company will need to make improvements and abide by a timetable for verifying that problems have been addressed. You should also document progress in problem areas and take preventive action to avoid a recurrence.

## CODE 3: THE GLOBAL COMPACT

(full text at http:www.un.org/partners/business)

At a World Economic Forum in Davos, Switzerland, then UN Secretary-General Kofi A. Annan challenged world business leaders to "embrace and enact" the Global Compact, both in their individual corporate practices and by supporting appropriate public policies. These principles cover topics in human rights, labor and environment. For business, they include:

- Being more in touch with markets, customers and consumers by better understanding the opportunities and problems of the social context.
- The advantages of a good social reputation.
- A greater chance of a stable and harmonious atmosphere in which to do business.
- A reduction of damaging criticism, which may ultimately lead to lost investment, contracts or customers, leading to the long-term benefit of a more stable and peaceful society in which investments can prosper.

The recent volatility of international financial markets, along with cultural and social side-effects that often are perceived negatively, has set off a backlash against liberalization. A return to market protectionism and unnecessary barriers against technical and commercial innovation is all too possible. A clear demonstration that basic and popular social values are being advanced as part and parcel of the globalization process will help to ensure that markets remain open, and will truly bring the people of the world closer together.

## CODE 4: US DEPARTMENT OF COMMERCE—MODEL BUSINESS PRINCIPLES

Recognizing the positive role of US business in upholding and promoting adherence to universal standards of human rights, the US Government encourages all businesses to adopt and implement voluntary codes of conduct for doing business around the world that cover at least the following areas:

### ■ PROVISION OF A SAFE AND HEALTHY WORKPLACE

Fair employment practices, including avoidance of child and forced labor and avoidance of discrimination based on race, gender, national origin or religious beliefs; and respect for the right of association and the right to organize and bargain collectively.

### ■ RESPONSIBLE ENVIRONMENTAL PROTECTION AND ENVIRONMENTAL PRACTICES

Compliance with US and local laws promoting good business practices, including laws prohibiting illicit payments and ensuring fair competition.

Maintenance, through leadership at all levels, of a corporate culture that respects free expression consistent with legitimate business concerns, and does not condone political coercion in the workplace; that encourages good corporate citizenship and makes a positive contribution to the communities in which the company operates; and where ethical conduct is recognized, valued and exemplified by all employees.

In adopting voluntary codes of conduct that reflect these principles, US companies should serve as models and encourage similar behavior by their partners, suppliers and subcontractors. Adoption of codes of conduct reflecting these principles is voluntary. Companies are encouraged to develop their own codes of conduct appropriate to their particular circumstances. Many companies already apply statements or codes that incorporate these principles. Companies should find appropriate means to inform their shareholders and the public of actions undertaken in connection with these principles. Nothing in the principles is intended to require a company to act in violation of host country or US law. This statement of principles is not intended for legislation.

## Why Should Businesses Follow Such Codes At All?

The platitudes expressed in the sample codes are all well and good, and they seem like the right thing to do. But can a business case be made for taking such actions? If you look at the long term, the answer is yes.

### BASIC QUESTIONS AND ANSWERS

Following are some basic questions and answers about why businesses should follow the guidelines set out in the codes described above.

QUESTION: Why should a business eliminate forced labor?
ANSWER: The abolition of forced labor is an effective way of promoting economic and human development. Forced labor degrades the human capital and social stability necessary to achieve sustainable economic development and secure investments. Forced labor robs societies of the opportunities to apply and develop human resources for the labor market of today and to develop the skills in education of children for the labor markets of tomorrow.

QUESTION: Why should a business promote the abolition of child labor?
ANSWER: Basically, the abolition of child labor promotes skilled and healthy workers for tomorrow. The effective abolition of child labor is a goal in itself, but it is also a powerful way of promoting economic and human development. Child labor degrades the human capital necessary to achieve sustainable economic development. The poverty-child labor cycle results in scores of under skilled, unqualified workers. If child labor is allowed to continue today, badly needed skills might be in short supply tomorrow. Children who do not complete their primary education (assuming it is available) are likely to remain illiterate and never acquire the skills needed to get a job and contribute to the development of a modern economy.

Also, the use of child labor can ruin a company's reputation. This is especially true in the case of transnational supply and service chains, where the economic exploitation of children, even by a business partner, can damage a brand image and have strong repercussions on profit and stock value.

QUESTION: Why should a business eliminate discrimination?
ANSWER: Discrimination in employment and occupation lowers the level of productivity in the workplace, and slows economic growth for society as a whole. The lack of a climate of tolerance results in missed opportunities for development of skills and infrastructure to strengthen competitiveness in the global economy. It can also narrow the labor pool from which a company hires.

QUESTION: Why should businesses adopt a precautionary approach to its environmental matters? That is, act to preempt potential damage caused by operations?

ANSWER: It is more cost-effective to take early actions to ensure that irreversible environmental damage does not occur. Adopting a precautionary approach makes sound business sense. While it is true that preventing environmental damage entails both opportunity and implementation costs, correcting environmental harm after it has occurred can cost much more (e.g. treatment costs, company image).

Also, avoiding risks makes a better investment. Investing in production methods that are not sustainable, deplete resources and degrade the environment has a lower, long-term return than investing in sustainable operations. In turn, improving environmental performance means less financial risk, an important consideration for insurers

QUESTION: Why should business promote greater environmental responsibility?

ANSWER: Better environmental management is a key source of competitive advantage for businesses. A wide range of benefits accrue from improved environmental performance, ranging from reduced effluent charges to better community relations. Better environmental management and better management are the same thing: a company that manages its impact on the environment well is a well-managed company. Finally, companies today find that maintaining financial performance and improving it over the long-term requires a balancing of three types of capital—social, economic and environmental.

QUESTION: Why should business develop, use and diffuse Environmentally Sound Technologies (EST)?

ANSWER: Production processes and technology that do not use resources efficiently generate residues and discharge wastes. For companies responsible for treating and storing the pollutants this represents on-going costs. Also, technological innovation creates new business opportunities for companies. Implementing ESTs helps a company reduce the use of raw materials leading to increased efficiency and overall competitiveness of the company. ESTs reduce day-to-day operating inefficiencies, emissions of environmental contaminants, worker exposure to hazardous materials and risk of technological disasters. Technologies that use materials more efficiently and cleanly can be applied in most companies with long-term economic and environmental benefits.

CHAPTER 6

# Ethics and the Boardroom

*Assume a virtue if you have it not.*
*– Shakespeare*

THE DRAMATIC RISE IN CROSS BORDER capital flows and international investments has created a sense of urgency to develop global standards of business ethics. As equity markets continue to globalize, companies throughout the world are being forced to look at various standards of corporate governance that affect their activities. Corporate governance is a term that describes how those entrusted with day-to-day management of a company's affairs are held responsible by shareholders, the community, governments, customers and employees. It is also concerned with communication and how a company presents itself to the wider world and corporate stakeholders including shareholders, employees, potential investors, customers and regulators.

Essentially, corporate governance is about the exercise of control over corporate entities. It is concerned with the structure and processes of the governing body (often the board of directors) and of the directors' relationships with shareholders, regulators, auditors, top management and any other legitimate stakeholders.

## Strong Support For International Standards

A strong system of ethical corporate governance can produce major benefits for societies—not the least of which is the prevention of large-scale banking and financial crises (witness what poor corporate governance practices did to Asia during the financial collapse of 1997-98). Strong corporate governance rules and procedures also prevent insiders from stripping any remaining value out of an insolvent firm, leaving workers and minority shareholders holding the bag.

Corporations throughout the world have become increasingly dependent on open market equity to finance their expansion. Cross border sales and purchases of bonds and equities by US investors have risen from the equivalent of 9 percent of gross domestic product in 1980 to more than 170 percent in the mid 1990s. Daily foreign exchange turnover is up from US$15 billion in 1973 to US$2 trillion by 2008. The volume of cross-border financial transactions in London, Tokyo and New York alone is over US$1 trillion per day. All this adds up to a shifting of economic clout to investors with equity stakes. Increasingly, these investors are foreign to the country of the firm's registry, and thus, governance structures are under pressure from cross-border investors to be more transparent.

On average about 35 percent of the stock of companies on the French stock exchange is foreign-owned; the comparable percentages are 25 percent for Germany, 35 percent for Spain and 40 percent for the Netherlands. Many of these investors are ignorant of the local governance procedures that oversee their investments.

How strong is the sentiment for a global standard of corporate governance practices? A survey of major institutional investors found that 25 percent in the US, 60 percent in France, 52 percent in Australia and 25 percent in Britain said that the realization of that goal was extremely important to them and considered a top priority.

## Board Secrets

Most boards of directors prefer to operate out of public view. This is not because they are necessarily doing anything illegal but because they deal with proprietary information. Management runs the business, but it is the directors who ensure that it is being well run and properly strategized. This holds true regardless of the company location. Be it New York, Beijing, Moscow or London, investors rarely get to see what actually goes on inside the boardroom. Indeed, the board meeting remains for some one of the business world's greatest unsolved mysteries.

The operative words in governance today seem to be preventive maintenance. After a decade in which one seemingly strong company after another stumbled—Enron in the United States, Daewoo in South Korea, Mitsubishi in Japan, Barings in the UK—governance is now focused on stopping corporate downfalls before they happen.

In boardrooms across the world, directors are struggling to redefine the rules under which they should—and shouldn't—operate. In the past a directorship was a relatively simple task. Directors had to attend the occasional meeting (often for a fee), vote on a proposal or two put forth by the company CEO, perhaps ask a few questions about forward strategy, set a pay scale for senior managers and have lunch afterwards. That has changed. Around the world, legal actions are being brought against companies, boards and, in some cases, individual directors alleging negligence, abuse of power or infringement of the rights of minority shareholders.

## What Should Directors Do?

Directors have the ultimate responsibility to monitor the activities of the top management of a corporation and to act if not satisfied. The primary duty of a director, in law, is to act honestly and ethically in good faith for the benefit of all the shareholders, giving them equal, sufficient and accurate information on all issues that could affect their interests. Directors may not treat the company as though it existed for their personal benefit (though some clearly do, even in countries that pride themselves on enlightened governance rules and high ethical standards).

The board of directors is the overall decision-making body in the modern corporation. Yet most directors, and there are thousands of them around the world, have never had any formal training for their work as directors. This situation is somewhat similar to the position of corporate managers in the 1950s, before the growth of management training, management theories and business schools.

The basic duties of the board of directors can be summed up as follows:

- Determine the organization's mission and objectives.
- Select the executive staff and guide the hiring process.
- Provide ongoing support and guidance for management.
- Ensure effective strategic planning.
- Provide adequate resources and oversee allocation.
- Determine the organization's operations.
- Assist in devising and enhancing the organization's public image.
- Provide judgements on internal company disputes.
- Monitor the ongoing performance of operations and management.

## Not All Boards Act The Same

While most transnational companies have an international flavor on their corporate boards, the prevailing business culture of the home country usually plays a major role in how the board acts and guides the vision of its members. Nor surprisingly, a survey by the international consulting and executive search firm Egon Zehnder International found only one characteristic common to boards worldwide: a commitment to making a profit. The boards of all 188 companies in 24 nations surveyed in Europe, Asia, Latin America and North America ranked this as their top priority. This is certainly not surprising since that is the point of entering into a "for profit" business. However, even the boards of non-profit organizations are also concerned with cash flow.

Besides that one single issue, the priorities, behaviors and visions of corporate boards varied widely according to geography.

- STOCK OWNERSHIP BY DIRECTORS Among North American companies, 54 percent require board members to own shares. Australia came in second with 47 percent. Asia trailed the field with 10 percent.
- CEO SUCCESSION While an important issue in North America, where 47 percent of the companies said their boards discussed possible successors to the corporate top manager, boards elsewhere rarely discussed CEO succession. Less than 25 percent of boards worldwide outside of North America discussed it.
- OUTSIDE DIRECTORS 82 percent of the companies in Australia and 74 percent of those in North America said their non-executive directors met independently of the managers sitting on the board. In Latin America, the percentage fell to 5 percent. Are CEOs told what was discussed at such meetings? "Always," reported 61 percent of North American companies. "Sometimes," according to all the Latin American companies.
- NUMBER OF BOARD MEETINGS PER YEAR Six to eight is fairly common. However, 33 percent of the Latin American companies held a dozen meetings or more; only 2 percent in North America made such a claim.
- THE TIME IT TAKES A DIRECTOR TO GET UP TO SPEED About half of all companies said it took six to 11 months. But 43 percent of the Asian companies said their directors could do the job within five months, versus 7 percent in North America. In seeming contrast, in Asia only 5 percent of the companies offer formal training for board members versus 58 percent in North America.

## Is Asia An Exception?

Indeed, Asian companies have unique circumstances that represent potential challenges to the adoption of international standards of corporate governance. This Asian market environment, where corporations are often clan-based and secrecy is a cultural custom, has different ownership structures and business practices. These create alternatives to the types of corporate governance standards that Western investors, particularly those in the UK and North American countries, are accustomed to observe. Anomalies in corporate governance practices in Asia, however, are likely to exacerbate investor caution and skepticism. The bottom line is simple: if Asian companies wish to attract Western investors (and not all of them do), these companies will face greater investor pressure to either conform to or reconcile their practices with Western standards.

## The Facts of Life

In this era of highly mobile equity and volatile capital markets, there are three key facts of life that are forcing companies and boards of directors to adopt higher ethical standards when it comes to how they are governed—in essence driving the corporate world toward a set of international governance standards.

- US INSTITUTIONAL INVESTORS Compared to the rest of the world, US institutional investors are truly the big kids on the block. US institutional investments dwarf those for all other countries, giving the type of corporate governance activism and demands for greater transparency in financial dealings that are common in the United States great potential influence over global investments and companies.
- SOPHISTICATED TRANSNATIONAL INVESTORS Companies participating in global equity markets are increasingly encountering transnational investors who are evaluating their performance according to an evolving set of global governance standards.
- BROAD EQUITY PARTICIPATION The "old boy network" of cross holdings and closely-held shares common outside of the United States is dissolving. As major blocks of these once closely-held shares are unwound in favor of broader equity participation, minority shareholders are insisting that their position must be improved in regard to fairness of voting rights and ability to provide appropriate input to management.

## Unwinding the Investment Web

At the turn of the century, the US economic model resembled current models in Germany, France and Japan. Capital expansion was accomplished with retained earnings, loans from a closely-knit banking community and through substantial long-term equity raised via extensive and virtually permanent corporate cross-shareholdings. Gradually, the US developed a broad and highly liquid equity market with dispersed ownership. This model is now being emulated around the world as countries rely more on equity market expansion in place of traditional patterns of highly concentrated ownership among founders, families, or small numbers of dominant institutional or corporate shareholders.

In the US and the UK, institutional investors have long held the lion's share of stock in the largest 25 corporations (57.2 percent and 57.7 percent, respectively). By comparison, the largest 25 companies in France, Germany and Japan have much less ownership by such institutional investors and a greater amount is closely held by banks and other corporations with direct links to the firm. But the situation is changing rapidly.

- In France, closely held ownership is close to 30 percent.
- In Germany, closely held ownership is lower at 18 percent.
- In Japan, closely held ownership is even lower at 14 percent.

NOTE: Just 10 percent of Germans hold company shares compared to 50 percent of Americans. The number of Germans holding shares could explode as more closely-held German company shares are made available and pension law reform creates individual stock retirement accounts for German workers. However, the Germans are much more risk averse than Americans, making it more likely that the Germans will opt for bonds.

## Changing European Equity Culture—But at a Price

Perhaps the most pressure for aligning corporate governance procedures is being felt in Europe because of the adoption of the Euro as a common currency and the increase flow of outside capital from the US.

Within Europe there is strong evidence of a convergence of governance and corporate cultures which is the direct result of market forces. For centuries there have been two very different and competing business cultures present in Europe. The US/UK model (a.k.a. Anglo-Saxon) is characterized by large, liquid capital markets, a growing concentration of shareholding power by institutional investors and a market for corporate control via takeover bids. The contrasting "continental" model is characterized by less liquid markets and a greater concentration of shareholder power with banks, "old money" families and governments. In France, the business system is built upon an elite group of like-minded managers (most of whom were educated at the same universities) who have honed their business skills by serving for a few years in a government ministry. Italy has a similar structure of business elite known as the *SALOTTO BUONO*. These systems are very different from the one that operates in more liberal market-oriented economies such as the US, Canada and Britain.

However, in recent years there has been a perceptible convergence of two different European cultures. In Britain, the shift is away from short-term profit horizons on the part of management and investors, towards a commitment to enhancing long-term shareholder value. This will be accomplished by paying more attention to all stakeholders, not just shareholders, through a more serious approach to ethics and corporate social responsibility. In continental European countries, there is a gradual merging of long- and short-term aims caused by the need to raise external financing on world markets and by privatization programs.

After centuries of very different business cultures, the fact that corporations are moving toward some standardization in the area of corporate governance practices is testimony to the impact of globalization. One of the first major continental European corporations to take the plunge was Daimler-Benz of Germany, which was required to adopt American accounting standards in order to list its shares in New York. When it did so, it was accused of treachery by other German firms because the system of US accounting required for the listing was more open than the German system. Within a few short years of that move, at least nine German companies were listed on the New York Stock Exchange along with 19 Dutch, 16 French, 11 Italian and 10 Spanish companies.

But all this upheaval in continental Europe is coming at a heavy social price. Because the banks and corporations used to hold each other's stock, there was little pressure from such investors to meet tough bottom line performance measures. For decades following the end of World War II the system worked. German companies had two advantages: stable sources of capital and patient shareholders. Now, facing more short-term pressures to return dividends, the big employers are no longer so benevolent. In the first six months of 2001, some of the biggest corporations that started to broaden their stock ownership announced worker layoffs: the electronics maker Siemens AG fired 6,000 workers, Grundig AG, the maker of televisions and radios, laid off 900, and steel maker Thyssen Krupp AG dismissed 3,200 workers.

## America's Way or the Highway

Many international business people will argue that when talking about the globalization of business standards, people really mean the Americanization of such standards. In some cases this may be true. The area of corporate governance is one such case, and in the view of the largest global investors it is justified given the place of the US in the world economy.

Outside of the US, there is significant pressure to bring disclosure of information to the investing public up to US standards. Although currently meant only for US corporations, Regulation Fair Disclosure (Regulation FD) is expected to shape the style and methods of communication between shareholders and corporations internationally as well.

Regulation Fair Disclosure which was adopted by the SEC in August 2000 and became effective in October of that same year, will have a profound impact on disclosure and corporate communication practices worldwide. By barring companies from disclosing material, nonpublic information to a select group and requiring the same information to be issued to the public either through a press release or through an SEC filing, the regulation is geared toward creating a level playing field for all market participants.

In many sophisticated European investment circles, there is concern that American interests carry disproportionate weight, that European companies may go too far in trying to accommodate a different business culture.

## Ethics Figure in Investment Decisions

For an expanding number of institutional investors, the attitude of the management of a company toward corporate governance is a crucial factor in whether an investment makes sense. Open and free financial disclosure and transparency are also key issues.

A survey by the international consulting firm PriceWaterhouseCoopers found that investment decisions are still generally based on "hard" quantifiable factors as opposed to "soft" corporate governance type issues. Still, some of these "soft" factors are growing in importance. Among them are clear and consistent accounting practices, providing reliable and accurate information for analysis, and conducting high quality and trustworthy communications with investors. While profit growth remains a key factor in investment decisions, it is increasingly the quality of those profits that are meaningful to investors and will draw their investment cash.

Investors do seem to be more likely to invest in well-run companies with high standards of both corporate governance and business ethics. The PriceWaterhouse-Coopers survey, which focused on companies in Asia, found that more than one in three investors would not invest in a company if they were not satisfied with the existence of a code of corporate governance and business ethics; three in five investors would not invest in a company if they were dissatisfied with the level of disclosure in the company's accounts; and a significant number of investors would not invest if they were dissatisfied with a company's relationship with its regulators (34 percent) or in a company that attracted negative public or press comment (25 percent).

## Keeping Score

Acknowledging the importance of corporate governance in investment decisions, and the difficulty obtaining honest information on some company structures, the international investment rating company Standard & Poor's launched a Corporate Governance rating system; it gives its opinion about the extent to which a company conforms to contemporary international codes and guidelines of good governance practices.

The rating system analyzes a company's corporate governance standards and issues a corporate governance score based on two levels—country level and company level. The rating system was launched in Russia and rolled out in Asia and hopes to achieve comparability of governance practices on a global basis. The company says that while it understands why governance practices differ in various market environments, it will not compromise the fundamental assessment of how a company's specific governance practices and structures support the broad-and overarching-principles of fairness, responsibility, transparency and accountability. Corporate governance rating systems covering all listed companies have also been proposed in Hong Kong and the Philippines by other rating firms.

## Making Accountants Accountable

It is clear to international accountants, government regulators and global investors that if companies are going to be attractive to foreign investors, there is a need for a global accountancy standard. Many European companies, again under pressure because of the introduction of the euro, are beginning to see the benefits of adopting an internationally recognized accounting framework, such as those presented by the International Accounting Standards Committee (IASC).

This committee was formed for the purpose of bringing financial accounting and reporting standards into closer conformity on a global basis. The IASC has 14 voting members, which are made up of public accounting organizations, the International Association of Financial Analysts and the business communities of various countries or groups of countries. Over the years, the IASC has issued in excess of 30 standards while its recognition and acceptance are growing at an impressive rate. The acceptance of a set of global accounting standards would mean that companies, regardless of where they are based, could list their shares on any capital market on earth.

At present, each country has its own set of rules on ethics, disclosure and transparency that companies must meet to list shares on their markets. More than 50 nations—with the major exception of the US—have welcomed these global accounting rules. The US views the proposed global standards as less stringent than those already in place in the US. However, a study of eight multinational firms using the international rules found that the results they produced were very close to those received when using the US accounting procedures.

NOTE: European and American views on accounting are not all that far apart. There is a difference in the way assets are revalued during the period in which a company owns them. Americans keep the original (historical) value on their books while most EU firms regularly revalue their assets. This is none too surprising since European firms often hold some assets for centuries rather than decades. The European accounting standards are also more akin to guidelines than to "hard and fast" rules. The stringency of American accounting was held to blame for the Enron implosion since static rules tend to invite circumvention. The vagueness of Europe's rules led to the scandals at Italy's Parmalat and the Dutch grocery retailer Ahold.

## The Need Is Clearly There

The development of high-quality international accounting standards is important because discrepancies in methods of accounting for identical transactions undermine the transparency and comparability of financial statements—and thus, inhibit potential investment.

The widely reported Daimler-Chrysler situation is a case in point—when reporting under US accounting standards, the company reported a loss; under German standards, the company regularly reported profits. When accounting experts cannot agree on what constitutes a "fair and true" picture of a company's results of operations, what message is sent to the investing public? Investors simply aren't sure which set of results to believe and are unable to judge a company's true financial health.

There is the argument that since business traditions and national laws vary country by country, different accounting and reporting treatment for different circumstances may be justifiable. However, different accounting and reporting treatment for the same facts and circumstances is confusing and a disservice to the investor. International harmonization should, by definition, solve these issues. International accounting standards would provide for a number of alternative treatments of accounts.

---

NOTE: Part of the problem surrounding the adoption of a single standard is the requirement set forth by the Security and Exchange Commission in the United States for public disclosure. The rules demand a considerable baring of the corporate soul and even require firms to disclose problems they "think" might happen. Some European cultures and almost all Asian cultures are not comfortable with this process of "doing one's laundry in public."

---

## Private Sector Push

While the adoption of a set of international standards in most areas of business is usually the work of governments or multinational political bodies, such as the United Nations, in the area of corporate governance it is the private sector that is pushing towards a set of global standards and practices. Though governance laws and regulations are moving to higher standards in countries all over the world, transnational investors (who are generally far more attuned to finance than government representatives) are demanding even higher standards than required by home country law.

Most investors recognize the effects of local governance practices when assessing companies abroad. However, certain minimum standards have begun to emerge that clearly influence transnational investor expectations around the world. The global rule of thumb seems to be that greater disclosure and transparency in how a company is run leads to higher valuations. Research clearly shows that investors are prepared to pay substantial premiums for companies that can show good corporate governance.

In recent years, increasing numbers of institutional investors—certainly in the US and to a lesser extent in the UK—have begun to publish their corporate governance principles. For investors who hold stock in hundreds of companies, this is a practical way to convey their governance philosophy to the management of each company in which they invest. Company boards ignore these rules at their own risk.

For example, Hermes, the largest British pension fund investor, holds stock in all of the largest 900 companies in the UK. Every year it sends its governance principles to the chairman of each company. Hermes stresses that this does not mean that it takes a "one size fits all" approach; it recognizes that each company should be treated separately because the goal of long term shareholder value may be achieved in different ways in different companies.

The organization demands, however, that if a company thinks it should be an exception to Hermes' basic rules, they had better contact Hermes and be ready to explain why they should be an exception, and to debate the issues. Obviously, if a company is performing well, Hermes will give them a certain amount of leeway; but if a company is performing poorly, then Hermes will put the squeeze on them to conform to its own governance rules.

## An Elusive Goal

The actual achievement of a global ethics standard or a set of international corporate governance or accounting practices is probably still a long way off. The devil, as always, is in the details. But there are signs of progress. In December 2000, the European Union Council of Ministers agreed on a draft text to establish a European Company Statute—30 years after it was first proposed. The statute would give companies operating in more than one European country the option of being established as a single company under EU law. This would allow the company to operate throughout the EU with one set of rules and reporting systems rather than being forced to operate according to the different national laws of states where the company has a subsidiary.

While this may seem to be a good sign, no one realistically expects rapid passage by the European Parliament. Consider this: when the EU set up a commission in the early 1990s to come up with a common electrical plug for all Europe, the idea was met with great enthusiasm. After six years of meetings, debates and engineering experiments, Europe still has eight different plugs and sockets. No one was willing to give up their current design.

EDITOR'S NOTE: Cultural differences regarding accounting do not just dwell on matters of format. Sometimes the very intent of the process is intrinsically different. As a French accountant remarked to the editor recently, "In the US, accounting is designed to facilitate business. In France, it is designed to facilitate the taxman."

## International Corporate Governance Codes of Conduct and Ethics

The number of suggested corporate governance codes has exploded in recent years as key investors—and in some cases, governments representing those investors—attempt to level the playing field in international capital markets. Most sets of these guidelines provide details about the functions of the board in protecting the company, its shareholders and its stakeholders. These include concerns about corporate strategy, risk, executive compensation and performance, as well as accounting and reporting systems. The following sets of guidelines provide a representative look of standards offered by organizations around the world.

### OECD PRINCIPLES

The OECD (Organization of Economic Cooperation and Development) brings together 30 countries sharing the principles of the market economy, pluralist democracy and respect for human rights. The original 20 members of the OECD are located in the Western countries of Europe and North America. Next came Japan, Australia, New Zealand and Finland. More recently, Mexico, the Czech Republic, Hungary, Poland, Korea and the Slovak Republic have joined.

The OECD guidelines are somewhat general and both the Anglo-American system and the Continental European systems would be quite consistent with them. However, there is growing pressure to put more enforcement mechanisms in the guidelines.

### OECD Code of Conduct and Ethics

In summary, they include the following elements.

1. THE RIGHTS OF SHAREHOLDERS

These include a set of rights, including secure ownership of shares, the right to full disclosure of information, voting rights, participation in decisions on sale or modification of corporate assets, including mergers and new share issues. The guidelines specify a host of other issues connected to the basic concern of protecting the value of the corporation.

2. THE EQUITABLE TREATMENT OF SHAREHOLDERS

Here the OECD is concerned with protecting minority shareholders' rights by setting up systems that keep insiders (including managers and directors) from taking advantage of their roles. Insider trading, for example, is explicitly prohibited and directors should disclose any material interests regarding transactions.

3. THE ROLE OF STAKEHOLDERS IN CORPORATE GOVERNANCE

The OECD recognizes there are other stakeholders in companies in addition to shareholders. Banks, bond holders and workers, for example, are important stakeholders in the way in which companies perform and make decisions. The OECD guidelines lay out several general provisions for protecting stakeholder interests.

4. DISCLOSURE AND TRANSPARENCY

The OECD also lays out a number of provisions for the disclosure and communication of key facts about the company, ranging from financial details to governance structures—including the board of directors and their remuneration. The guidelines also specify that annual audits should be performed by independent auditors in accordance with high quality standards.

5. THE RESPONSIBILITIES OF THE BOARD

Here the OECD spells out the key functions for boards of directors, the basics of sound corporate governance and the duties and responsibilities of individual directors. It urges complete transparency in relations between the board and company management.

## International Corporate Governance Network

In order to ensure that corporate governance strategies would be shared across markets, an association of global institutional investors, stock exchanges and governance experts formed the International Corporate Governance Network (ICGN). During one of its earliest conferences, the ICGN adopted the world's first best practice standards for cross-border share voting.

Adopted at the annual conference in Frankfurt, Germany, the ICGN developed its own set of corporate governance principles based on those of the OECD. However, the ICGN felt the OECD lacked detail: "While the ICGN considers the OECD Principles the necessary bedrock of good corporate governance, it holds that amplifications are required to give them sufficient force. In particular, the ICGN believes that companies around the world deserve clear, concrete guidance on how the OECD Principles can best be implemented." The ICGN Statement on

Global Corporate Governance Principles, therefore, provides what it calls a "working kit" of corporate governance criteria.

1. CORPORATE OBJECTIVE

The overriding objective of the corporation should be to optimize, over time, returns to shareholders. To achieve this objective, the corporation should endeavor to ensure the long-term viability of its business and to manage effectively its relationships with stakeholders.

2. COMMUNICATIONS AND REPORTING

Corporations should disclose accurate, adequate and timely information in particular meeting market guidelines where they exist, so as to allow investors to make informed decisions about the acquisition, ownership obligations and rights and sale of shares.

3. VOTING RIGHTS

Corporations' ordinary shares should feature one vote for each share. Corporations should act to ensure the owners' rights to vote. Fiduciary investors have a responsibility to vote. Regulators and law should facilitate voting rights and timely disclosure of the levels of voting.

4. CORPORATE BOARDS

The board of directors or supervisory board as an entity, and each of its members as an individual, is a fiduciary for all shareholders, and should be accountable to the shareholder body as a whole. Each member should stand for election on a regular basis.

Corporations should disclose upon appointment to the board, and thereafter in each annual report or proxy statement, information on the identities, core competencies, professional or other backgrounds, factors affecting independence, and overall qualifications of board members and nominees, so as to enable investors to weigh the value they add to the company. Information on the appointment procedure should also be disclosed annually.

Boards should include a sufficient number of independent non-executive members with appropriate competencies. Responsibilities should include monitoring and contributing effectively to the strategy and performance of management, staffing key committees of the board, and influencing the conduct of the board as a whole. Accordingly, independent non-executives should comprise no fewer than three members and as much as a substantial majority.

Audit, remuneration and nomination board committees should be comprised wholly or predominantly of independent non-executives.

5. CORPORATE REMUNERATION POLICIES

Remuneration of corporate directors or supervisory board members and key executives should be aligned with the interests of shareholders.

Corporations should disclose in each annual report or proxy statement the board's policies on remuneration—and, preferably, the remuneration of individual board members and top executives—so that investors can judge whether corporate pay policies and practices meet that standard.

6. STRATEGIC FOCUS

Major strategic modifications to the core business(es) of a corporation should not be made without prior shareholder approval of the proposed modification.

Shareholders should be given sufficient information about any such proposal sufficiently early, to allow them to make an informed judgement and exercise their voting rights.

7. OPERATING PERFORMANCE

Corporate governance practices should focus board attention on optimizing, over time, the company's operating performance. In particular, the company should strive to excel in specific sector peer group comparisons.

8. SHAREHOLDER RETURNS

Corporate governance practices should also focus board attention on optimizing, over time, the returns to shareholders. In particular, the company should strive to excel in comparison with the specific equity sector peer group benchmark.

9. CORPORATE CITIZENSHIP

Boards that strive for active cooperation between corporations and stakeholders will be most likely to create wealth, employment and sustainable economies.

10. CORPORATE GOVERNANCE IMPLEMENTATION

Where codes of best corporate governance practice exist, they should be applied pragmatically. Where they do not yet exist, investors and others should endeavor to develop them.

CHAPTER 7

# Shareholder Activism: Keeping Corporations on Their Ethical Toes

*IT IS BETTER TO LIGHT A CANDLE THAN CURSE THE DARK.*
– ANCIENT CHINESE PROVERB

WHEN IT CAME TO HOLDING STOCK in one of the world's major corporations, it used to be a case of love it or leave it. Shareholders of all stripes who didn't like the deal corporate management set up, or objected to an investment in a country where human rights were routinely violated, or simply were offended by the way a company treated its employees, had a single option. They had to follow what some have called the first "Wall Street Rule": when disenchanted with management, sell your holdings.

## Developing Ethical and Financial Responsibility

Today, the relationship is very different. Investors from the United States to Europe (and even Japan) are attempting to make corporations more ethically and financially responsible through shareholder activism. This often confrontational attitude by shareholders in the governance of companies is a relatively recent development.

In the past, walking away often meant selling big chunks of a company's stock, which could drive the share price down. Virtue had a price. Depending on the size of the investment, it may actually be more expensive to walk away from corporate stock than to work with company management to change corporate behavior. In some cases, even walking away wasn't really an option. Large institutional investors (such as pension funds, trusts, mutual funds and endowments) all have only one thing in common: they manage assets on behalf of someone else. They also frequently hold indexed portfolios, which preclude the sale of a specific stock, regardless of its performance indicators or its underlying corporate ethics. The only route for change left was from within.

Public opinion has begun calling for boards of directors to exercise their powers in the interests of the many people who can be affected, rather than solely in the interests of shareholders and the bottom line. Shareholders now have much more information with which to challenge the board on both financial and ethical issues. The premise behind shareholder activism is that organizations can use their investment strength to bring about social justice through social change. Shareholder activism (or advocacy) describes the actions many socially aware investors take in their role as owners of corporations. These efforts include discussions with companies on issues of concern and submitting and voting proxy resolutions. Socially responsible proxy resolutions are generally aimed at influencing corporate behavior toward adapting a more responsible level of corporate citizenship, steering management toward action that enhances the well-being of all the company's stakeholders and, most importantly, improving financial performance over time.

Most institutional investors agree that regular engagement, or "turning up the heat from time to time," is the best form of intervention. This may involve attending annual meetings and voting on the issue, or voicing their views to the press. Publishing corporate governance guidelines and making corporate management aware of these demands has also proven to be an effective weapon for shareholder activists.

The institutional activism movement has not lacked for skeptics. Business leaders and politicians have argued that large pension funds lack the expertise and ability to serve as effective monitors of corporate performance and lack the understanding of long-term corporate strategy. Their interference in the governance of companies can actually hurt performance or skew priorities.

---

WARNING: Shareholders must be wary of having their financial power hijacked by organized stakeholder groups who are less concerned about the long-term financial welfare of a firm than the cause they represent. The cause (e.g., child labor, worker's rights) may seem virtuous on the surface, but investors must look at the motivation for raising an issue before they throw their considerable financial weight behind it. Some stakeholder groups are actually anti-capitalist groups in "sheep's clothing" and have their own ethical issues that need to be resolved.

---

## The Roots of Activism

The roots of activism have taken hold in the changing nature of world investment patterns. As institutional investors amass a burgeoning percentage of corporate equity, so have they gained shareholder power.

The phenomena had its origins in the US. It became formalized during the hostile takeover period of the early 1980s when corporate management appeared to have lost touch with the concerns of common shareholders, instead focusing on purely managerial concerns—especially when it came to lining individuals' pockets. Conflicts of interest became so common—and obvious—they were impossible to ignore. Corporate raiders (or corporate strategists, depending on your outlook) used junk bonds to take many public companies private, broke them apart and then resold the assets in pieces. Often, the result was socially devastating in the form of factory closings and lost jobs.

---

NOTE: Many of the companies that were treated in this manner were, admittedly, unhealthy or burdened with overpriced union contracts. It was the methodology used, not the underlying problems, that incensed activists.

---

## Institutional Dissent

Prior to the 1980s, shareholder activism was confined to a smattering of individuals with political axes to grind and a distrust of corporate power. Publicity was their main goal; they also hoped that the public spotlight would create outrage among the general public and other shareholders who would then pressure management or legislators to change corporate policy. Other goals included efforts to create a more self-conscious business community and to simply to make life miserable for management.

## Churches

Religious groups have been longstanding members of the shareholder activism movement. They grounded their activism in a religious commitment to social justice and they often used selective investment screens to avoid "sin" companies; many still do not invest in entertainment companies, such as casinos or those producing military technology, tobacco or alcohol products. A clear win for religious groups in the early 1980s was the adoption of World Health Organization (WHO) guidelines on the sale of infant formula in developing countries by global commodity companies.

## Shareholder Activists: Whiners or Winners?

Shareholder activism is not just about confrontation and challenge. In fact, it is more a process of negotiation and compromise. Though the world media has focused on the filing of proxy resolutions aimed at changing corporate behavior, such resolutions are really a last resort. Shareholder activists usually file resolutions only after they have failed to reach an agreement on contentious issues through negotiation with management.

Shareholder actions usually begin with an attempt to engage management in a dialogue on a specific issue. A proxy resolution is the "stick" that makes palatable the "carrot" of discussion. Even after a resolution is filed, compromise may occur and the resolution may be withdrawn. If it does go to a vote, it is rare for a shareholder resolution to pass. While on the surface it may look like a defeat for activists, it has served the purpose of rousing public interest, and sometimes, publicly embarrassing corporate management and inflicting damage to the corporate reputation—the latter is something that may eventually hurt the long-term bottom line, so these activists may back off. The reality is that once on the table, the issues raised by shareholder resolutions rarely go away on their own. Consequently, management tends to resist even simple revisions fearing that such action is the "thin edge of the wedge" of a much greater level of interference.

## Investors of the World Unite!

On issues of intervention, many institutional investors take different approaches domestically and internationally. In their home countries, they may tend to hold larger percentages of company stock and have more intimate relationships with company management, allowing them more direct intervention. When they invest abroad, they may have smaller stakes in companies and only a superficial understanding of the local market, forcing a more indirect approach.

A striking development is the extent of communication among institutions around the world. Institutional investors abroad are able to give support to local investors and learn about key issues in their particular markets. When possible, they also try to forge alliances with local investors to share knowledge and expertise, creating a world of global investors with similar concerns.

This trend became clearly evident in the mid 1990s when TIAA-CREF—a US pension fund and the largest private pension plan in the world, with more than US$260 billion under management, extended its corporate governance initiatives to Europe.

While most of these initiatives involve private meetings, one European corporate governance initiative was widely publicized, and that involved a French company called Eramet.

The French government, which in addition to CREF was a major stockholder in the company, intended to give one of the company's nickel mines away to resolve an outside dispute. TIAA-CREF objected on the grounds that the mine belonged to the shareholders in common; it argued that the government should buy the mine first from Eramet before giving it away. TIAA-CREF introduced a resolution that won enthusiastic support from Société Générale (a leading French bank soon to face its own ethical problems in 2008), and other investors. The resolution not only led to changes in Eramet's management, it also raised the issue of corporate governance among business leaders in Europe.

## As Global Capital Moves, So Do Investors

As investor activism spreads, more and more Europeans buy shares and European companies must be more respectful of the rights of minority investors. One example: A Paris court blocked Schneider Electric's proposed US$7.1 billion takeover of Legrand, a rival maker of electrical equipment, following a suit by minority shareholders in Legrand, who argued that the terms of the deal discriminated against their class of holdings.

The message to French companies was clear: they can no longer treat their investors, especially minority shareholders, with disdain. Rather, they must fairly weigh the interests of all their owners when considering mergers. It is a message that companies across continental Europe are increasingly having to heed.

Shareholder activism has even come to Japan—a country where the questioning of authority and open protest in business are rare. The MAC Japan Active Shareholder Fund was launched as the country's first mutual fund dedicated to better corporate governance through shareholder activism.

NOTE: Japan has also had another tradition of "shareholder" activism in which members of criminal gangs (*yakuza*) bought company shares and then threatened to disrupt corporate meetings. They blackmailed management to avoid the disruption. Many global corporations find little difference in the methods (if not motivation) of the yakuza and those of shareholder/stakeholder activists in getting their way. The violence that often accompanies anti-globalization rallies does not help to discredit the comparison.

## Executive Pay On Display

There is one area of corporate policy where shareholder activism can claim global success. It is in the area of public disclosure of senior executive pay. Shareholders had reason to be upset. In the US, for example, CEO compensation increased by 212 percent in the 1990s, as opposed to factory workers who saw their earnings increase by only 54 percent. In Japan, by contrast, the average CEO makes 17 times what the average worker makes—versus 85 times for CEOs of major American corporations. Europe is not far behind the US when it comes to executive pay excess. The typical European CEO now earns about 75 percent of the average US CEO.

Due to shareholder protests and demands, many governments throughout the world have forced disclosure of management pay rates, bonuses and retirement packages. In the early 1990s, not a single large French, German or Japanese company chose to disclose remuneration details for individual top executives. That is beginning to change. In Britain, the government is closer to requiring companies to put an annual resolution to shareholders to approve the report of the board remuneration committee. In France, the government drafted statute changes that would require release of details of the remuneration awarded the top two officers in a company. In Germany, the Socialist party (which strongly promoted full disclosure of individual pay while in the opposition through most of the 1990s) is considering legislation requiring release of such figures. In Japan, one company announced that it had formed an advisory panel of outsiders to provide recommendations on executive pay; another small firm—People Co—became the first listed corporation in Japan to disclose pay details for individual directors and top executives.

NOTE: General Electric was forced to review and reduce the retirement package of its legendary former CEO, Jack Welch after the exorbitance of the benefits came to light. Other CEOs scurried to either renegotiate or protect their own "golden handshake" retirements.

## A New Trend: Mandated Ethics

In the US, shareholder activism is already heading to a new frontier: activists are pressuring the US government to restrict foreign access to the US stock and bond markets. If successful, the move would have a major impact on global businesses, especially for those dealing in nations seen as having a less-than-exemplary record on social responsibility.

Their target is the growing practice by foreign firms with questionable ties to rogue nations of raising money on Wall Street. Though the US has banned trade and other financial dealings with some nations, its capital markets have always been accessible to any foreign company that meets its investment standards. Now, this may all change, making a company's ethical practices just as important as its financial potential.

The number of foreign firms registered with the US Securities and Exchange Commission tripled in the 1990s to more than 1,200.

The issue came to the fore when a subsidiary of the China National Petroleum Company (CNPC) sought to sell shares on the New York Stock Exchange.

CNPC has a major oil project in Sudan, an African country whose regime is accused of waging a religious war in which millions have been killed. The US has banned trade, loans or aid to Sudan because of the government's support of terrorism and poor human rights record.

But the anti-investment campaign goes well beyond Sudan. Legislation has been introduced in the US Congress to screen any foreign-based company that wants to sell shares in the US for questionable activities or ownership ties. The US government has resisted pressure from human rights groups, citing its concern that restricting access would raise doubts about the US commitment to free markets and open flow of capital.

But the effort has triggered a debate over the appropriate role of financial markets in a global economy and whether society can afford to turn a blind eye to the social or political consequences of unrestricted flows of money. US officials and financiers argue that tampering with capital markets could backfire. Companies can take their business to dozens of other stock exchanges, from London's and Tokyo's to Hong Kong's. And foreign governments could retaliate, banning US firms from their markets. Piety, it seems, has a price.

CHAPTER 8

# Socially Responsible Investing: A New Trend Where Ethics DO Matter

*WE MUST MAKE THE WORLD HONEST BEFORE WE CAN HONESTLY SAY TO OUR CHILDREN THAT HONESTY IS THE BEST POLICY.* – GEORGE BERNARD SHAW

FOR MANY INDIVIDUAL INVESTORS WORLDWIDE, it is no longer enough to know *if* a company makes money, but rather *how* it makes money. Socially Responsible Investing (SRI), virtually unheard of 30 years ago, has grown into an important component of global capital markets. According to the nonprofit Social Investment Forum, over US$2 trillion, or one dollar out of every eight dollars managed professionally, is invested according to some social criteria. SocialFunds.com reports that there are now almost 200 mutual funds utilizing social screens to select investments.

## Shareholder Activism as an Important Economic Tool

Proponents of SRI use social or moral criteria when researching and selecting investments. SRI considers both the investor's financial needs and an investment's impact on whatever the investor uses as the ethical base. SRI incorporates three main strategies that work together to promote socially, ethically and environmentally responsible business practices, which, in turn, contribute to improvements in the quality of life throughout society. The three strategies are: screening companies for morally or ethically objectionable practices; engaging in shareholder activism to persuade companies to change certain behaviors; and community investing, which involves direct investment in disadvantaged communities.

Screening is the practice of including or excluding publicly traded companies from investment portfolios or mutual funds based on social, ethical and environmental criteria. Generally, social investors seek to own profitable companies that make "positive" contributions to society. Buy lists include enterprises with outstanding employer-employee relations, excellent environmental practices, products that are safe and useful and respect for human rights around the world. Conversely, they avoid investing in companies whose products and business practices are construed as harmful.

WARNING: Terms like "positive," "excellent" and "outstanding" listed above are relative to each culture or economy while the term "human rights" is considered by many Asian and African societies to be an invention of the West. For most of the world's poor, responsible investing is a rich person's game they may never get to play.

Community investment provides capital to people who have difficulty attaining it through conventional channels or are underserved by conventional lending institutions. Of course, community investment means different things depending where you are in the world. Perhaps the best known community investment program in the world, micro-credit, originated two decades ago in Bangladesh with the Grameen Bank (winners of the Nobel Prize in 2006). The program targets landless/assetless borrowers (women are given preference and make up 90 percent of total borrowers). The loans, usually small (between US$25 and US$75), are collateral-free, and usually have a maturity of 50 weeks with weekly repayments. Borrowers have full freedom to choose the activity to be financed by the loan, which are mostly rural activities with short gestation and daily sales, such as poultry farming, petty trade and shop-keeping, cattle raising or handicrafts.

And if you are not looking to invest in the stock market, Australia's Bendigo Bank has come up with what it claims to be the first "Ethical Investment Bank Account." The unique option of this account: you can increase your support for the work of Oxfam Community Aid Abroad by electing to forego all or part of the interest on your savings. These proceeds are paid by the Bendigo Bank to The Ethical Investment Trust which then sends the funds to Oxfam Community Aid Abroad.

## A Brief History of Socially Responsible Investing

The origins of ethical investing go back millennia. Early Jewish, Christian and Islamic laws laid down directives on how to invest ethically while Hindu and Buddhist doctrine dealt extensively with issues of wealth and its use. More specifically, Socially Responsible Investing grew out of opposition to US involvement in the Vietnam War. Many chemical and weapons companies were targeted by political campaigns because of their manufacture of weapons used by US forces. Also, during that decade, a series of social and environmental movements from civil rights and women's rights to environmental movements captured media attention and raised issues about the social responsibility of world businesses. These concerns broadened to include management and labor issues as well as anti-nuclear sentiment.

The concept of social investing attracted even more media attention when it focused on ending apartheid (a formalized system of racial segregation) in South Africa. The South African divestment campaign, supported by both academic and international governmental institutions, eventually forced major multinational corporations out of South Africa. Soon after, partly because of this economic pressure, apartheid ended and democracy was brought to South Africa. SRI, which until then had been considered by big business to be nothing more than "feel-good investing," finally matured into a major global investment phenomena.

The next step was logical. Investors began asking themselves if they could apply these same tactics to force change or divestment from corporations that were polluting, fostering abusive work regulations or supporting oppressive political regimes.

## The Global Growth and Role of SRI

There are now at least three major stock indices that track the performance of global stocks that meet specific requirements for socially responsible investors. The best known and oldest of the three is The Domini 400 Social Index—a market capitalization-weighted common stock index. It monitors the performance of 400 US corporations that pass multiple, broad-based social screens. The Index consists of approximately 250 companies included in the Standard & Poor's 500 Index, approximately 100 additional large companies not included in the S&P 500 but providing industry representation and approximately 50 additional companies with particularly strong social characteristics.

Second, the Dow Jones Sustainability Index was launched in 1999 as a group of indices (Dow Jones Sustainability Group—DJSG) that tracks the performance of the top 10 percent of the leading sustainability-driven companies in the Dow Jones Global Index of 2,000 firms. Corporate sustainability is a business approach that creates long-term shareholder value by embracing opportunities and managing risks deriving from economic, environmental and social developments.

In each of the 64 industry groups, the top 10 percent of companies in the investable universe is selected according to their sustainability performance score. The investable stocks universe consists of the 2,000 largest capitalized companies in the Dow Jones Global Index. Alcohol, gambling and tobacco companies are excluded. Also excluded in all DJSG indices are companies with more than 50 percent of sales derived from weapons and armaments (their weighting in the index is reduced in case 5-50 percent of sales are derived from weapons and armaments).

Finally, ARESE (a Paris-based investment firm that conducts research on corporate social, environmental and sustainability performance) recently announced the introduction of the ASPI Eurozone, which will track the financial performance of companies in the Eurozone that are leaders in sustainability. The Eurozone comprises the European Union member countries that have adopted the Euro.

## Japan Gets in on the Act

A growing niche sector within the Japanese fund management industry is the so-called eco-fund market. Five major funds have so far attracted 190 billion yen (about US$1.75 billion), and their rate of growth is even faster than SRI funds in the US and Europe. The Japanese eco-funds, however, are not true SRI funds. Asset managers do not apply full social and environmental criteria in selecting companies for investment.

What selection that does occur is based on a combination of two criteria. In the first place, within an initial 600 Japanese company investment universe, the Nikko Eco Fund, for example, in co-operation with Good Bankers Co., applied a financial screen aimed at assessing the companies which show the best long term growth perspective. Secondly, an "ecological" screen was applied, comprising two appraisals. The first one rated the company according to its "positive contributions to the environment" while the second one estimates to what extent—and how successfully—the company was "engaged in activities oriented towards environmental protection." At the end of the process, the Nikko Eco Fund selected less than 100 of 150 companies considered as "candidates for investment."

So far, none of the eco-funds in Japan have stated that they will shun certain sectors or companies on ethical grounds (e.g. tobacco, nuclear power, labor abuse). However, as competition in the eco-fund market heats up and differentiation becomes increasingly difficult, it is likely that ethical funds of varying themes will emerge in Japan.

## Does it Cost You Money to be Socially Responsible?

There is no clear answer as yet. The fund rating service known as Morningstar analyzed 47 US mutual funds claiming to have socially responsible records of at least three years. Of those, 19 funds—or 40 percent—received a rating of four or five stars. Only 32.5 percent of all funds make it into these top two categories. US Domestic SRI funds returned 12.32 percent, beating the average US fund by 11.34 percent in a five year study ending in 1995. Also, the Domini 400 Social Index occasionally outperforms the S&P index.

But the results are not as compelling or as impressive as they may seem. The difference in performance of the Domini funds does not signal an inherent superiority of SRI funds but rather reflects the results of different industry "bets" implicit in the social screening process the index uses. If the Domini index had been re-weighted so that it matched the S&P 500's macro-economic and industry exposures, the result would have been the same.

---

NOTE: Of course, the statistics above do not include the foregone opportunity costs of not investing in some very profitable, but possibly questionable, firms. People pursuing an SRI strategy turn a blind eye to this cost in the name of virtue -- just like other investors do when a stock they <u>didn't</u> invest in does well.

---

## SRI and God: Investing Methods Based on Religious Values

Socially Responsible Investing now encompasses practically every set of values on the planet. There are funds for Christian Scientists (which don't invest in pharmaceuticals), for orthodox Muslims (no investing in banks, due to Islamic principles proscribing the charging of interest), for conservative Christians (which avoid companies involved in pornography and abortion) and funds that screen for the more obvious "sin" industries, like traditional tobacco, alcohol, weapons, and gambling concerns, as well as for companies that fall short of various environmental, labor, and diversity criteria.

## Islamic Investing

Islamic investing is a complicated business based on Islamic ethics and the body of law called *SHARI'AH*. Those ethics prohibit money going into companies involved in alcohol or gambling, for example. Also excluded are companies that make profits from interest (usury) payments, such as banks and insurance groups. That means 16 of the 30 stocks on Wall Street's Dow Jones Industrial Average fall outside *SHARI'AH*.

Islamic investing, however, is probably the fastest-growing area of faith-based investing in the world. Islamic mutual funds worldwide are worth over US$500 billion and increase annually by 10-15 percent. Nearly half of them have been launched in the last 10 years. Dow Jones launched its own Islamic Market Index to track *SHARI'AH*-compatible companies and Germany's No. 4 lending institution, Commerzbank, has launched its AlSukoor European Equity Fund, targeting Muslims in the Middle East as well as those living in Europe. AlSukoor raised US$50 million in its first three weeks alone.

Perhaps not so coincidentally, Islamic investing products are a suitable alternative for investors of other faiths, especially conservative Christians. Islamic funds avoid the same so-called sin stocks: alcohol, tobacco and pornography. They also avoid most conventional financial companies because Islamic law prohibits collecting interest on debt, and the ban extends to making money from a company that acts as a lender or a borrower.

---

NOTE: Some of these Islamic funds faced their own ethical dilemma when it was discovered that some of their participants had links to terrorist organizations. A good faith attempt at ethical behavior often raises a new and unexpected ethical question.

---

Islamic funds avoid companies with debt-to-asset ratios higher than 33 percent and accounts-receivable-to-asset ratios above 45 percent. In addition, to be considered as an investment candidate, a company's combined interest income and income from what Islamic law calls "inadmissible revenue"—revenue from sinful activities—must not top 5 percent of total revenues. That limitation necessarily excludes a lot of popular companies; Apple Computer and IBM Corp., for instance, carry too much debt. But it leaves roughly 650 global companies, worth nearly US$10 trillion, to choose from in the portfolio. A little sin is tolerated, but not too much.

Because of the prohibition on interest associated with debt, Islamic markets are also beginning to come up with alternatives to traditional bond investments. One US management firm is working with leasing companies to develop securities backed by operating leases, which don't pay interest but rather a share of the leasing revenues, and could therefore be bought by Muslims. Firms are also working to develop a US version of a *TAKAFUL*, a kind of mutual-aid society that serves as an alternative to conventional insurance for Muslims.

---

NOTE: A good deal of Islamic strictures on "usury" rely on a very flexible set of semantics. House and car loans, where no profit will ever be derived through generation of business revenues, are structured so that the would-be owner of the house or car "buys" the bank out of the loan over time. Unsurprisingly, the buy out includes additional money that bears a striking resemblance to interest. Ethics can be flexible.

---

## How an Islamic Mutual Fund Works

Islamic principles guide the US$24 million Amana Mutual Funds Trust Growth fund. Its return places it in the top 5 percent of Morningstar's large-cap growth category. The fund shuns investments in businesses such as liquor, pornography, gambling, and banks and avoids bonds and other fixed-income securities. Any company dealing with pork or pork-related products is banned. All stock picks are submitted to a board of Islamic experts for review.

Muslims are encouraged by their faith to invest for the long-term, but Islamic ethics demand that Muslim investors pay *ZAKAT*—money or charitable works, which a Muslim of means must distribute among the poor every year. While its intention—to foster in Muslims the qualities of sacrifice and rid them of selfishness and greed—is highly noble, *ZAKAT* can play havoc with Muslim investment portfolios, especially if their portfolio gains may not be realized for years. Islamic jurists have agreed that to distribute *ZAKAT* sooner rather than later it is allowable to consider the difference in the market value of a portfolio from the beginning to the end of each Gregorian calendar year and pay 10.3 percent (10 percent for lunar calendar) of the gain, if any, as *ZAKAT*. There are dozens of *ZAKAT* calculators available on Islamic investing Web sites. The amount of *ZAKAT* an investor actually distributes remains an individual decision and most Islamic funds will allow investors to transfer shares directly into a charity's account.

## Values-based Investing: Down with Cultural Polluters

Values-based Investing is a strategy for people with a strong sense of religious or social belief wishing to invest in companies that operate in line with their personal values. For example, if pornography is offensive to you, would it bother you to learn that one of the companies in your portfolio was distributing pornography through a subsidiary business? What if you owned stock in a company that sounded harmless, but was actually a hard-core porn company?

By applying Values-based Investing filters to an investment strategy, an investor can rest assured that their portfolio is as clean as their conscience.

One of the better known filters is The Investigator. It began as a tool for investment professionals when the Institute for American Values Investing, an independent research firm, discovered that there were no opportunities for investors to screen their investments according to their values. The Institute defined the "negative" issues most important to the investors they represented. It identified pornography, abortion, anti-family entertainment and the active promotion of non-marriage lifestyles.

CHAPTER 9

# The Personal Ethics Battle

*ALL THAT IS NECESSARY FOR EVIL TO TRIUMPH IS FOR GOOD MEN TO DO NOTHING.* – EDMUND BURKE

CORPORATIONS ARE MADE UP OF PEOPLE, of course, and ultimately it is the individual that will be forced to come up with a methodology for making a decision based on balancing ethics and profits. Despite the proliferation of corporate ethics codes, the urge to cheat to win business or increase profits still remains widespread. Each and every day society pays a heavy price for the choices—both ethical and unethical—of its members.

## The Person and the Personal

Tough choices don't always involve professional codes of conduct or criminal laws. Nor do they always involve headline-size issues. They often operate in areas that laws and regulations don't reach. Ethical decision-making is highly complex. While people generally want to do the right thing, a wide range of factors influence them: culture, peers rules, regulations, fear, policies and what has gone on before.

In organizations, ethics can be understood as sets of formal and informal standards of conduct that people use to guide behavior. These standards are based in part on principles derived from core values such as honesty, respect and trust. In practice, standards of ethical behavior are also learned directly from the actions of others. For example, what we see our peers and managers do in the workplace may influence our views of what is acceptable and unacceptable behavior.

Ethical decision-making requires more than a belief in the importance of ethics. It also requires sensitivity to perceive the ethical implications of decisions, the ability to evaluate complex, ambiguous and incomplete facts and the skill to implement ethical decisions without unduly jeopardizing your career.

## Ethical Choice, Cultural Quagmire

A British engineer recalls her introduction to the competitive and dynamic world of international business and the classic problem faced by altruistic individuals in business: you need to make your numbers and you need to make a difference.

She had joined the business development team of a large multinational corporation and was immediately assigned to help develop and implement a series of projects in East Africa. After several months on the job, she was part of a team that presented the company's development plan to the finance and health ministries of one of the subject countries.

"I thought we were miracle workers. We had a great cost-efficient plan that in just three or four years would have a positive impact on the health and safety of a large portion of the population. I was so pleased with myself. I mean here I was doing a job I liked and had trained for and we were also going to do some good for all these people," she says.

The "feel good" didn't last long. Though the presentation did go well, it was suggested a few days later by some lower level government functionaries that the "go ahead" for the projects would require a "contribution" to the individual ministers involved.

"I just never thought of it," the engineer says. "No one in my company ever mentioned that this sort of thing happened—that this is part of doing business in this particular culture. I just didn't know what to do, or who to turn to.

"Then one of the government representatives said my company always paid to speed decisions along and I shouldn't worry about it. Still I was afraid that I might risk my job if I paid, or I might get fired if I lost the deal. No one prepared me for this and I was angry."

The dilemma faced by this young British engineer is typical of the personal ethics battles managers face in international business. The expectation of bribes or kickbacks is just one of the challenges. Often, the rules of what is proper, responsible behavior may be subject to differing interpretations. In fact, the lack of a universally accepted understanding of what constitutes ethical corporate behavior can put an individual in a difficult position. Learning how to make decisions in such situations—what factors one should consider and what process one should undertake to reach an ethical decision—is an important but often overlooked international business skill.

Because of cultural differences, local laws and social norms can deviate from what you consider ethical. It is necessary to constantly examine your own standards to ensure that they are reasonable and well-founded and live up to standards that are reasonable and solidly-based.

## How Bad Is It?

Research paints a rather bleak picture of ethics, practices within companies and corporations. The result has been that employers are seeing an enormous amount of white-collar crime and unethical behavior in the workplace. Survey snapshots cite the seriousness of the problem that can be traced directly back to poor personal ethics in the workplace for both labor and management.

In a survey by the Society of Human Resources Managers and the Ethics Resource Center Business Ethics Survey it was found that during a one-year period more than half (54 percent) of the 747 human resource professionals surveyed had observed workplace conduct in violation of the law or in violation of the organization's standards of ethical business conduct. Symptomatic of the poor state of personal ethics in the workplace is the volume of employee theft and pilfering, which is an equal opportunity curse that affects virtually all businesses and cuts across all job classifications from janitor to CEO.

TYPES OF MISCONDUCT OBSERVED

- Lying to supervisors—45%
- Abusing drugs or alcohol—36%
- Lying on reports or falsifying records—36%
- Conflicts of interest—34%
- Stealing or theft—27%
- Employees receiving gifts/entertainment in violation of organization policy—26%
- Misusing organization's assets—24%
- Altering results of product or service testing—16%
- Misusing insider information—14%
- Employees engaging in fraud—12%
- Employees giving gifts in violation of organization policy—10%
- Employees receiving kickbacks—10%
- Improperly obtaining competitors' proprietary information—7%
- Violating environmental laws or regulations—7%
- Violating antitrust laws—3%
- Employees taking bribes—2%
- Crime in the workplace—2%

## Why Employees Steal: It's a Material World

According to social scientists, in most cultures today, individuals have an uncontrollable psychological disposition to attain personal material wealth. Here, the forces that drive humans to steal are explained by an evolutionary pressure to satisfy personal needs that if not countered will dominate the person's will.

Similarly, employee theft has been attributed to the anthropological belief in the survival of the fittest. Proponents claim that the battle of the fittest in our current era is no different than the battle of the fittest described by Darwin many years ago. Today, however, the fittest is no longer determined by physical dominance, but rather by one's material wealth. Accordingly, amassing material wealth is a sign of triumph. Another rationale for employee theft is that employees see stealing as a form of additional compensation to lessen the gap of social inequality.

## Countering The Problem

The introduction of a formal ethics program is considered to be an effective countermeasure. Usually, regardless of the culture, issues of employee theft are addressed in a negative and reactive way. Companies must:

- Keep criminals or potential thieves out of their employ.
- Use resources to detect crime.
- Take action once an employee is caught stealing.

Recommended pro-active steps that can help rebuild a corporate culture to improve ethics, give employees a better basis for making ethical decisions and eventually curtail unethical behavior and theft include:

- The creation of an ethical environment which starts from the top down and focuses on fairness and ethics. This includes a commitment to a set of values by the employer.
- Development of a company mission statement by a process which involves everyone in the organization.
- Implementation of a personal ethics training program.
- Implementation of an employee feedback system.

In the world of work, improving ethical decision-making in your organization can reduce incidents of fraud, theft and the costs associated with unethical conduct. More importantly, an organization built on character and solid ethical principles will quickly earn a reputation for integrity and credibility with its customers. Even if this move towards ethics does not attract new customers or improve sales, profits would increase as theft and fraud are reduced.

## Personal Decisions: The Personal as Cultural

Most people have convictions about what is right and wrong based on religious beliefs, cultural roots, family background, personal experiences, laws, organizational values, professional norms and habits. These may not be the best values to make ethical decisions by, not because they are unimportant, but because they are not universally accepted. All adults are morally autonomous beings with the power to choose their values; but it does not follow that all choices and all value systems have an equal claim to be called ethical.

Each person has an "operational value system" that reflects how one ranks competing values in deciding how to act. A personal value system encompasses all values—core beliefs and attitudes that guide and motivate behavior—and, therefore, it includes personal convictions about right and wrong, sometimes called "personal moral values." The fact that everyone has a personal value system that includes opinions and beliefs about what is right and wrong, however, does not mean that ethics is purely a personal matter.

To a situationalist, nothing is always right or always wrong and sometimes it is acceptable, even good, to lie. Have no doubt about it, the notion of situational ethics exists in the business world. People in positions of responsibility need to take many things into consideration. The day-to-day practical problems in business are linked to moral philosophy, but ethics cannot be confined to philosophy.

### CHOOSING ALTERNATIVES

Ethical decision-making refers to the process of evaluating and choosing among alternatives in a manner consistent with ethical principles. The really tough choices in the business world don't always involve right versus wrong. They often involve right versus right. They are genuine dilemmas precisely because there may be several right answers ethically—and no wrong ones.

The common "right versus right" conundrums faced most frequently by business managers:

- Truth versus loyalty.
- Individual versus community.
- Short-term versus long-term.
- Justice versus mercy.

### SO WHAT'S A PERSON TO DO?

Most major corporations have a code of conduct or formal policy statements to assist employees and managers in coping with these international challenges. But if the issue is not dealt with through these resources, management often is the best source of guidance. In addition, the legal or human resources department can be contacted, depending on the issue at hand and the amount of time available. Most large companies also have an ethics office or ombudsman set up as an alternate support channel.

If you are not in a situation where you can easily turn to someone for advice, you can employ the simple "headline test" for a quick perspective. How would the issue look if it was displayed on the front page of tomorrow's newspaper (e.g., "Employee of [your company] bribes Minister of Finance to Secure Investment Approval")? If you suspect they might react negatively to the news, then, in all likelihood, it is not a good move.

### OTHER PERSONAL TESTS AND AIDS

Few companies supply their employees with pamphlets and reminders on what to consider or what questions they should ask themselves when faced with an ethical dilemma on the job.

Here is an "Ethics Quick Test:"

1. Is the action legal?
2. Does it comply with our values?
3. If you do it, will you feel bad?
4. How will it look in the newspaper?
5. If you know it's wrong, don't do it!
6. If you're not sure, ask.
7. Keep asking until you get an answer.

## Making An Ethical Decision: What Is Involved?

While there are no magical processes that will ensure an individual will arrive at an ethical decisions in business, there are some basic and generally agreed upon guidelines to point individuals in the proper direction. No matter what process is followed, an individual must be prepared to be honest with him/herself and take the time to think about the pros and cons of their actions. Some basic guidelines:

### THE BIG PICTURE

Decisions should take into account the interests and well being of all those who will be affected by your decisions. Failing to do so will obviously lead to a biased and potentially unfair decision that benefits only some.

Do not subordinate ethical values to non-ethical or unethical values. While this may seem obvious, the danger that lurks here is that an individual may try to rationalize a situation into one perceived as involving competing ethical principles rather than ethical and an unethical motives. For example, consider a person who is contemplating paying a bribe to close a deal. The person (erroneously) sees the choice as one between integrity—not paying the bribe—and responsibility—a commitment to putting food on the table for his family. Often, other ethical ways are available—though they may be less obvious and more costly in reaching for noble goals. In many cases, ethical means of reaching worthy ends only require a little more work and sacrifice.

### PERSONAL WARNING SIGNS

If you find yourself using one of these common cliches/excuses in the workplace, stop and think about your behavior. These phrases can act as early earning signs that what you are considering doing is unethical:

- "Well, maybe just this once."
- "No one will ever know."
- "It doesn't matter how it gets done as long as it gets done."
- "It sounds too good to be true."
- "Everyone does it."
- "We can hide it."
- "No one will get hurt."
- "What's in it for me?"
- "This will destroy the competition."
- "We didn't have this conversation."

---

NOTE: Universities in both the UK and the US have sought ways to drive home the importance of business ethics on the international stage—and the potential personal penalties for acting unethically. Both Pepperdine University in California and St. Andrews in Scotland regularly take the best and the brightest in their graduate business programs on tours of prisons—housing former businessmen convicted of "white collar" crimes. Pepperdine developed the "Ethics in Business" program for its executive MBA program in the 1980s. Its purpose is to make students personally confront ethical issues and to show them what can happen to business executives lacking ethical or moral grounding. Participation in the prison trip is required for graduation.

---

## Are Ethics Practical?

While issues such as human rights, corruption, labor practices and the environment may grab headlines, the challenges faced by international managers is more often concerned with reconciling differing expectations of "proper" business conduct in different cultures. Consider the ethical dilemmas posed by the following examples:

1. GIFT GIVING While it is customary in some cultures to exchange expensive gifts, the headquarters of many multinationals (not to mention government ethics watchdogs) may interpret the exchange of significant gifts as an attempt to buy influence.
2. CONFLICT OF INTEREST It is common in many Asian, Middle Eastern and African societies to hire relatives and conduct business with companies owned by one's family. However, most Western companies have conflict of interest and anti-nepotism policies and restrictions to prevent favoritism and to encourage objective decision-making.
3. CONTRACTS VERSUS HANDSHAKE In a number of cultures, there is a history of building business relationships based on trust and friendship, where a handshake rather than a written contract seals business arrangements.

Many corporations are globalizing their business practices standards to show greater sensitivity to cultural differences. At the same time, a number of societies are reevaluating prevailing practices. For example, among Japanese companies, Nissan and Hitachi have implemented policies banning gift giving. Business conduct also has drawn close scrutiny in Indonesia, which is cracking down on cronyism and nepotism. Through such incremental changes—both within societies and on the part of multinational corporations—a gradual convergence of views is developing on what is deemed acceptable and appropriate behavior on the part of businesses. For example: the Malaysian Anti-Corruption Agency has exceptionally strict laws against bribery, but allows for the practice of gift giving. But giving a gift that seems too generous may be interpreted as a bribe and could get you in trouble with the authorities.

WARNING: Ethics provides many more shades of gray than black or white.

## Practical Ethics: The Art Of Gift Giving—And Refusing

Gift giving is one of the oldest social traditions known to man. In cultures that are high context and relationship driven (as opposed to low context, task driven cultures), business is built upon personal relationships and gifts are an integral part of those relationships.

Gifts should never replace the basics of good business practices and etiquette. They are a supplement, not a substitute for, a sound business proposition, regardless of the culture. Of course, a gift should never take on the appearance of a bribe, even in countries where such practices are commonplace. A gift is just that—a gift to show appreciation or respect. A bribe—well, that is part of the cost of doing business in some places in the world.

NOTE: Like education, bribes can be a matter of degree! A lot about which cultural influence is the strongest also depends on who is the buyer and who is the seller.

## Where Gift Giving Matters—And Doesn't Matter

- HIGHLY IMPORTANT IN BUSINESS: Japan.
- IMPORTANT, BUT NOT CRITICAL TO BUSINESS: Asia/Pacific Rim, the Middle East, Africa.
- SOMEWHAT IMPORTANT, MORE AS A COURTESY: Latin America, Eastern Europe/ Russia.
- NOT IMPORTANT OR EXPECTED IN BUSINESS: United States, Canada, Australia, most of Western Europe.

### REFUSING GIFTS

Actually refusing a gift is fairly rare in international business circles. With the movement towards common global ethics standards, however, it is likely to become a little more common. (It is important to distinguish between a proper gift of appreciation or respect and a bribe masquerading as a gift). In American culture, it is perfectly acceptable to refuse a gift and, under certain circumstances, it is even mandatory. An American executive is more likely than any other global executive to return a gift to a giver because it is considered too extravagant, has sexual implications or might be misconstrued as a bribe.

In the US, company policy frequently states that an employee, regardless of rank, is not allowed to receive a gift of any size. As a courtesy to international colleagues, most companies and company executives will mention this up front to avoid any embarrassment to the giver. If you have any doubt about a company policy towards gifts, by all means ask the company's representative you are dealing with. By the same token, any executive working for such a company should inform a foreign colleague as early as possible of the company gift policy. Politely let others know either beforehand or at the time the gift is offered that you appreciate the gesture, but are prohibited by company policy from accepting. It is good manners and should never create hard feelings.

When US and European companies started doing a lot of business in Japan, many Western businesspeople thought that the practice of gift giving might be wrong rather than simply different. To them, accepting a gift felt like accepting a bribe. As Western companies have become more familiar with Japanese traditions, however, most have come to tolerate the practice and to set different limits on gift giving in Japan than they do elsewhere.

## Ethics Self Assessment Test

The following is an example of a self-assessment test dealing with personal ethics:

### THE WORLD BANK ETHICS KNOWLEDGE ASSESSMENT TEST

1. Should the private sector primarily focus on maximizing profits over other goals?
2. Should the private sector be concerned with their effect on civil society?

3. Is an organizational code of ethics the same thing as a company mission statement?
4. Do sound ethical business practices encourage a foundation for profits?
5. Does an organization's attention to ethics take away resources from other, more profitable, uses?
6. Is financial performance the primary factor in determining investor interest?
7. Is being an ethical person sufficient to be a "good" manager?
8. Has the rise of instant media and global news had an impact on the ethical conduct of business?
9. Can employees rely on conscience alone to make sound ethical decisions?
10. Do ethics training seminars for employees affect their ethical decision-making?
11. Do people behave ethically because of their personal ethical integrity or because of the influence of an outside entity such as the State or an employer?
12. How important is a commitment from the leadership of an organization for creating an ethical climate?
13. Can an organization be in full legal compliance with all of its decisions, and still be unethical?
14. Should an organization expose to the outside world an incident of unethical behavior?
15. Should an organization be responsible for the unethical conduct of its employees?
16. Since senior management is primarily responsible for the "ethical behavior" of their companies, do boards of directors bear much responsibility in this area?
17. Should the primary focus of an organizational ethics program be on legal compliance?

## The Answers

### QUESTION 1

Answer: No.

Milton Friedman's "the business of business is business" maxim aside, there are many arguments as to why organizations should focus on other factors besides profit maximization. Business has learned in recent years that it has many duties that are first owed to civil society before they can start worrying about profit. And besides, good citizenship and ethics can have a positive impact on the bottom-line of a business.

### QUESTION 2

Answer: Yes.

More and more business success is influenced by non-market relationships, particularly those with governments and their respective agencies, NGOs, the media and civil society in a broader sense. Sound business practices and good corporate citizenship reduces exposure to lawsuits, damaging legal sanctions and restrictive government regulations.

### QUESTION 3

Answer: No.

A mission statement is an expression of the company's current and future business scope. The emphasis, therefore, is on what the company does and will do. On the other hand, a code of ethics focuses on how the company does what it does.

### QUESTION 4

Answer: Yes.

Although this may sometimes be counter-intuitive, more and more companies find that sound ethical principles and high organizational integrity are a foundation for corporate excellence and can lead to greater profits. Evidence suggests that organizational integrity and business ethics are linked to economic performance.

### QUESTION 5

Answer: No.

In fact, a sound ethics system and culture in a corporation can lead to greater productivity and lower employee turnover. Sound value systems help companies achieve and sustain outstanding functional performance. A sound values systems can:

- Provide a focus for organizational efforts.
- Provide a source of organizational identity.
- Increase the motivation and commitment of the employees.
- Facilitate the achievement of long-term objectives.
- Facilitate organizational flexibility and adaptability.
- Lead to a leaner organizational structure and a decentralized decision-making process.

### QUESTION 6

Answer: No.

Sound business practices can make an important contribution to a company's reputation in the marketplace. Research shows that investors are willing to pay a premium for companies that have solid corporate governance and a strong ethical reputation. Bridgestone-Firestone Tires experienced a huge and well-documented loss of investor confidence because of their ethical problems. Nike suffered many of the same kinds of problems when they were implicated in the sweatshop working conditions of their contracted shoe manufacturing plants. Investors may see ethics as an ounce of prevention well worth the price.

### QUESTION 7

Answer: No.

Ethical managers are just as likely to make management mistakes as anyone else. Ethics is only one component of what makes a manager successful. An unethical manager, however, would have a hard time claiming long-term success.

## QUESTION 8

Answer: Yes.

With advances in global communications, news about company business conduct travels easily around the world. Business scandals in one country can become headline news in many other countries within a matter of minutes. This also puts pressure on local companies to improve their commitment to ethical business practices in case they want to establish business relationships with the world's leading companies. Stiffer demands from world governments about compliance has also had an impact.

## QUESTION 9

Answer: No.

Although managers should start with an assumption of human decency, they should also launch appropriate corporate ethics initiatives. Even truly decent people are fallible. Furthermore, even if all the employees of an organization are perfectly ethical, the structure of the organization could contribute to various pressures that compromise overall ethical standards.

## QUESTION 10

Answer: Yes.

Ethics training, if done properly and supported by the actions of senior management, can have a major positive impact on corporate behavior.

## QUESTION 11

Answer: Both personal and external influences motivate ethical behavior.

Although business ethics is highly influenced by the overall practices of an organization, it is also dependent upon an individual's value system. On the other hand, an individual's value system is also a reflection of the value system of the society within which the corporation operates. Society sets the overall ethical framework within which management and employees have to work out their own codes of conduct. Therefore, society also has to accept responsibility for setting the standards against which corporate decisions are evaluated.

## QUESTION 12

Answer: It is of key importance.

Many researchers have found a close relationship between leadership, values and business ethics.

## QUESTION 13

Answer: Yes.

Legal compliance often implies meeting minimal standards for regulation. Being in compliance does not automatically mean an organization is acting ethically. It's also true that the interpretation of legal language changes over time, which means there is no guarantee that what is legal today will be legal tomorrow. This makes it rational to have an ethics program to prevent costly litigation. There are many other reasons not to count strictly on the law to ensure ethics.

## QUESTION 14

Answer: Yes.

Even if there are no legal consequences for not taking appropriate action once unethical behavior is disclosed, management could suffer a serious loss of confidence among employees, creditors, shareholders, suppliers and customers. Undisclosed instances of unethical behavior that become public can often have catastrophic effects on an organization. For example, the Bridgestone-Firestone Tire incident is a case in point.

## QUESTION 15

Answer: Yes.

It is management's responsibility to institute systems that reduce the probability for misconduct and to detect and punish legal violations. It is also the responsibility of management to deeply integrate a shared set of values and guiding principles throughout the organization. However, holding the corporation accountable does not exclude individual accountability.

## QUESTION 16

Answer: Yes.

Boards of directors can be held responsible if they neglect their fiduciary duty to supervise management in the area of ethical conduct.

## QUESTION 17

Answer: No.

A "compliance-based" ethics program is not enough. Sound ethics practices cannot be achieved without a comprehensive program that focuses on avoiding illegal practices; this should be combined with managerial responsibility for ethical behavior as well as reinforcing the company's guiding values, culture aspirations, philosophy and patterns of thought and conduct. This is called the "integrity-based" approach.

Source: World Bank

CHAPTER 10

# Building An Effective Corporate Ethics Code

*SET YOUR EXPECTATIONS HIGH; FIND MEN AND WOMEN WHOSE INTEGRITY AND VALUES YOU RESPECT; GET THEIR AGREEMENT ON A COURSE OF ACTION; AND GIVE THEM YOUR ULTIMATE TRUST.*

– JOHN FELLOWS AKERS (CHAIRMAN, IBM)

THE WORLD TODAY has thrust a new role on multinational corporations—that of a conveyor of moral values. It may be an unwanted or unfamiliar role, but it is no less a real responsibility. Any company doing business across borders must be prepared to accept moral scrutiny. It should be able to point to an ethical corporate culture and a formalized code should the spotlight fall on them—if only for the purpose of maintaining a good image.

A code of ethics fulfills many purposes within an organization. It increases the ethical sensitivity and judgment of employees, strengthens support for individuals' moral courage, helps to hone an organization's sense of identity, supports the firm's public image and wards off potential legal challenges. To compete effectively, global companies must ensure that their ethics codes and codes of conduct are culturally coherent to all employees. This is much harder than it sounds.

## Strategic Justification For Codes

Companies do not build an ethics code just for fun. In the past it often took a trauma-inducing event, either within the company itself or within the company's industry sector, to get the ball rolling. With the growing recognition that a company has social responsibilities and strict policing of ethical standards by governments and non-governmental organizations, the incentives for creating an ethics code are many. Typical incentives and justifications include:

### LEGAL INCENTIVES

- Changing legal requirements.
- Growing involvement in regions with different cultural and political traditions.
- An incident that hurt the company.
- Growing media scrutiny.
- An incident that hurt the industry.

BUSINESS JUSTIFICATION

- Establish core principles for global operations.
- Promote employee professionalism.
- Limit legal risk.
- Enhance company reputation.
- Limit public relations risks.
- Control quality of suppliers.

## Act Locally, Profit Globally

In remote foreign locations, local management often gives its own interpretation of a company's values and ethics codes. This can be dangerous in some cases, creating an inconsistency of application and behavior that can ruin a corporation's global reputation and leave employees confused. The way to prevent this from happening is to cross-fertilize—that is, to send individual managers from the head office to local offices to promote a central set of corporate ethics. Local country employees should be moved to other company locations throughout the world so they begin to understand that the corporate ethics program is indeed a global one; the program should be consistent in application with room for some local interpretation so long as that interpretation is consistent with overall corporate values.

Codes of conduct must be explicit to be useful, but they must also leave room for managers to use their judgment in situations requiring cultural sensitivity. Host country employees shouldn't be forced to adopt all home country values while renouncing their own and vice versa. Managers living and working abroad who are not prepared to grapple with moral ambiguity and tension should pack their bags and go home. The view that all business practices can be categorized as either ethical or unethical is too simple.

## Context Must Help Shape Codes

Context must shape ethical practices. For example, wages paid by wealthy foreign firms to locals in emerging markets may be considered low by rich country standards, but in developing nations these wages may be considerably higher than local standards.

Similarly, when cultures have different standards of ethical behavior—and different ways of handling unethical behavior—a company that takes an absolutist approach may be making a disastrous mistake. Managers cannot operate in another culture without being aware of the host culture's attitudes toward local ethics as well as the ethics of the foreign guests.

While consistency is considered a vital component of a successful global ethics policy, more enlightened corporations will encourage managers to use common sense in its application. Certain circumstances require codes of conduct to be flexible.

Consider the case of a British manufacturing company with a subsidiary in India. Local company policy gave first preference for jobs to the children of employees, once the child had reached a certain level in school and was, of course, of legal working age in India. The company honored this commitment even when other applicants were more qualified than an employee's child. The perk is extremely valuable in a country where jobs are hard to find, and it reflects the Indian culture's belief that Western nations have gone too far in allowing work demands to erode family structure. However, in Britain, such a practice would be a clear case of nepotism and in violation of ethical principles and possibly employment law. In a country like India where nepotism is viewed as an acceptable aspect of the extended family culture, providing such a perk for employees may be the right thing to do. To ban it might create employee disloyalty.

---

NOTE: There is a thin line between adaptation and rationalization.

---

Managers failing to understand that local values and cultures play an important role in the development of a set of corporate ethics for global use may find that they:

1. Impose the cultural values of company headquarter's culture without regard for how those values are perceived in other cultures—hindering potential business success in those regions.
2. Create a global ethics program that is too narrow and based on compliance issues related to the headquarter's home country.
3. Fail to address the core elements of their programs in terms that resonate with the culture of the countries or regions in which they work.
4. Fail to address the ethical needs of a diverse workforce resulting in a potentially less effective and efficient workforce.
5. Be unaware of or unresponsive to what local societies and customers may expect from local business operations of a transnational company.
6. Not pay enough attention to the issue of corporate values as guidelines of decision-making and the application of policies, procedures and practices within local operations.

---

WARNING: Global managers should never lose sight of the fact that in ethics it "takes two to tango" when it comes to establishing a foreign/local ethics regimen. Neither side can impose its will and still garner long-term success.

---

## Not So Very Worldwide

Despite all the talk about the importance of corporate ethics, few corporations actually have a written code of conduct and ethics. In Australia, for example, 71 percent of companies do not have a written code and in Japan the figure is 70 percent. In Germany, France and Britain fewer than 60 percent have a written code. (Though still low, it is a big improvement from less than 20 percent in 1984.) However, even those large multinational corporations that do have written codes rarely take the time and care to ensure that they are coherent across cultures. As a result, little attention is paid to them outside of the head office. In the meantime, however, the marketplace and activist stakeholders are demanding that a lax attitude toward an ethics code be replaced by a functioning code that can be seen by consumers as having an impact on how a company operates.

## Beware the Poorly Conceived Corporate Code

Not everyone agrees that having a corporate ethics code is such a good idea. Critics point out that there is a clear danger if employees are not well versed on the details of the ethics code; a firm's employees can be scared away from doing business in circumstances where the morality of a country or business partner are ambiguous.

They say business ethics initiatives can impair business success because ethics codes do not fully acknowledge:

1. The need for tolerance of diverse practices and customs that are essential for doing business in the global marketplace.
2. The advantage gained by less scrupulous competitors.
3. The danger that employees will not take advantage of business opportunities because of potential ethical problems. Some employees will simply avoid such places all together.

## Proactive Ethics

Successful ethics programs are rooted in corporate culture rather than mandated by law and the need to maintain a company's reputation. There needs to be a culture of compliance in any company. The mere presence of systems and controls within a company is not enough. In fact, Australian law requires "an environment of compliance operating within a company." A company can be criminally liable if it fails to maintain a corporate culture that requires compliance with the law or if the corporate culture directs, tolerates or leads to non-compliance with the criminal provisions proscribing the bribery of foreign public officials.

Some corporate culture factors that are critical include:

- Consistency between ethics and compliance policies and action within the organization.
- Leadership attention to ethics.
- Employee perception of fair treatment.
- Openness and discussion about ethics and values within the organization.
- Employee perceptions of the objectives of ethics management efforts.

## What Is Corporate Culture and Why Is It Important?

Corporate culture is the glue that holds an organization together. It incorporates an organization's values, norms of behavior, policies and procedures. Like a national culture, corporate culture has some basic components that make up the whole. While national cultural components include such things as language, religion and humor, the components of corporate culture are more utilitarian. No one single component can reveal the true internal makeup of a corporation, but when taken together as a whole, they present a clear picture of a company's values and goals.

The key corporate cultural components are:

1. THE SYSTEM OF REWARDS What type of employee behavior is appreciated and rewarded? Do risk-takers move up in management ranks or does the corporation reward loyalty and long-term service instead?
2. HIRING DECISIONS The type of individual a company hires says much about its culture. Is a company ready to grow and accept new ideas by hiring a diverse workforce or is it content to keep hiring the same type of individual to build a homogenous workforce?
3. MANAGEMENT STRUCTURE Is the corporation rigidly formed in a hierarchical structure? Is it managed by an executive committee or a dominating chairman?
4. RISK-TAKING STRATEGY What is a corporation's view of risk? Does it encourage taking chances, trying new products and markets? Or is it content with well-established markets and products?
5. PHYSICAL SETTING Is the office an open plan that encourages communication, cooperation and a sense of egalitarianism? Or are offices segregated to encourage individual achievement? Is headquarters a monument to ownership or a functional working environment?

While it would be impossible to say what the perfect type of corporate culture should be for a global company (it depends on the culture you are operating in, the industry and basic cultural components stated above), there are basic traits that an effective global corporate culture should incorporate to be successful:

- It needs to develop a sense of accountability among staff and employees.
- It needs to be coherently transmitted across cultures. For instance, if it is Asia-centric, European employees simply won't buy in.
- While flexibility is important, there must be a consistent application of principles across cultures, such as the granting of religious holidays.
- It must be attuned to the competitive requirements of the world market and be able to adapt to new market conditions.

## The Difference Between Ethics and Compliance

Not addressing nor understanding the difference between a compliance program and a true values-based ethics program can be disastrous. The compliance approach is geared toward preventing unlawful conduct and criminal misconduct. The value-based integrity approach, in comparison, has a more lofty goal: to achieve a desired conduct across-the-board, even if not required by law. Companies with a compliance approach put lawyers at the helm while value-based ethics program let company managers lead.

Businesspeople are forever making ethical decisions about questions that the law does not answer. For example, US privacy law gives little guidance as to what companies may do with the data they collect on individual customers. In contrast, European law reflects a deep concern about the misuse of information about individuals. Business ethics policies should go beyond the minimum of law, set expectations higher and establish a corporate culture that goes beyond mere compliance.

Compliance codes are straightforward statements of do's and don'ts. Many ethics codes are nothing more than compliance codes aimed at meeting the barest of legal requirements. By their very nature they are local and impossible to translate into a global context (after all, company subsidiaries are subject to local laws and as such it is necessary for each local unit to have its own "compliance code"). The major difference is that compliance codes deal solely with meeting legal regulations while true ethics codes go beyond legal compliance to incorporate corporate values and social goals.

Organizations that do not differentiate between ethics codes and compliance codes run the risk of:

1. Introducing what they may call a values-based ethics code that is really a compliance code providing only a limited set of guidelines that do not allow employees enough latitude to solve everyday ethical dilemmas. The notion of compliance is not terribly responsive to many day-to-day concerns managers and employees face.
2. Providing a legal compliance program that is not very exciting and runs directly counter to employee motivation. This can create unfilled expectations among employees.
3. Relying on best practices developed in compliance programs that may not effectively support value-based ethics programs.
4. Failing to recognize that value-based and compliance programs require different definitions of success.
5. Finding themselves being held accountable for a questionable, but legal company action that might be viewed as "unethical" or "unfair."

## A Comparison Of Compliance and Value-Based Ethics Programs

### COMPLIANCE

ETHOS: Conformity with externally imposed laws and standards.

OBJECTIVE: Preventing unlawful conduct.

LEADERSHIP: Lawyer driven.

BEHAVIOR ASSUMPTIONS: Autonomous beings guided by a fear of wrong-doing.

### VALUE-BASES ETHICS STRATEGY

ETHOS: Self-governance according to chosen standards.

OBJECTIVE: Enable responsible conduct.

LEADERSHIP: Management driven.

BEHAVIOR ASSUMPTIONS: Social beings guided by material self-interest, values, ideals and peers.

## The Basic Elements of a Corporate Ethics Code

The corporate ethics code plays a key role in creating an environment of predictability and consistency for the behavior of employees and suppliers. Codes also address the relationship between organizational control and an individual's moral judgment. Codes in use by international business organizations typically contain provisions about the following:

1. A general statement of the values of the organization and its guiding principles.
2. Definitions of what constitute both ethical and corrupt conduct.
3. Competence requirements and professional standards.
4. Directives on personal and professional behavior.
5. Affirmations of fairness, equity and equal opportunity.
6. Stipulations on gifts and conflicts of interest.
7. Restrictions on the use of organizational facilities for private purposes.
8. Guidelines on confidentiality, public comment, whistle-blowing and post-separation use of company/organizational information.
9. Identification of different stakeholders and other interested parties and their rights.
10. Mechanism for enforcing the code.
11. Advocates personal responsibility.
12. Advice on interpreting and implementing the code.

## Writing The Code

A corporate ethics code needs to be more than the rules of the road; it should include a statement of the company's core values. If the company does not have such a statement, then the first words they put on paper should be this statement of core values. The code should be organized around the core values.

Codes of conduct must provide clear direction about ethical behavior when the temptation to behave unethically is strongest. The pronouncement in a code of conduct that bribery is unacceptable is useless unless accompanied by guidelines for gift-giving, payments to get goods through customs—and "requests" from intermediaries who are hired to ask for bribes.

---

WARNING: Being too general, overly sensitive or politically correct will only exacerbate the problem. Ethics is a serious business requiring direct and specific forms of address and redress.

---

Obviously any person or team charged with writing a corporate ethics code should know the ethically sensitive areas within their operation. But writing a code involves much more than simply putting words on paper. How the code is written and developed, is probably just as important as the final product. Code writers must develop a process that ensures "buy in" from every part of the company, how the code will guide practice and how the code will be used to teach good practice.

## OVERLOOKED ISSUES

While most companies that have written and implemented a global code of ethics have tales of employee skepticism and resistance to the introduction of the code; most of these can be traced to a single common element or failure that goes back to the process of development—namely, employees were not consulted in its formation. The most effective way of obtaining employee "buy-in" of the code is to ensure that employees have a big say in how it was developed. They need to be consulted and encouraged to participate in the drafting of the principles underlying the code.

The code should go through several drafts before it is finalized and each draft needs to be circulated among employees with a clear mechanism to register their input. Employees should feel they have had a part in drafting the code; they cannot feel that unless they have actually had a part in drafting it. They must see the code changing in response to their input.

## MAKE IT USER-FRIENDLY

A code needs to explain to all employees and managers how they can use it. A pamphlet explaining options and where to go to get advice is a good start. A "hotline" employees can call to ask questions and get interpretations of the code is essential. There should be guidelines on how someone can raise the issue of an ethical breech and a procedure for suggestions for how a code can be updated or changed. The code should also include an ethical decision-making model and case studies.

In a nutshell, the code should be:

- Easy to read.
- Practical and relevant for each business or geographic market.
- Sufficient but not excessive in detail.
- Well written and accessible in tone.

Obviously, business ethics policies vary widely in format, such as printed brochures or manuals or publication on a company's intranet. While the exact content may vary, effective policies address key business relationships: employees, customers, vendors, competitors and the public. The individual topics often directly state standards for complying with laws, avoiding conflicts of interest, protecting company property and confidential information, maintaining health and safety in the workplace, avoiding discrimination and harassment and respecting privacy. Some companies expect their contractors and suppliers to live up to the same ethics policy.

## QUESTIONS TO ASK

Before sitting down to authorize the formation of a company ethics code, an organization's management should consider these questions:

1. What do we hope to achieve?
2. Why is this important to us?
3. What does success in this arena look like?
4. Who is the target audience?
5. Who are the persons or groups of persons affected by our organization or individual members of our organization, and how are they prioritized?

6. What are our organization's main areas of action?
7. What unethical decisions and actions would our organization like to prevent, and how could they be prevented?
8. What ethical problems are members of our organization most likely to encounter?
9. How can conflicting principles be resolved?

## WHAT CODES ADDRESS

A survey of major global corporations by The Conference Board, an independent business research organization, found that codes of conduct most often addressed these issues (in descending order of frequency):

1. Bribery, improper payments.
2. Conflict of interest.
3. Security of proprietary information.
4. Receiving gifts.
5. Environment.
6. Sexual harassment.
7. Antitrust.
8. Workplace safety.
9. Political activities.
10. Community relations.
11. Confidentiality of personal information.
12. Human rights.
13. Employee privacy.
14. Whistle-blowing.
15. Substance abuse.
16. Nepotism.
17. Child labor.

## MAKE SURE IT TRANSLATES

Attempting to transmit a code of conduct or ethics from one culture to another is a special challenges. An interesting case study, presented by the Paris-based European School of Management in its publication *Trends*, cites the Japanese manufacturing and trading company Matsushita Group's (Panasonic is Matsushita's best known corporate brand) attempt to introduce what it calls its Basic Management Objective and Seven Principles (a corporate philosophy and basic code of conduct) to the company's French workers. The challenge for management was to translate these rather spiritual principles—all of them based on Japanese culture and the importance of the group over the individual—into something relevant for French culture, which is far less group oriented. The Basic Management Objective places a heavy emphasis on group well-being while the Seven Principles attempt to create the type of employer/employee relationship found in Japan, rather than in France, which is heavily unionized.

### The Basic Management Objective

Recognizing our responsibilities as industrialists, we will devote ourselves to the progress and development of society and the well-being of people through our business activities, thereby enhancing the quality of life throughout the world.

### The Seven Principles

1. CONTRIBUTION TO SOCIETY We will conduct ourselves at all times in accordance with the Basic Management Objective, faithfully fulfilling our responsibilities as industrialists to the communities in which we operate.
2. FAIRNESS AND HONESTY We will be fair and honest in all our business dealings and personal conduct. No matter how talented and knowledgeable we may be, without personal integrity, we can neither earn the respect of others nor enhance our own self-respect.
3. COOPERATION AND TEAM SPIRIT We will pool our abilities to accomplish our shared goals. No matter how talented we are as individuals, without cooperation and team spirit we will be a company in name only.
4. UNTIRING EFFORT FOR IMPROVEMENT We will strive constantly to improve our ability to contribute to society through our business activities. Only through this untiring effort can we fulfill our Basic Management Objective and help to realize lasting peace and prosperity.
5. COURTESY AND HUMILITY We will always be cordial and modest, respecting the rights and needs of others in order to strengthen healthy social relationships and improve the quality of life in our communities.
6. ADAPTABILITY We will continually adapt our thinking and behavior to meet the ever-changing conditions around us, taking care to act in harmony with nature to ensure progress and success in our endeavors.
7. GRATITUDE we will act out of a sense of gratitude for all benefits we have received, confident that this attitude will be a source of unbounded joy and vitality, enabling us to overcome obstacles we encounter.

These principles would make perfect sense to a Japanese worker, but would be a tough sell to a French worker who does not share the same sense of hierarchical duty. The first problem they needed to overcome was in the physical translation of the principles from the Japanese into the French language. A verbatim translation probably would not have worked because many of the powerful allegories would be lost along with some of the uniquely Japanese ideological references. Instead, the company created a set of principles in French based not on the verbatim translation, but rather on one that stripped out the redundancies and non-transferable references in the original; it gave them more of a universal context that French workers would understand.

To implement the code of conduct, all workers were given seminars in the corporate philosophy as well as some examples from the French workplace to show how these concepts could be applied. The French workers were taught how to understand the corporate mindset of the company's Japanese managers in France and were encouraged to debate the value of the principles. The purpose of the seminars was to create a sense of ownership among the French workers for these "foreign" values. The key to the success of the project was that both senior French and Japanese management provided leadership in this area and demonstrated the use of the values in day-to-day practice. Instead of just being another management fad of the month, the seven principles have become a part of the everyday activities of employees.

## Guidelines for Ethical Leadership

Of course, any corporate ethics program is only as good as its leaders. A good leader is a person that others trust. How can a corporate CEO exhibit leadership in the development of an ethics program and promote a culture where good ethical behavior is the norm? Good leaders:

- Are actively involved in the creation and management of corporate ethics and compliance programs.
- Ensure that their involvement is highly visible.
- Communicate why ethics is a core business issue.
- Acknowledge the ethical issues involved in the making of critical decisions and detail how the decision addresses those issues.
- Insist that company managers talk through the ethics of their decisions in detail.
- Ensure that all company managers understand their impact on organizational culture and how the attention or inattention to the ethical dimension of their choices impacts the organization's culture.

## Reactive, Proactive or "No" Active?

Why are some companies able to successfully deal with an ethical crisis while others often compound the damage by adopting a mindset of denial and arrogance? Experts refer to The Seven Deadly Sins—types of behavior that are common among organizations that have failed to successfully handle an ethical crisis. In many cases the damage to corporate reputation was made exponentially worse by the handling of the crisis rather than the crisis itself.

The Seven Deadly Sins:

1. USE DAMAGE CONTROL Don't worry, the crisis will blow over in a day. It is better to say little or nothing rather than overreact.
2. DENY THE PROBLEM Call it an isolated incident; deny any further investigation is necessary.
3. BE PROUD OR ARROGANT Of course such a thing could never happen in a company like ours. It isn't our fault; it's the accuser who is to blame.
4. DON'T CONCERN YOURSELF WITH PEOPLE ISSUES There was no breach of corporate procedure so we must be in the right, regardless of the fairness of the situation.
5. DON'T BOTHER WITH MORALITY Never admit that a moral issue is more important than a business issue.

6. DON'T TAKE RESPONSIBILITY Simply refuse to acknowledge that you have an ethical responsibility to the community and other stakeholders.
7. DON'T APOLOGIZE—EVER.

WARNING: Some of these "sins" are not thought of as such in all cultures. Cultures with strict hierarchical structures or a heightened sense of privacy, for instance, would find many of the "sins" to be standard operating procedures of which every participant approves. Western firms touting complete transparency and the airing of company laundry in public will not find universal acceptance of the practices.

## Developing A Global Perspective In Managers

Learning to spot intolerable practices and to exercise good judgment when ethical conflicts arise requires practice. Creating a company culture that rewards ethical behavior is essential. The following guidelines for developing a global ethical perspective among managers can help.

- Treat corporate values and formal standards of conduct as absolutes. Whatever ethical standards a company chooses, it cannot waver on its principles either at home or abroad.
- Design and implement conditions of engagement for suppliers and customers.
- Allow foreign business units to help formulate ethical standards and interpret ethical issues. The French pharmaceutical company Rhone Poulenc Rorer has allowed foreign subsidiaries to augment lists of corporate ethical principles with their own suggestions. Texas Instruments has paid special attention to issues of international business ethics by creating the Global Business Practices Council, which is made up of managers from the various countries in which the company operates.
- In host countries, support efforts to decrease institutional corruption. Individual managers will not be able to wipe out corruption in a host country by themselves, no matter how many bribes they turn down. When a host country's tax system, import and export procedures and procurement practices favor unethical players, companies must take action.
- Exercise moral imagination. Using moral imagination means resolving tensions responsibly and creatively. Coca-Cola, for instance, has consistently turned down requests for bribes from Egyptian officials but has managed to gain political support and public trust by sponsoring a project to plant fruit trees. And take the example of Levi Strauss, which discovered in the early 1990s that two of its suppliers in Bangladesh were employing children under the age of 14—a practice that violated the company's principles but was tolerated in Bangladesh. Forcing the suppliers to fire the children would not have ensured that the children received an education, and it would have caused serious hardship for the families depending on the children's wages. In a creative arrangement, the suppliers agreed to pay the children's regular wages while they attended school and to offer each child a job at age 14. Levi Strauss, in turn, agreed to pay the children's tuition and provide books and uniforms. That arrangement allowed Levi Strauss to uphold its principles and provide long-term benefits to its host country.

## What is an Effective Ethics Program?

Having a written policy is only the first step. Training, monitoring and correcting are just as important. An effective ethics program should include these steps:

1. Establish corporate standards and procedures.
2. Appoint at least one high level individual in the business organization to oversee compliance (and use due care not to appoint someone with an already questionable set of ethics).
3. Require everyone in the corporation to participate in training or at least read the standards and procedures.
4. Implement regular monitoring and auditing systems.
5. Enforce the standards consistently; respond quickly to detected offenses and prevent further offenses.

## Is Your Program Effective?

How can you judge if your corporate ethics program is an effective one? Effective programs have these traits in common:

- The organization's values are consistent with each other so that expectations are clear.
- Employees at all levels understand the organization's fundamental values.
- Value statements are perceived as valid guidelines for decision-making in the absence of policy or precedent.
- Stated values address the actions of the organization as it deals with employees.
- Stated values address the organization's dealings with customers and suppliers.
- The rules for doing business stay the same in good times and when things are not going well.
- People know where to go for guidance when they need an interpretation of organizational values.
- Rewards for "whistle-blowers" when they are correct and punishment when they are proven false.
- The organization's stated values are consistent with the values and ethics of the business community.

## Measuring Success

Perhaps one of the most difficult aspects of maintaining a corporate ethics program is obtaining quantifiable measures of success (or failure). There are, of course, some obvious measures, such as fewer fines or legal suits, but they measure legal compliance performance as opposed to the true effectiveness of an ethics program.

It is best that companies do benchmark surveys of employees (and even vendors and customers) either before an ethics program is instituted or as soon as possible after its start. Benchmarking also can be effective in measuring the impact of changes in ethics codes, provided surveys are done before and after the changes. And finally, admit to the bean counters and corporate planners that some things only can be measured subjectively.

Some of the more subtle success measures include:

- Reduced unethical/illegal conduct.
- Improved employee awareness of legal issues.
- Employee willingness to look for advice.
- Employee comfort in bringing problems, failure and bad news to supervisors.
- Employee willingness to report violations.
- Employee commitment to the organization.
- Better employee decision-making.

## Six Steps For An Effective Ethics Program

1. Tailor standards to the company's business needs.
2. Designate high-level managers to oversee compliance.
3. Educate employees in the company's standards and procedures through publications and training.
4. Design a compliance system than includes auditing and monitoring procedures and a mechanism that encourages employees to report potential violations.
5. Enforce standards through consistent discipline.
6. Report all violations and take appropriate action to improve the program.

## Twelve Steps For Implementing A Code Of Business Ethics

1. INTEGRATION Produce a strategy for integrating the code into the running of the business at the time that it is issued.
2. ENDORSEMENT Make sure that the code is endorsed by the chairman, CEO or managing director.
3. CIRCULATION Send the code to all employees in a readable and portable form, and give to all employees joining the company.
4. BREACHES Include a short section on how an employee should react if he or she is faced with a potential breach of the code or is in doubt about a course of action involving an ethical choice.
5. PERSONAL RESPONSE Give all staff the personal opportunity to respond to the content of the code.
6. AFFIRMATION: Have a procedure for managers and supervisors to regularly state that they and their staff understand and apply the provisions of the code and raise matters not covered by it.

7. REGULAR REVIEW Have a procedure for regular review and updating of the code.
8. CONTRACTS Consider making adherence to the code obligatory by including reference to it in all contracts of employment and linking it with disciplinary procedures.
9. TRAINING Ask those responsible for company training programs at all levels to include issues raised by the code in their programs.
10. TRANSLATION See that the code is translated and properly localized into local languages used at overseas subsidiaries.
11. DISTRIBUTION Make copies of the code available to business partners (suppliers, customers, etc.), and expect their compliance.
12. ANNUAL REPORT Reproduce or insert a copy of the code in the Annual Report so shareholders and a wider public know about the company's position on ethical matters.

## Do Global Companies Really Exist?

What does being a truly global company mean? First, it requires new ways of thinking. It means going beyond just being a Swedish company with global products and foreign offices or a South Korean conglomerate with a manufacturing plant in Brazil. Most large companies that deal in the global marketplace are not yet truly global enterprises. Rather, they still think in compartments, viewing their home market as the driving force beyond their existence and new products. The average multinational company that thinks of itself as a global concern still produces more than two-thirds of its output and locates two-thirds of its employees in its home country. For example, although both operate worldwide, the culture of Ford Motor Company is distinctively American while that of Volkswagen identifiably German. Yet, there is no denying that multinationals are the main force behind worldwide flows of capital, goods and services.

## Company Codes: A Global Sampling

The following are a set of extracts of company ethics and behavioral codes from global corporations. One interesting contrast is the relative lack of specifics involved in the code for Japan's Mitsubishi Motors compared to companies based in Europe and the United States. The Mitsubishi statement, however, is in keeping with an Eastern view of ethics and is representative of the state of corporate ethics codes in that region.

Other interesting cases are that of Sara Lee Corporation's Supplier Selection Guidelines and Levi Strauss' Terms of Engagement Guidelines, which are clear in their purpose of forcing suppliers into ethical behaviors. Companies are finding out that, at least in the eyes of the public, you are really only as ethical as your least ethical supplier. (Just ask giant American retailers K-Mart and Wal-Mart, which have been forced in recent years to fight public relations battles relating to the supply of clothing from factories alleged to be using child labor in Latin America.)

## Unilever

Unilever is a global supplier of consumer goods in foods, household care and personal care product categories. It sells spreads, oils and cooking fats in more than 100 countries. The company's home care brands are also available in over 100 countries. The company's most popular international home care brands include Omo, Surf, Skip, All, Comfort, Wisk, Cif, Domestos and, in the UK, Persil.

### Unilever's Code of Business Principles

Unilever enjoys a reputation for conducting its business with integrity and with respect for the interests of those our activities can affect. This reputation is an asset, just as real as our people, factories and brands. Our first priority is to be a profitable business and that means investing for growth and balancing short-term and long-term interests. It also means caring about our customers, employees, shareholders and suppliers, and the communities in which we conduct our operations.

In the course of meeting our business objectives, we consider it essential that all employees understand and comply with our values and therefore share the Unilever way of doing things. It is very easy in the realm of business ethics to make high sounding statements of little practical value. The general principles contained in this Code are the bedrock; more detailed guidance tailored to the needs of different countries and companies already exists and will be further developed. This Code of Business Principles is a core Unilever statement.

- STANDARD OF CONDUCT: Unilever conducts its business with honesty and integrity and with respect for the interests of those with whom it has relationships.
- OBEYING THE LAW: Unilever companies are required to comply with the laws and regulations of the countries in which they operate.
- EMPLOYEES: Unilever companies are required to recruit, employ and promote employees on the sole basis of the qualifications and abilities needed for the work to be performed. Unilever is committed to providing safe and healthy working conditions for its employees worldwide. Unilever believes it is essential to maintain good communications with employees, normally through company based information and consultation procedures.
- CONFLICTS OF INTEREST: Unilever expects its employees to avoid personal activities and financial interests which could conflict with their commitment to their jobs. Steps are taken to ensure that employees receive appropriate guidance in areas where such conflicts can arise.
- PUBLIC ACTIVITIES: Unilever neither supports political parties nor contributes to the funds of groups whose activities are calculated to promote party interests. Unilever companies are encouraged to promote and defend their legitimate business interests. In so doing they may either directly, or through bodies such as trade associations, raise questions and discuss particular government actions or decisions. Where their experience can be useful, they are encouraged to cooperate with governments, individuals, agencies and other organizations in the development of proposed legislation and other regulations which may affect such legitimate interests. Unilever companies are also encouraged to respond to

requests from governments and other agencies for information, observations or opinion on issues relevant to business and the community in which we operate.

- PRODUCT ASSURANCE: Unilever is committed to providing products which consistently offer value in terms of price and quality, and which are safe for their intended use.
- ENVIRONMENTAL ISSUES: Unilever is committed to running its business in an environmentally sound and sustainable manner. Accordingly its aim is to ensure that its processes and products have the minimum adverse environmental impact commensurate with the legitimate needs of the business.
- COMPETITION: Unilever believes in vigorous yet fair competition and supports the development of appropriate competition laws. Employees receive guidance to ensure that they understand such laws and do not transgress them.
- RELIABILITY OF FINANCIAL REPORTING: Unilever accounting records and supporting documents must accurately describe and reflect the nature of the underlying transactions. No undisclosed or unrecorded account, fund or asset will be established or maintained.
- BRIBERY: Unilever does not give or receive bribes in order to retain or bestow business or financial advantages. Unilever employees are directed that any demand for or offer of such bribes must be immediately rejected.
- APPLICATION: This Code applies to Unilever companies throughout the world. Where Unilever companies participate in joint ventures the application of these principles will be actively promoted; this will significantly influence the decision to enter into or to continue in any joint venture.
- COMPLIANCE: It is the responsibility of the Board of Unilever to ensure that the principles embodied in this Code are communicated to, understood and observed by all employees. An independent Internal Audit function supports the Board in monitoring compliance with the Code. The Board of Unilever will not criticize management for any loss of business resulting from adherence to these principles. Equally, the Board of Unilever undertakes that no employee will suffer as a consequence of bringing to their attention, or that of senior management, a breach or suspected breach of these principles.

In this Code the expressions "Unilever" and "Unilever companies" are used for convenience and mean the Unilever Group of companies comprising Unilever N.V., Unilever PLC and their respective subsidiary companies. The Board of Unilever means the Directors of Unilever N.V. and Unilever PLC.

## Mitsubishi Motors

Japan's Mitsubishi Motors Corporation announced the introduction of a revised set of corporate principles for member companies of the Mitsubishi Motors group both in and outside of Japan. "Mitsubishi Motors' Corporate Principles" (Japan) and the English-language version "The Spirit of Global Mitsubishi Motors Way" (worldwide) reflect the spirit of the "Innovation in Motion" corporate policy for 1998 that replaces the "Corporate Principles" introduced in June 1980.

### Mitsubishi Motors' Corporate Principles (Japan)

- To realize Innovation in Motion, always for the benefit of the customer.
- To be constantly innovative, from a truly global perspective.
- To conduct oneself with integrity, as a member of a company that is above-board and ethical in its dealings.

### The Spirit of Global Mitsubishi Motors Way (worldwide)

- Customer satisfaction.
- Speedy and simple.
- Innovative and creative.
- Fair and open.

The revised corporate principles aim to provide all concerned with appropriate guidelines in their efforts to:

- Realize Innovation in Motion. This goal will be achieved by improving customer satisfaction and building up long-running relationships with customers through on-going innovation in the company's activities and an ongoing questioning and appraisal of what constitutes excellence from the viewpoint of what value means to the customer. This will enable the company to provide in a timely manner the kind of products and service that are readily acceptable to the customer.
- Make meaningful contributions to environmental conservation and to development of the world community. These contributions are to be made from a global perspective.
- Become a company with a presence. In other words to become, from a corporate ethics viewpoint, a company that is readily accepted by the community it operates in for the aboveboard and ethical manner in which it conducts itself. Giving precedence to human and social qualities, the company must conduct itself with integrity and remain true to its principles, as epitomized in "Shoji komei" [integrity and fairness], the words of Iwasaki Koyata—4th president of the old Mitsubishi organization.

"The Spirit of Global Mitsubishi Motors Way" is a simplified version of the new code of conduct that uses keywords to capture the essence of the concepts in the Japanese version and is written in English for group companies outside Japan. It takes into consideration, differences in culture, climate and ways of thinking.

*1: To create products which distinguish themselves by excellent quality and innovative engineering. To put our customers' viewpoint first both in thought and action. To unite all our physical and mental resources in a cooperative effort to serve our company and society at large.

## Sara Lee Corporation

Sara Lee Corporation is a global manufacturer and marketer of high-quality, brand-name products for consumers throughout the world. With headquarters in Chicago, USA, Sara Lee has operations in more than 40 countries and markets branded products in more than 170 nations.

## Sara Lee Corporation
## Supplier Selection Guidelines

The global expansion of the Sara Lee Corporation's business activities into more countries and diverse cultures requires a commitment to the procurement of products and services in a manner which:

- Is conducive to global good citizenship.
- Will enhance the company's reputation and the image of all Sara Lee brands.
- Will ensure the achievement of Sara Lee's commercial success.

### OBJECTIVE

Sara Lee's objective is to utilize the corporation's purchasing power to influence those from whom the corporation procures products and services to:

- Embrace high standards of ethical behavior.
- Comply with all applicable laws and regulations.
- Treat their employees fairly, and with dignity and respect, so as to promote their welfare and improve their quality of life.
- Be socially responsible citizens in the countries and communities in which they operate.

The following sourcing guidelines have been established to ensure a uniform and consistent approach with all suppliers as Sara Lee pursues these objectives. Operating management is charged with the responsibility to conduct appropriate due diligence with all suppliers before entering into any business relationship. "Suppliers" include contractors, joint venture partners and suppliers of goods and services, including raw material suppliers.

### SUPPLIER SELECTION GUIDELINES

1. ETHICAL STANDARDS

Sara Lee believes in doing business with those suppliers who embrace high standards of ethical business behavior and who demonstrate commitment to those standards through rigorous practices.

2. LEGAL REQUIREMENTS

Sara Lee is committed to full compliance with all laws and regulations in the locations where the corporation operates and conducts business, and will not knowingly operate in violation of any such law or regulation. Sara Lee will not knowingly use suppliers who operate in violation of applicable laws and regulations.

Sara Lee believes in doing business with those suppliers who recognize and respect the right of employees to exercise their lawful rights of free association, including joining or not joining any association.

3. ENVIRONMENTAL REQUIREMENTS

Sara Lee believes in doing business with those suppliers who share the corporation's commitment to the environment, and who pursue practices which conform to applicable environmental standards. Sara Lee expects suppliers to promptly develop and implement plans and programs to correct any non-compliant practices.

4. EMPLOYMENT PRACTICES

A. WORKING HOURS: Sara Lee will not knowingly use suppliers who fail to comply with the legal maximum working hours as specified by each country's standards and laws.

B. CHILD LABOR: Sara Lee will not knowingly use suppliers who employ workers in violation of the local mandatory school age, or under the legal employment age in each country. In no case will Sara Lee procure goods or services from firms employing non-family workers under age 15.

Additionally, Sara Lee will favor those suppliers who are proactive in contributing to the continued education and betterment of its employees.

5. FORCED LABOR Sara Lee will not knowingly use suppliers of either raw materials or finished product that have been produced by forced labor, or services provided by such labor.

6. DISCRIMINATION Sara Lee believes that people should be employed on the basis of the ability to do the job, rather than on the basis of personal characteristics or beliefs. Sara Lee will favor doing business with those suppliers who practice this principle.

7. DISCIPLINARY PRACTICES Sara Lee will not knowingly do business with suppliers who employ any type of corporal punishment, or other forms of mental or physical coercion

8. HEALTH & SAFETY Sara Lee believes in doing business with those suppliers who have demonstrated concern for and commitment to the health and safety of their employees. Additionally, this same guideline applies to those suppliers who provide housing to employees.

## Nokia

Finland's Nokia Corporation is a mobile phone manufacturer and a supplier of mobile, fixed and Internet Protocol networks and related services as well as multimedia terminals. Nokia supplies its products in over 130 countries.

### Nokia's Code of Conduct

Nokia has always recognized that its own long-term interests and those of its various stakeholders depend on compliance with the highest standards of ethical conduct and applicable law. The code of conduct has been approved by Nokia's Group Executive Board and is introduced and reinforced to Nokia employees through induction, training and internal communications.
(The term "stakeholders" refers to employees, customers, suppliers, shareholders, governmental and non-governmental organizations, the communities in which it does business and other parties that have influence over or are influenced by Nokia.)

The code of conduct is reflected in the Nokia Values and Nokia Way of working, and every Nokia employee is expected to conduct himself or herself, and his or her business, in line with this code without exception. Stricter guidelines or more detailed instructions may be appropriate for certain regions or countries, but they should not contradict this Code. Nokia periodically reviews this code of conduct and is committed to making changes in its content and implementation when changes or further clarification so demand.

- ETHICS AND LAW Nokia is strongly committed to the highest standards of ethical conduct, and full compliance with all applicable national and international laws. This includes, for example, those relating to antitrust and promoting fair competition, corporate governance, preventing bribery, illicit payments and corruption, publicly traded securities, safety in the intended use of the products and services Nokia delivers to customers, labor laws and practices, the environment, human rights laws and internationally recognized standards, and protecting copyright, company assets and other forms of intellectual property. Nokia's goal is not mere minimum legal compliance, but as an industry leader to be among the world's best in corporate responsibility, practicing good corporate citizenship wherever it does business.
- HUMAN RIGHTS Nokia will respect and promote human rights. Nokia recognizes, with the international community, that certain human rights should be considered fundamental and universal, based on accepted international laws and practices, such as those of the United Nations' Universal Declaration of Human Rights, International Labour Organization and Global Compact principles.

  Among those rights that Nokia views as fundamental and universal are: freedom from any discrimination based on race, creed, color, nationality, ethnic origin, age, religion, gender, gender reassignment, sexual orientation, marital status, connections with a national minority, disability, or other status; freedom from arbitrary detention, execution or torture; freedom of peaceful assembly and association; freedom of thought, conscience and religion; and freedom of opinion and expression. Nokia will not use child or forced labor. Nokia will not tolerate working conditions or treatment that are in conflict with international laws and practices.
- CONFLICTS OF INTEREST, GIFTS & BRIBES Nokia employees must avoid activity that leads to a conflict of interest. This includes, but is not limited to acceptance and giving of personal gifts or hospitality, to or from Nokia stakeholders, other than gifts of nominal value or reasonable hospitality given in the ordinary course of business. Any agreement or understanding regarding favors or benefits in exchange for the gifts must be avoided. Gifts of other than nominal value may not be accepted without full disclosure to and prior relevant clearance from the employee's supervisor. Nokia and its employees will not pay or offer to pay bribes or illicit payments to government officials or candidates, or other parties, in order to obtain or retain business. Nokia does not provide financial support to political parties or other political groups.

  (Nominal value is defined as EUR 100, though local and national laws take precedent if stricter. A company-wide standard operating procedure on gifts and hospitality exists to give employees further instructions. Stricter regional or national policies may be adopted where appropriate.)
- WORKPLACE PRACTICES Nokia employees must respect and encourage Nokia Values at work, promoting teamwork, individual responsibility, and the strength that comes from diversity. Nokia will strive to pay fair compensation, and provide a safe and healthy workplace for employees. Nokia is committed to equality of opportunity in all its employment practices, policies and procedures.

Job requirements fulfilled, no employee or potential employee will, therefore, receive less favorable treatment due to their race, creed, color, nationality, ethnic origin, age, religion, gender, gender reassignment, sexual orientation, marital status, connections with a national minority, opinion, disability, membership or non-membership of a trade union. Nokia will continue to invest in the personal and professional learning and growth of Nokia's employees. Nokia will encourage its employees to lead balanced personal and professional lives.

- ENVIRONMENT Nokia's environmental activities are based on life-cycle thinking. The goal is to reduce adverse environmental effects during our product life cycles. This is done by managing our own operations and our supplier network, incorporating Design for Environment (DfE) into our product development, processes and service design and supporting sound End-of-life practices.

  Nokia does not use any endangered species for any business purpose and furthermore requests that its suppliers avoid raw material procurement from an origin where there are clear human or animal rights abuse, or the method of procurement or distribution is illegal.

- SUPPLIERS Nokia will do its utmost to contract only with subcontractors or suppliers who themselves adhere to international human rights and environmental laws and practices. Nokia commits to monitoring the ethical performance of its suppliers and to taking immediate and thorough steps in cases where the ethical performance of its suppliers comes into question.

- IMPLEMENTATION The compliance commitment in this Code extends to all matters, including decisions relating to trade, investment, subcontracting, supplying, business development, and in all other business and employment relationships. Nokia's approach to implementing this Code of Conduct will be active, open and ethically sound.

  Although difficult questions of interpretation may arise in specific instances, particularly regarding the need to sensitively balance local customs and requirements with global standards and guidelines, Nokia recognizes that the above commitment means that Nokia will do its utmost to identify ethical, legal, environmental, employment, and human rights issues and resolve matters consistent with this Code of Conduct.

  It is the responsibility of each Nokia employee to promote this Code. Questions about the application or meaning of any provisions of this Code, or potential violations of the Code are to be reported to superiors. Where serious allegations are concerned, fair and comprehensive investigations will be conducted by those senior Human Resources, Security and line management closest to the issue. If this is inappropriate, more senior managers or global heads of these functions should be notified.

  Acts inconsistent with this Code must be promptly corrected and are subject to disciplinary action up to and including termination of employment. Nokia will ensure that there will be no adverse work-related consequences as a result of an employee bringing complaints of violations of this Code.

---

NOTE: Although the guidelines presented above go a long way towards addressing the ethics issue, none are perfect nor could they be applied easily in every society. The reader will observe that each is burdened with its own "headquarters country" cultural bias.

CHAPTER 11

# Managing an International Corporate Ethics Program

*THOUGH ETHICS REQUIRES TRAINING AND RATIONAL CAPABILITY, IT CAN LARGELY BE LEARNED AND APPLIED BY JUST ABOUT ANYBODY.* – PLATO

IF YOUR AIM IS TO TEACH bad people to be good, you are doomed to failure. But any company that has somehow managed to exclusively hire a staff of "bad" folks is probably in trouble anyway—or will, at least, soon be. Though the development of a person's moral judgment and character is an ongoing and continuous process, transforming an individual with little moral character into an honest employee is, most often, an insurmountable challenge. The bottom line—a corporate ethics training course won't save you if you employ dishonest people, but it sure can help others make the right decisions to help your business.

NOTE: Some unethical decisions have been made due to inexperience or ignorance and not through any premeditated malice.

## Can You Teach Old Dogs New Tricks?

Experts can't emphasize enough that ethics training isn't really about teaching somebody to be an honest or good person. Beware of the consultant that promises otherwise. The reality is that those values and good traits should have been learned at home, in school or through normal social interactions. The aim of an ethics-training program is to reinforce existing personal values and tie them into "the big picture" values of the company.

Personal character really does matter in the workplace. Employees don't leave their character at home when they head for the workplace. It is clearly apparent in all social interactions and constantly relied upon when making decisions at work.

One British ethics training officer for a large service industry organization not-so-fondly recalls a time in the mid 1990s when she was sent to Moscow to introduce a training program explaining her company's ethics code. Since opening in Russia a year earlier, her company had lost hundreds of thousands of pounds of merchandise and physical stock to pilfering.

"I knew pilfering rates in Moscow were high, but ours were even worse than most," she says. "The first thing I did was look at employee records. Most locals had worked for service industries under the old Soviet system. This was a bunch that came as close to having virtually no ethics when it came to workplace behavior.

"I didn't even try to teach a course there. Instead I flew back to London and suggested that the only way we were ever going to end the pilfering and introduce any semblance of ethics in our organization there was to fire the lot. I can teach people how to deal with ethical dilemmas and how to match their personal values with our corporate values, but I can't teach a bunch of dishonest people how to be honest. That's society's role."

The training officer eventually went back to Moscow more than a year later—after most of the local staff had been replaced with a younger, less-Soviet crowd.

"The training course got a very good reception and we now have pilfering rates that are even below average—and they continue to drop. But I will be honest, it wasn't really the course that changed the situation, it was the personal ethics of the new staff. We just showed them how to apply what they already knew and felt and showed them the rewards of ethical behavior."

## Ask Before Hiring

So how does a company ensure that the person they are hiring has at least some grounding in ethical business behavior? Of course, if you ask a potential employee outright if they are an honest, ethical employee, invariably they will answer, "Yes." After all, wouldn't you do the same? There are, however, more subtle methods to judge a potential employee's ethical maturity.

Interviewers say it pays to be alert to how a person responds to a tough question. For example, you might ask the job candidate: "Give me an example of a tough ethical dilemma you've experienced in your career." Or you could ask: "Suppose you come into our company and you find yourself working for a boss and you've got questions about his or her ethics. What would you do?"

---

HINT: In employee interviews, always give the candidate plenty of time to answer a difficult question without interjecting or "helping" them with an answer.

---

The key is asking questions that don't necessarily have a right or wrong answer, but enable you to see how a person responds. For instance, are they comfortable with the ethics issue? And do they have the ability to talk about it without getting nervous. If they say, "I never thought about that before," that may be telling you something about their ethical awareness—and their lack of experience as well.

---

WARNING: This direct approach is very difficult to apply in high privacy or high context cultures. Simply asking a direct question does not always bring a direct, or even true, answer even in cultures that revel in transparency. Interview situations often result in applicants saying what they think the interviewer wants to hear. Direct questioning is best used at upper management levels rather than with line employees.

---

## Teaching Ethics Means Raising Awareness

If "good" and "bad" behavior can't be easily taught, what can be taught is the ability to recognize ethical issues and problems in the workplace, the importance of the corporate ethics code and what actions one needs to take to arrive at a decision that complies with that code.

Before designing a training course, management needs to consider three basic facts of life:

1. Employees should be held accountable for their actions.
2. They cannot be held accountable for rules that are vague or unclear.
3. Employees are basically trustworthy, but may not be able to make good decisions in circumstances that are confusing.

Employees need to be armed with the knowledge to analyze and resolve ethical dilemmas so that they aren't paralyzed. In fact, the word "training" can be misleading when applied to corporate ethics programs. No company, regardless of its geographic location or home culture, can train employees to act ethically in the same way that it can provide training in specific job skill courses like computer software or accounting methods. After all, employees come to a job with a personal set of moral standards and values already in place.

With this perspective in mind, the role of ethics training should be to raise awareness about business ethics issues and educate employees about proper business conduct standards and the core values of the organization. The goal should be to provide employees with the guidance and tools they need to apply these standards and values in the workplace and make sound ethical business decisions.

The goals of a corporate ethics training program can be summarized as follows:

- Enhance staff knowledge on legal requirements.
- Enable staff to understand and realize ethical standards set by their company.
- Equip staff with skills to handle ethical dilemmas.
- Equip management with skills to detect early warning signs of corruption, fraud and malpractice.
- Enable staff to abide by the company's code of conduct.

---

NOTE: Most firms, especially retailers, make adjustments to their forecasts and pricing to allow for employee theft of goods and misuse of company time. Managers readily accept the existence of these ethical lapses, but become concerned when theft exceeds expectation.

---

## Training Benefits

The 750 members of the Ethics Officers Association are thoroughly convinced about the benefits to their organizations of the job they do—and they seemed to have convinced those that hold the pursestrings that ethics training does have company-wide benefits. In a 2000 survey of ethics officers, 99 percent responded that they believed their company's commitment to ethics will increase or at least remain the same in the next five years.

As for benefits, an effective training program can:

- Improve performance by linking corporate values to individual success.
- Enhance overall organizational effectiveness by encouraging mutual respect and trust.

- Increase responsiveness to competitive challenges by fostering candor and willingness to learn from mistakes.
- Strengthen organizational culture by encouraging, recognizing and rewarding values-based behavior.
- Help create an honest, trustworthy and ethical staff that are valuable assets of a company and the community as a whole.
- Enhance the reputation and brand name of a company.

## Desired Outcomes: First Know The Rules

Before beginning a training program it is essential that an organization define exactly what it wants to achieve through the training. Experts suggest some rather broad but worthy goals.

### ALL EMPLOYEES SHOULD:

- Know the rules and understand why they are in place for the company as a whole as well as in their functional area.
- Act responsibly.
- Use decision-making resources and skills.
- Apply the rules appropriately.
- Know how and where to get help.

### ADDITIONAL GOALS FOR MANAGERS:

- Know how to resolve gray areas.
- Exhibit and encourage responsible behavior.
- Identify areas of risk and areas of compliance.
- Set values and provide vision.

## Persuade, Don't Dictate

Teaching ethical behavior is more than supplying a list of do's and don'ts. No adult likes to be told what to do in an authoritarian, demeaning manner. In many cultures, especially those that value the independence of the individual, such an approach is likely to encourage potentially disastrous resistance to the ethics effort. It is a matter of not what you teach, but how you teach it.

Many large multinational corporations have shifted the emphasis of their training programs away from passive employee compliance toward a focus on accountability and active employee commitment to living out corporate core values.

The reason for this shift is simple. In the past, ethics training took on a dictatorial "thou shalt not" tone that alienated employees. Now in vogue is a more positive approach, one that stresses individual responsibility, gives employees the tools to understand corporate standards and values and make sound ethical decisions that put those values into action. Ultimately, the role of ethics training has become the empowerment of each and every employee to make ethical decisions.

While a training course cannot always offer employees the clear-cut answers they may seek about ethical matters, it can reinforce a core set of standards and values that will enhance their abilities to make sound ethical decisions on behalf of the company they represent.

## Typical Training Packages

In large corporations, there is no one single training method that is guaranteed to be successful. Most rely on a variety of educational methods, precisely because employees have different learning styles that need to be addressed. Methods include videotapes, live action dramas that present questionable behaviors, ethical case studies and face-to-face meetings. Computer-based interactive multimedia training provides an opportunity to communicate a consistent message to all employees.

Face-to-face discussion and dialogue are perhaps the most important part of any ethics training initiative. Also useful in large firms is an ethics hotline—a confidential telephone number with dedicated trained employees that people can use 24 hours a day, seven days a week, to ask confidential questions and raise concerns about business conduct issues.

One key for success is to obtain input from employees about their most pressing concerns and use that information to design training programs. A training effort is much more effective when it addresses issues that are meaningful to employees. Companies can actually use their hotlines and training sessions as a channel for gathering information about the topics employees most want to discuss.

## A Phased Introduction: One Company's Experience

Through trial and error, corporations have learned that introducing a corporate training program is best done though phases with management being trained before the rank and file. Here is how one large telecommunications company handled the introduction of its ethics training program.

All management employees from senior officers to first-line supervisors were required to take an Ethics Awareness Workshop. They experienced a training package designed to help employees understand the importance of using the ethics code and to encourage dialogue about ethical issues and decisions they might face on the job. Having equipped management with the fundamental tools, the company then included line employees through meetings with their supervisors.

The next building block enhancement, designed to bring awareness to a new level, was Values and Ethics in the Workplace—a course developed for managers to reinforce the company's core values and help managers learn how to put those values into action in their organizations. The cornerstone of this training was an ethical decision-making model—a structured step-by-step guide for employees who face an ethical dilemma.

The other type of training program was a more targeted effort addressing specific topics or a particular job level or work function with a cluster of related concerns. One course dealt with employees working with government officials and employees. The training used hypothetical case studies to help employees refine their abilities to think through ethical issues.

When the company's ethics code was rewritten, the company devised a new training program; it featured a 30-minute videotape accompanied by a leader's guide to help supervisors frame discussions about the video with their work teams. The tape included three real-life vignettes, each dramatically portraying a key ethics issue employees might face in the workplace—respecting others in the workplace, the accuracy of company reports and safeguarding the privacy of customer records.

After initial training modules helped employees gain a general understanding of the importance of ethics in the workplace, the company refined the training to help employees make daily job decisions using the company's core values as a framework.

## The Basic Elements of an Effective Ethics Training Course

In the late 1990s, KPMG's Business Ethics Institute and the Center for the Study of Ethics and Behavior in Accounting at Binghampton University surveyed 41 multinational firms to determine essential tools for ethics training. In addition to senior management's genuine commitment to ethical behavior, the following are the most important elements of an effective training course:

1. Training that focuses on improving decision-making and reasoning skills rather than preaching legal compliance or rule adherence.
2. Live instruction and face-to-face interaction and dialogue among peers.
3. Small classes of no more than 25 people to allow employees to interact and role play more freely.
4. Executive endorsement. Ethics training programs receive more support among employees when senior managers make personal visits, provide a video-taped message and generally promote the importance of ethical behavior within the global marketplace.
5. Follow-up communication within six months of the first ethics course. Various follow-up approaches include an ethics article in the company newsletter, organizing an employee network and informal ethics focus groups to discuss case materials in person or via the company intranet.
6. Other key features of an effective ethics training program include realistic case materials, the use of a professional trainer, at least four hours of training, a separate course on compliance and an awareness program for new employees.

## Essentials for Ethics Training

Experts agree that five elements are essential for an effective training program:

1. A phased approach.
2. Multi media messages and multiple delivery systems.
3. Decision-making resources (written code, help-line).
4. Case discussions.
5. Multimedia ethics games and simulations.

## Ways to Deliver the Ethics Message

- Videos.
- Brochures.
- Posters.
- Newsletters.
- Novelties.
- Intranet.
- Management actions—"walking the talk."

## Keep the Message International

The term "ethics" is a culturally loaded and international companies need to be careful when devising a training program for all, lest they tap into a deep well of resentment. When devising a training program it is important to make sure that the ideas and concepts included in the program are not too deeply imbedded in any particular culture. While virtually all multinational organizations translate their ethics code, fewer actually translate their training materials—a silly mistake. When including videos in a training program, use subtitles whenever possible. It makes your international staff feel that you are interested in making ethics a transnational program. Do not staff all international ethics positions with individuals from your home country. Choose representatives and trainers who are native to the region in question—someone who knows the local language, customs and culture.

## Training to the Rescue: Hong Kong Emergency

Over 80 percent of business managers and young workers responding to a 2000 Survey of Young People's Attitude Towards Work Ethics commissioned by the Independent Commission Against Corruption (ICAC) said the ethical standards of working youth in Hong Kong were deteriorating. Besides, 40 percent of the respondents rated the work ethics of young people as low or very low.

The findings concurred with results of annual ICAC surveys over the past three years, which indicated Hong Kong's youngsters were comparatively more tolerant of corruption than older generations who had witnessed or suffered from this rampant evil in the 1970s.

Worries over these findings prompted the Conference on Work Ethics of Young People, held at the Hong Kong Convention Center. About 450 people from 250 organizations in various fields—youth, business, education and social services—gathered to map out strategies to improve ethical standards of young people through training. Their answer: introduce ethical training in schools and companies.

## The Ethics Office

In some organizations the ethics officer has often been seen as a policeman, enforcing conduct, doing formal audits and disciplining wrongdoers. However, this vision has changed in recent years, partly because corporate ethics programs have become more comprehensive (and subtle) and the ethics officers themselves realized that they were becoming more isolated within their organization. (No one wants to have lunch with a guy who may be spying on them.)

Today, the basic mission of the ethics office in a major corporation goes beyond simple enforcement and punishment. It must integrate organizational values and integrity throughout all operations to help the organization and its employees live their values with every decision and action.

The ethics officer needs to interact across all functions from legal to human resources to security to corporate governance. The role can be summarized as follows:

1. To ensure that business policies and practices continue to be aligned with ethical principles.
2. To clearly communicate ethical expectations.
3. To provide multiple channels for feedback through which people can ask questions, voice concerns, and seek resolution to ethical issues.
4. To oversee ethics training.
5. To oversee investigations.

## The Ethics Officer Profile

According to the Ethical Officers Association, the typical ethics officer in a large multinational corporation:

- Has been in his/her position for 3.2 years.
- Has been at his/her company for 14.2 years.
- Is 49 years old.
- Has a background in the Legal or Human Resources departments.
- His/her key responsibilities are:
- Developing ethics policies and procedures.
- Overseeing organization-wide ethics and compliance communications, including external reporting.
- Overseeing investigations, training.
- Risk assessment.

Above all, an ethics investigator must be a good listener.

## Ethics Investigations

The first step in any workplace investigation, regardless of where on the planet it is taking place, is to prevent the situation from getting any worse. If merchandise is going out the back door in Moscow, Idaho USA or Moscow, Russia, the reaction should be the same—get a better lock. If an employee is complaining about sexual harassment in New York or New Delhi, you should react the same in both cases—make sure that no further incidents occur while the investigation is taking place.

The reality of the international business world today is that no ethics program, no matter how well designed or implemented, can prevent all wrongdoing. But how seriously a company regards violations and pursues an investigation may dictate the severity of any legal sanction.

Every nation has its own set of laws governing privacy issues and every culture has its own set of norms regarding management intrusion into areas of personal privacy. Unions, too, will maintain their own versions of what management can and cannot do in an investigation. It is important that an investigation take these basic facts of international life into account—and every investigative team should have at least one individual who is aware of the cultural and legal intricacies of the region. Five basic rules of thumb for investigators, regardless of their geographic location, are:

1. First impressions aren't always correct.
2. One new piece of information can change the whole perspective.
3. One small misunderstanding can take you down the wrong path.
4. Listening and trying to understand others helps to see the whole picture.
5. Good communication is essential in solving problems.

## Common and Uncommon Investigation Techniques

The most common investigative techniques used in an ethics investigation in international businesses are not too dissimilar from those many local police departments would use, though investigators working for a corporation have an easier time getting access to some materials, such as computer disks, voice mail and e-mail.

Some of the basic techniques used by corporations in their ethics investigations include:

- Document reviews of the transaction in question.
- Examination of personnel records.
- Examination of travel and expense records.
- Interviews with witnesses and other affected employees.
- Retrieval of electronic data such as e-mail and computer disks, including network drives.
- Retrieval of telephone records.
- Examination of voice mail.
- Examination of records of entry into the premises.
- Public records searches (to establish possible motives or personal agendas).
- Criminal background checks.
- Confrontational interviews with the individuals in question.

Depending on the size and scope of the investigation and the potential impact on a corporation's reputation or bottom line (potential fines for violation of laws), more intense techniques are sometimes employed. These include:

- Physical surveillance.
- Eavesdropping, such as telephone taps.
- Desk, file and locker searches.
- Police intervention.

- Personal trash searches.
- Personal credit reports and review of bank records.
- Paying informants for information.
- Polygraph tests.
- Undercover sting operations.

## Tips For Handling An Ethics Investigation

- Take each complaint seriously (but don't assume the first story is the whole story).
- Thoroughly understand all the factors involved.
- Think though the steps that are required.
- Uphold promises of privacy and confidentiality.
- Act in a timely fashion.
- Meet with the accused.
- Document the investigation.
- Suggest both internal and external remedies.
- Implement a follow-up procedure to avoid future problems.

## What Actually Is Being Investigated These Days?

According to a survey by the Ethics Officer Association, the typical ethics office staff launched an average of 59 investigations in a single year. For global companies with revenues over US$10 billion, the average was 120 investigations.

The most frequently investigated categories were:

1. Misuse of resources.
2. Conflict of interests.
3. Sexual harassment.
4. Discrimination.
5. Theft.
6. Bribery.

## Investigation Pitfalls

An ethics investigation is not just about catching the malefactor at any cost. Sometimes, how the investigation is conducted has as big an impact on employee morale and trust. A botched ethics investigation may have far worse implications for a company than the unethical practice under investigation. Investigators will face significant dilemmas:

- Should the accused be made aware of the investigation and told who has leveled the accusation(s)?
- When are civil authorities brought into the process?
- Should "whistle-blowers" have their integrity questioned or taken at face value?
- Should "whistle-blowers" be punished if the accusation(s) is proven false?

Experts in the field of ethics investigations cite the following as the most common errors of ethics investigations in the workplace:

- Corporate policies are not clear or non-existent.
- Roles of parties involved in the investigation are not clearly established.
- Investigators are not objective.
- Investigators suffer from an over-zealous mindset. Instead of assembling information for corporate managers to make a decision, they seek to "prove" guilt.
- Confidentiality is violated.
- Rights of the accused are violated.
- Limits to the investigation are not set or not maintained.
- Companies fail to consider the potential impact on customers of the investigation process.
- Inexperienced managers don't know how to react.

---

WARNING: Ethics investigators must be careful not to violate an employee's legal rights during an investigation. Improper procedures may subject the company to legal liability and bad publicity.

---

## Helplines/Hotlines: They Don't Work In All Cultures

When it comes to managing a global corporate ethics program, the use of telephone hotlines or helplines can be a major component of success—or a major cultural no-no, depending on how and where they are used.

Contrary to popular wisdom, international corporations view their ethics hotlines primarily, not as "snitch lines" for anonymous accusations and tips, but rather as a communications tool to help employees with questions about ethics policy or specifically how to deal with a specific ethical dilemma.

A survey of large multinational corporations by The Conference Board found that over half maintained a telephone information and reporting service related to their ethics program. The main purpose was two-fold: to report potential irregularities and to help employees seek clarification of company ethics and business conduct policies. One-in-five of the companies that maintained these hotlines said they had encountered significant resistance in some countries and cultures.

In some cases, employee resistance may be based on historical events, in others it is the national culture that causes helplines to go unused. Companies report significant resistance to the notion of telephone hotlines in Europe. Indeed, resistance to the idea of anonymous accusations, informers and telephone tip-offs about alleged wrongdoing seems too close to Soviet tactics of using such techniques to denounce enemies and neighbors.

In Latin America and Asia, where the individual comes second to the group and society has a rigid hierarchical culture, the use of a hotline to anonymously report a problem or a perceived ethics violation, is viewed as an act of great disloyalty. It is also considered wrong to deliberately cause a superior to lose face.

And in India, it is highly important who answers the telephone. Callers need to have complete confidence that the person on the other end will keep things confidential. For hotlines to work in India, a culture with great respect for office and authority, the person receiving the complaint must be identified as relatively high up in the organization (ideally, even the CEO). He/she should also be well respected within the organization.

International companies have found that in many cultures confidentiality is often a more important aspect of a hotline than anonymity. Disclosure of confidentiality is essential to the preservation of workplace morale; but anonymity can offer employees a dangerous temptation to make malicious or irresponsible accusations. In some cultures where personal vendettas are common, an ethics hotline program can be easily abused.

Companies should not pursue anonymous calls unless there is a clear cut and urgent concern about a threat to life or property. Finally, regardless of the country or culture they operate in, companies should never offer bounties for information. This action is almost universally disdained in the workplace.

To try and overcome this resistance, many international companies have learned to emphasize the advisory role and personal help in understanding the corporate code that hotlines offer. At the same time, they de-emphasize the "informer" aspects. This tactic will only work, of course, if the organization has an overall system of open and honest communication with its employees and a reputation for fairness and honest treatment.

## Noble Whistle-blower or Venomous Informer?

As part of its international campaign against corruption, the European-based Business and Industry Advisory committee and the Trade Union Advisory Committee to the OECD issued a joint communiqué in December 1999 that recognized a key role for whistle-blowing in anti-corruption programs.

The two committees said that the real impediment to whistle-blowing in Europe was not lingering effects of the informant culture of World War II and the Cold War, but rather the absence of a context of procedures, protections and assurances for whistle-blowers and for those who might be injured by malicious accusations. The two committees said it was far better for systems to be put in place which encourage staff to raise worries within the organization than to place this same staff in a position where they felt they had to approach the media to vent concerns.

To have an effective program in Europe, the committees advised companies to:

1. Communicate a clear statement that malpractice is taken seriously and to give a list of examples of what a company considered to be unethical behavior.
2. Provide assurances of confidentiality for staff raising concerns and an opportunity to raise concerns outside the line management structure.
3. Institute penalties for false and malicious accusations.
4. Give employees a road map on the proper way in which concerns can be raised outside of the organization if they are not answered within the organization.

## Setting The Proper Tone For Global Employees

Baxter International is a large global manufacturer of health and medical products with 45,000 employees in more than 110 countries at more than 250 facilities. Headquartered in Deerfield, Illinois, the company had sales of more than US$6.9 billion. This is how Baxter presents its helpline to its global employees, emphasizing the assistance it can provide them:

"The Business Practices Helpline was established as an independent channel of communication to raise issues and open communications about Baxter Business Practices. Employees, customers, suppliers, and other Baxter constituencies may use this communication vehicle to seek guidance, discuss concerns, or report issues relative to Baxter's business practice standards.

The Business Practices Helpline was established by the Corporate Responsibility Office and is managed by the Business Practices group. A dedicated Business Practices Counselor is available to assist you. You can reach our Counselor during normal business hours. If you are calling after normal business hours please leave a message in our confidential voice mail box and our Counselor will call you back the next business day.

Persons calling the Business Practices Helpline may choose to remain anonymous. There are no caller identification features attached to this line. Our objective it to encourage open communication regarding business practice issues. We are encouraged to see the number of calls we get asking for guidance have increased over time and now far exceed the number of calls we get reporting potential violations!"

CHAPTER 12

# Business/Corporate Intelligence and Ethics: Temptation Abounds

*HE THAT FAILS IN HIS ENDEAVOURS AFTER WEALTH OR POWER WILL NOT LONG RETAIN EITHER HONESTY OR COURAGE.* – SAMUEL JOHNSON (1709-1784)

SUPPORTERS OF "COMMERCIAL INTELLIGENCE" GATHERING say it is just as an essential part of a large corporation's business plan as the sales and marketing functions. Its detractors say it is a dirty business akin to spying. It is an ethically fuzzy area for some and a fact of life for others. It may be hard to trust a business service that has given the world such euphemisms as "waste archeology"—a term that is used to describe sifting through trash for financial, product or marketing secrets.

What is certain these days is that the market for business or corporate intelligence services is mammoth—and growing every year—in every region of the globe. International corporations can't compete these days without employing some elements of "CI," as it is known in the trade.

According to industry associations and government estimates, the market for business intelligence is worth about US$2 billion a year worldwide. A survey by the Society of Corporate Intelligence Professionals found that 25 percent of the hundreds of large corporations interviewed said their company's total corporate intelligence spending in 2000 topped US$100,000. Almost 14 percent said their company spent over US$500,000.

Another survey by The Futures Group found that 82 percent of companies with annual revenues over US$10 billion had an organized system for collecting information on rivals while 60 percent of all companies had an organized intelligence system.

Regardless of the intentions and promises to remain ethical, the reality is that where big money and competitive advantage is involved, the temptation to cross the lines of ethical conduct increases exponentially.

## What is Corporate Intelligence?

Call it what you like, but don't call it corporate espionage, say practitioners. While some managers prefer to cloak it in the relatively harmless sounding veil of "research," the activity of collecting, analyzing and using information regarding any aspect of countries, industries, companies, institutions, and even individuals, to help make informed business decisions is "competitive or business intelligence."

Corporate Intelligence activities run the gamut of the ethical spectrum. At one extreme is blatantly illegal activity, such as theft of trade secrets. At the other end (and what business intelligence is really about) is digging into public information, obscure government records, research papers and trade journals to keep abreast of a competitor's moves. It's the stuff in the middle (hiding identities to get competitor's information or tricking an employee of a rival firm to spill secrets) that constitutes the ethically gray area. Such tactics, though not illegal, tread on ethically thin ice.

More formally, the Society of Competitive Intelligence Professionals (SCIP) defines competitive/business intelligence as the process of monitoring the competitive environment. It enables senior managers in companies of all sizes to make informed decisions about everything from marketing, research and development and investing tactics to long-term business strategies. Effective CI is a continuous process involving the legal and ethical collection of information, analysis that doesn't avoid unwelcome conclusions and controlled dissemination of actionable intelligence to decision-makers.

Business intelligence is provided by many different types of firms, from "cloak and dagger" investigative companies to the world's largest accounting and auditing firms.

## The Business Case for Corporate Intelligence

Global power is no longer purely a military issue for politicians. Strength today is defined as economic power, which, in turn, is defined by the ability of nations—and the corporations headquartered in those nations—to be first with technological innovations. The front line is no longer some geographical boundary, but rather the field of research and development. Former allies are now direct business competitors—with a much harder edge than when they united against a common enemy. In some cases, Great Britain and France, for example, now see themselves more as economic rivals than as true military and strategic allies.

Resources previously used exclusively for military intelligence gathering are now being expanded to gather intelligence on commercial technological innovations, on mergers, investments and other financial transactions. The military generals have been replaced by the captains of industry—CEOs and corporate presidents and directors. Victory is defined in financial terms like "market share" and "first to market" with a new or improved product. Nowadays, the "flag follows commerce," in a reversal of the time-honored adage.

Because of the speed of innovation, the growth of giant multinational corporations and the globalization of competition, business executives can no longer afford to rely on instinct or intuition when making strategic business decisions. Too much now is at stake. In many industries, the consequence of making one wrong decision could mean bankruptcy.

Robert Flynn, the former CEO and chairman of NutraSweet, says that corporate intelligence gathered by his firm against competitors allowed his firm to make smart, fact-based decisions, contributing up to US$50 million each year to his company's bottom line.

## Avoiding Potential Disaster

Today, corporate intelligence gathering plays an important role in "due diligence" searches during mergers and acquisitions—especially international ones. The explosion of cross-border mergers and lack of any meaningful global financial reporting standards or transparency requirements means that companies need to go well beyond publicly available records and company statements to find assurances that they are associating with a legitimate business—not one run as a front by some money-laundering global mafia. Does the notion of a global mafia running a legitimate front business sound far-fetched? It shouldn't—such things have been around for centuries.

Fuelling the growth of such due diligence investigations is the large pool of private capital (merchant banks, venture capital firms, private equity firms) that is pursuing global opportunities and putting money into businesses that do not trade on recognized securities markets and face less stringent reporting and corporate governance rules.

### BRUSH WITH DISASTER

A German executive recalls his company's close brush with disaster in its attempt to acquire a Hungarian manufacturing concern.

"On the surface everything looked good. The company was private but had a healthy balance sheet audited and approved by a legitimate accounting firm. My company was ready to move, but one of our senior officers said he felt something just didn't seem right. He had met many Hungarian business executives in the course of his dealings and something just did not mesh about the behavior and business knowledge of the president of the Hungarian firm we are going to take over.

"We contracted an investigative firm in Germany and asked them to look deeper into the company. What they came back with after just one month was eye-opening and confirmed our suspicions. They said yes, the business was legitimate in most ways. Its productivity was not in question, but we learned that the company was founded by members of the Russian mafia with money it was trying to launder from the drug trade. The company was founded on loans from shell venture capital firms in Russia.

"We have had some incidents with Russian mafia types in our dealings inside Russia and we wanted no part of them. We killed the deal—and saved ourselves some huge potential embarrassment and even possible blackmail. Sometimes you cannot be too careful or investigate deep enough."

## The Costs: Expensive Trade Secrets Out The Back—And Front—Door

The potential costs of lost trade secrets and intellectual property is staggering. Surprisingly, most of it stems from secrets leaked by insiders—not by outside spies snooping through company records.

Surveys by security organizations in the United States have shown that a third of large corporations admit they have discovered cases in which employees passed confidential information to someone outside the company; one-in-five have discovered a security system violation from the outside in the last year. Perhaps more alarming, among 20,000 job applicants, three-in-ten admitted that they could be tempted to steal from their employer.

In a survey of Fortune 500 companies, the American Society for Industrial Security estimated that US corporations sustain losses of more than US$45 billion per year from the theft of trade secrets. Companies reported that on average, each had suffered 2.5 incidents of unauthorized appropriation of proprietary information. The average estimated loss per incident was calculated to be over US$500,000, with most incidents occurring in the high technology and service sectors. Of course, someone's loss is another's gain.

In another study, Pacific Northwest National Laboratory in the US, under contract by the FBI, developed an economic loss model in an attempt to assess economic damage from intellectual property theft. This model determined that the misappropriation of intellectual property resulted in over US$600 million in lost sales and the direct loss of 2,600 full-time jobs in the United States per year.

To stem losses, the US Congress enacted the Economic Espionage Act, which provides stiff jail terms and fines for individuals and companies guilty of stealing trade secrets. But more importantly the act also broadened the definition of a trade secret to include an idea of a process that has potential to make substantial profits for a company. Previously, a trade secret had to be an idea or process that had been patented, copyrighted or already in use. The US government has prosecuted dozens of cases of major corporate or industrial espionage; according to Congressional testimony, over 800 cases of economic espionage—both domestic and international—are under investigation each year.

---

NOTE: This is not just an American problem. The European Parliament issued a report that said European commercial firms lost several billion dollars as a result of corporate espionage. Other cultures, notably China, have little regard for intellectual property. Company secrets, proprietary information and even software are, for the Chinese, mere "thoughts" to be freely exchanged.

---

## Costly Failures And Ethical Lapses: Some Examples

For companies who may still doubt the value of either using competitive intelligence or the need to guard against those that employ it, here are some real life examples of costly intelligence lapses, some of which honestly have more to do with naivete than cloak-and-dagger spying.

Xerox failed to guard against its competitors using technology it invented. It actually invited competitors to a demonstration in the hopes of coming up with a universal standard for Graphic User Interface (GUI) technology, the basis for Mac and Windows software. The competitors came and watched and then scurried home to build their success on Xerox's invention.

Johnson and Johnson's (J&J) Tylenol is the world's largest non-generic over-the-counter headache remedy; but it was Bristol Meyers that once had the lead in the race to replace the common aspirin. Bristol Meyers had beaten Johnson and Johnson to the punch with the development of a drug called Datril. J&J, however, eventually beat Datril to the market by using competitive intelligence. Knowing that Bristol Meyers usually test marketed new drugs in the cities of Albany, New

York and Peoria, Illinois, J&J flooded the test market area and learned of the marketing plans for Datril. J&J managed to leap ahead in its marketing plan for Tylenol, and the rest is history.

José Lopez de Arriortua was hired away from General Motors by Volkswagen of Germany. When he left the US automaker, GM brought suit because it believed that Lopez had absconded with proprietary documents, computer disks and records of suppliers and costs. The case was settled out of court after more than three years of wrangling. It cost Volkswagen US$100 million in damages. Lopez, who resigned from VW (apparently VW management did not want him to leave), was indicted in Germany for industrial espionage. Despite his ethical shortcomings, Lopez later set up a consulting firm and managed to attract an impressive client list.

## Ethics In Action: P&G, Unilever Trash Each Other

A recent example of a costly ethical lapse is the case of the giant consumer goods manufacturer Proctor and Gamble (P&G), maker of Pampers diapers and Tide washing powder, and its admission that it, or rather an outside competitive intelligence firm in its employ, had taken documents from trash cans outside the Chicago officers of Dutch rival Unilever (Lipton Tea, Dove soap).

P&G agreed to pay Unilever US$10 million in cash and allow an outside auditor to investigate the firm's product development and marketing procedures; this was to ensure it would not take advantage of what intelligence it may have learned from the 80 pages of marketing plans and development details for new hair care products pulled from Unilever's trash.

P&G explained that the documents were obtained by outside contractors. Though the technique did not violate any laws, it did violate P&G's internal ethics code. Three staff members were fired as a result and industry experts subsequently praised P&G for coming forward on its own to admit the ethical lapse.

Corporate intelligence insiders say that many large global corporations regularly rely on subcontractors to do their dirty work. The subcontractor can come back with a report and the main contractor doesn't inquire how the subcontractor got the information. It allows companies to deny they are violating either their own ethical standards or the law. This technique provides "plausible deniability."

Oddly enough, this was not P&G's first embarrassment in the area of business intelligence gained from a competitor. A P&G employee bribed a worker for Lever Brothers in the 1940s to steal several bars of a soap under development called Swan. P&G used the formula to improve its own Ivory soap and ended up paying Lever US$5.7 million for infringing on its patent. (That's the equivalent of US$58 million today.) The case between Lever Brothers and P&G in 1943 went through a trial and appeal before being privately settled. While providing an eerie parallel to the current dispute, it also shows the impact corporate espionage can have. Using the patent technology P&G acquired and then paid millions of dollars for, Ivory soap became one of the company's standard-bearers and most familiar brand names in the world. Lever Brothers' Swan would never prove a serious threat to Ivory.

Was it worth the fines and embarrassment for P&G? It would seem so. "Despite Lever's monetary victory in the courts, Ivory won in the marketplace," reads the P&G-approved corporate history, *EYES ON TOMORROW*.

## Beyond The Private Sector—Governments And Commercial Espionage

It would seem that in the global business community virtually everyone is gathering intelligence on everyone else. In the post Cold War world, the global governmental sector has started to focus its attention on commercial espionage.

The United States has the NIS, France has the DGSE, Germany has the BND, Israel has the LAKAM, and South Korea has their NSP. Russia has the GRU, which is the industrial espionage arm of the former spy agency, the KGB. They have one thing in common: they all gather intelligence on foreign corporations.

The FBI says it is aware of 23 countries conducting operations targeting US trade secrets. It has been widely reported that France, for example, routinely bugged Air France flights and French hotel rooms to obtain economic and technical information from selected foreign passengers and guests. China has thousands of technology intelligence analysts trying to better understand how they can leverage the worldwide body of technology knowledge to assist in their transition to a hybrid market economy.

French universities have even developed master's degree programs to train corporate intelligence specialists for both state-owned and private companies.

The European Parliament investigated charges that the United States and its National Intelligence Service (NIS) were using Echelon, a secret operation established during the Cold War and operated by the US, Britain, Canada, Australia and New Zealand, to intercept international telecommunications traffic and secretly collect intelligence on European commercial firms. It claimed that the US used Echelon to beat the European consortium, Airbus Industries, to a major aircraft deal with Saudi Arabia in 1994.

Even though former CIA head James Woolsey admitted in the Wall Street Journal that Echelon was used to gather intelligence against European firms—it was mostly associated with catching those firms engaged in bribery—the European Parliament concluded there was no hard evidence linking Echelon and corporate espionage. Many skeptics were not convinced.

## Different Countries, Different Attitudes Towards Corporate Espionage

While the notion of government-supported business intelligence gathering may be horrific to some businesses, such a partnership between the government and private sector to further national goals is common in many cultures. In fact, the adversarial relationship between business and government found in the US is much more the exception than the rule in the global business arena.

## JAPAN

The government and businesses in Japan have refined the act of corporate intelligence gathering to an art—partly because of Japan's culture and partly because of historical accident. Still, the Japanese are the recognized leaders in creating a public-private partnership to "spy" on rival foreign commercial enterprises.

Following its defeat in World War II, the victorious Allies imposed tough restrictions on Japan's military and potential rearmament. Japan could never use more than one percent of its GNP (Gross National Product) for defense. Barred from effective participation in the military arena, Japan shifted its focus to economic development. The country's intelligence service, *KEMPEI TA*, was likewise barred from gathering intelligence to support military operations. *KEMPEI TA* instead focused its energies on commercial intelligence, gaining a several decades lead on most other national intelligence services.

Culturally, Japanese businesses see no problem in partnering with government to forward their joint long-term agenda of national economic security and power. Many Japanese businessmen take a course in commercial spycraft at the government-run Institute for Industrial Protection, which teaches the latest techniques in business intelligence gathering.

The gathering of business intelligence in Japanese industry is as respected a function as marketing or financial planning. Innovation, not generally associated with Japanese business culture, is much appreciated, however, in Japanese business intelligence circles. The Japanese have in fact pioneered many of the current practices. Their measures are generally much more active than passive.

For example, Japanese firms will often purchase small and medium companies engaged in design or production of technologies where the Japanese are weakest from a developmental or competitive point of view. Often, they will acquire minority shares in such companies to avoid host government restrictions on foreign ownership of firms developing technologies with potential military applications. Another target for Japanese firms are foreign banks that specialize in lending to high-tech companies. This has been effective in the volatile high-tech markets of the new century. Because high-tech firms need to inform potential lenders of their economic potential and new products to win investment cash, Japanese firms that own the lending banks end up getting access to the high-tech intelligence.

## FRANCE

The French also have no aversion to public-private partnerships when it comes to gathering business intelligence. French companies supplement governmental commercial spying by buying up major, but not majority, interests in foreign firms. In 1990, for example, France spent over US$12 billion in acquiring American businesses, for the first time surpassing the totals of both the British and Japanese.

The spotlight fell on French government activities in the early 1990s when the French intelligence service Direction Général de la Sécurité Extérieure (DGSE) tried to recruit spies at the European branches of IBM, Texas Instruments and other US electronics firms on behalf of the ailing French computer firm Compagnie des Machines Bull—which, incidentally, is owned in large part by the French government.

### BRAZIL

A big player in a big hurry with big ambitions in an emerging market, Brazil has placed former intelligence officers in many state-run commercial ventures that have dealings with foreign corporations. Again the national business culture encourages close cooperation between the private and public sectors.

## Ethical Issues in Intelligence Gathering

Some experts in the field of business intelligence say it is not necessary to use illegal or unethical methods to gather good intelligence. The Society of Corporate Intelligence Professionals says that, in fact, using illegal means is a failure of business intelligence—because almost everything decision makers need to know about the competitive environment can be discovered using legal, ethical means.

Practitioners point out that there is a huge difference between business or corporate intelligence gathering and commercial espionage, even though most laypeople tend to lump them together. Espionage is the use of illegal means to gather information.

### ETHICAL BREACHES

The most common ethical breeches in the industry occur in these areas:

- Misrepresentation.
- Covert surveillance.
- Theft.
- Attempts to influence the judgment of those with important information, i.e., bribery.

### CLEAR RULES

To maintain an ethical intelligence gathering program, companies need to establish clear rules governing these areas:

- Deception (such as posing as an MBA student working on a marketing project) should never be used in the process of collecting information.
- Undue influence occurs when an employee or their hired agent provides favors, such as a job or cash, to individuals in possession of desired information.
- Covert collection methods, such as aerial photography of the construction site of a competitor's new manufacturing plant, that require a competitor to develop excessive security measures is inappropriate.
- Unsolicited intelligence, such as receiving a copy of a competitor's strategic plan, should bring about immediate contact with your company lawyer; the plan should not used in your decision-making process.

## Preventing Ethical Lapses

Convinced of the importance of gathering business intelligence, how can corporate managers ensure that they remain within ethical boundaries? Here are a few tips for executives:

1. Work with professionals who abide by a recognized code of conduct in the industry. For example, the Society of Competitive Intelligence Professionals has a code of conduct that rules out the use of deception to gather information.
2. Clarify the hiring process. Encourage managers not to ask questions that can cause prospective employees to divulge trade secrets from a previous employer.
3. Ask about confidentiality agreements. If new employees are under such agreements with former employers, don't put them into jobs where they could only succeed by using such information.
4. Be clear on what you consider "trade secrets."
5. Don't assume these losses happen only at headquarters. Your company's operations around the world are subject to infiltration. The seven areas with the greatest loss potential have been identified as the United States, China, Japan, France, Canada, Mexico and England. This is not because there are unscrupulous intelligence gathers at work in these regions, but rather they are where the valuable information often resides.
6. Respond with training. Training is a powerful deterrent in keeping your company from being a target for intelligence losses. It's also probably the best deterrent in keeping your company from being a deliberate or unwitting perpetrator of these actions against others.

## Personal Tips

When it comes to protecting your company's secrets, a little bit of paranoia can go a long way. Few international business travelers would have considered themselves targets while sitting in the first class section of transcontinental aircraft or in their hotel room. Yet, the French government has been accused of bugging seats in the first-class section of their airliners. Japanese have heard similar accusations about Tokyo hotel rooms frequented by executives. Some basic street-wise tips:

1. Lock your doors. Computer passwords alone won't keep determined infiltrators from stealing secrets. Make it as difficult as possible to access the hardware as well.
2. Encrypt sensitive computer files.
3. Shred all paper documents not required for legal records before trashing them.
4. Don't discuss company secrets in unsecured environments.
5. Make sure your translators for international negotiations are on your payroll, not that of your counterpart.
6. Don't assume your consultants and temps are working on your behalf.

## A Code of Ethics for Intelligence Gathering

The Society of Corporate Intelligence Professionals (SCIP) is a nonprofit global membership organizations dedicated to helping members develop expertise in business intelligence gathering. SCIP currently has over 7,000 members in 44 countries. SCIP has a code for its members that is a useful guide on how to do things ethically in what can easily become a fuzzy domain.

### The Society of Corporate Intelligence Professionals Code of Ethics

- To continually strive to increase the recognition and respect of the profession.
- To comply with all applicable laws, domestic and international.
- To accurately disclose all relevant information, including one's identity and organization, prior to all interviews.
- To fully respect all requests for confidentiality of information.
- To avoid conflicts of interest in fulfilling one's duties.
- To provide honest and realistic recommendations and conclusions in the execution of one's duties.
- To promote this code of ethics within one's company, with third-party contractors and within the entire profession.
- To faithfully adhere to and abide by one's company policies, objectives and guidelines.

CHAPTER 13

# E-Ethics: Making It Up As They Go Along

*A SYSTEM OF ETHICS BUILT SOLELY ON THE GOALS OF COMFORT AND HAPPINESS WOULD BE SUFFICIENT ONLY FOR A HERD OF CATTLE.* – ALBERT EINSTEIN

THE EXPLOSION IN COMMUNICATIONS TECHNOLOGIES has created an ethical minefield for individuals and companies. The complete rules of Internet and e-commerce ethics have yet to be written, and those that have aren't always enforced. The perception that individuals, corporations and governments are making it up as they go along is not far from the truth.

With the growth of the Internet and e-commerce, concerns have arisen around online consumer privacy, workplace privacy, ethical marketing and the private use of workplace communications tools by employees. At the same time, many small and large companies operating in the New Economy have grown so fast that they have had little time—and many would say little inclination—to develop ethical processes.

Many blame the low (or non-existent) ethical standards of the new breed of Internet entrepreneurs, the so-called dot-comers for much of the problem. It appears that many Internet entrepreneurs were more interested in playing the capital markets for the quick buck than trying to build sustainable companies with long-term economic value. Fortune magazine said the fast-paced dot-com world created the context in which "ethically dubious behavior can seem almost normal"—maybe even requisite.

## Personal Cyber-Ethics: Invisible On The Web?

One perception that makes the use of the Internet and other modern communication tools so tempting for individual ethical lapses is that technology allows an individual to become almost invisible. While in truth people often leave "cyberfootprints" when using the Interet and e-mail, there are other cases when cloaked identity, the establishment of pseudonymous e-mail accounts, the use of the Anonymyzer (an Internet site that disguises your e-mail address and identity) or even the copying of software to your personal computer without the proper license gives individuals the feeling of being invisible. And being invisible often means people can be easily tempted into ethical lapses and even illegal behavior. But this is hardly a recently invented concept.

Consider the story of Gyges and The Ring—a parable that Plato often used 2,400 years ago to discuss the human inclination toward unethical behavior when unmonitored. The story goes like this:

Gyges was a shepherd who one afternoon came across a corpse laying in a cave wearing nothing but a gold ring. Gyges took the ring and wore it, taking it to the regular gathering of local shepherds held to discuss goings-on in the neighborhood. While playing with the ring, evidently during a rather boring part of the meeting, young Gyges discovered that by turning the signet of the ring inwards, he became invisible. When he did that, the other shepherds at the gathering spoke as if he had left the tent. Once he turned the signet around, he became visible again. This set his mind to thinking about the potential of this amazing power, and the wealth and respect he could achieve with it. Gyges wrangled himself an appointment to the king's court. When he arrived at court, he used his powers to seduce the queen, murder the king and take over the throne.

What Plato wanted to know is a valid question today when it comes to the invisibility of the individual on the Internet. Plato asked: Is there any human being so *JUST* that he would not take advantage of such a device? Is it only the surveillance of others that keeps us from running amok? Would a normally just man, given the opportunity, do what Gyges did? Glaucon, one of Plato's students argued this: "For all men believe in their hearts that injustice is far more profitable to the individual than justice..."

Socrates countered Plato's doom and gloom argument with the notion that there exists a true and eternal good, the sovereign good; and that the correct education will give rise to acceptance and understanding of this good, and thus, illicit ethical behavior from individuals. No, argued Socrates, not all men, in fact few, would do what Gyges did with his magical ring.

Socrates' counter argument is closer to today's reality. Despite the chance to be invisible on the Internet, most people use it ethically.

But Gyge's ring and the Internet are not exactly equal, at least, in the case of Internet use in the workplace. Employees are learning (often the hard way) that they are far from being invisible on the Web and in e-mail correspondence. It seems that major corporations have bought into Glaucon's argument. In the United States, for example, more than three-quarters of companies now monitor their employees' phone calls, e-mails, Internet activities and computer files. This figure has doubled in the last decade, driven by employers' concerns regarding productivity and liability—and perhaps, the fable of Gyge's ring. Consider the cases of the US-based chemical giant Dow Chemical that fired 40 employees for misuse of company e-mail, or Xerox that fired more than 40 employees for idling away up to eight hours a day on pornographic websites. The downloading of porn videos was so pervasive it choked Xerox's computer network and prevented employees from sending and receiving legitimate e-mail.

## Making It Personal

Certainly in the workplace, the Internet can be a dangerous—and a time-consuming thing. From a host of surveys published over the last three years, it would appear that employees at firms with Internet and e-mail access are taking advantage of these communication tools for personal use.

BusinessWeek magazine reported that 80 percent of workers say they use company e-mail to send and receive personal messages. The global employment Web site, Vault.com, cites that 90 percent of employees use the Internet for personal reasons while at the office. International Data Corporation reports that personal use of the Internet at work is attributable for 30 to 40 percent of lost workplace productivity.

According to the results of a SurfWatch survey, 24 percent of the time spent online by the employees of the participating companies was not work-related. SurfWatch determined that the three categories accounting for the largest portions of non-work surfing were general news, sexually explicit material and investment information. The ePolicy Institute states that 90 percent of US workers admit to recreational surfing on company time, accounting for nearly one-third of their online activity.

The Saratoga Institute, an Internet research group, also acknowledges that personal usage that gets out of control can cost companies a lot in lost productivity. In fact, a company with 1,000 Internet users who do personal Web surfing for one hour per day can lose more than US$35 million in productivity costs each year.

A good example of the potential costs of abuse: the consulting firm NetPartners estimates that businesses lost US$500 million in worker productivity when the US Congress released the final report of special prosecutor Kenneth Starr detailing online the investigation of US President Bill Clinton and his various peccadilloes. No less than 13.5 million workers logged on to get the report in a single day.

And it turns out that employees in government service are no more ethical when it comes to workplace Internet abuse than their counterparts in the private sector.

The US Internal Revenue Service found to its horror that over a seven-day period slightly more than half of IRS employees' time spent on the Internet was for personal use. Web sites viewed included those devoted to stock trading, chat rooms, streaming media, sports, sexually explicit content and gambling. In addition, almost half of 82,000 incoming e-mails reviewed were for non-business purposes.

One large British company was astounded to discover that it had 18,000 pages of pornography on its corporate server.

## E-mail—Ethical Implications

According to International Data Corp., over 130 million workers assigned to computer workstations send 2.8 billion messages each day. While it may sound that these employees are being highly productive, the reality is that a large percentage of these e-mails are for personal use. (Note: Worldwide, 183 billion emails of all types are sent each day.)

Besides abusing corporate e-mail for personal use, an unethical employee can use e-mail to anonymously accuse another employee of wrongdoing or to soil their reputation. Michael Eisner, chairman of Walt Disney, says that e-mail has served to increase the intensity of emotion within his company; it has become the principal cause of workplace warfare, mostly because individuals "shoot from the hip" and don't think about the tone of replies. Also, e-mail programs that hide the sender's identification tempt ethical abuse, providing the opportunity to defame an individual without being detected.

## Paying The Price

Allowing a corporate e-mail system to be abused by an employee can be a costly affair. The extent to which an employer may be held liable for a sexual harassment claim based on e-mail messages or sexually explicit Internet material generally depends upon the severity and pervasiveness of the conduct, the employer's knowledge and the employer's response. There are many examples of how misuse of e-mail or the Internet can lead to employer liability. For example, a subsidiary of Chevron Corporation had a list, "why beer is better than women" circulated throughout the company on its e-mail system. A hostile work environment sexual harassment claim was filed by female staff based on that e-mail. The claim was settled out of court for US$2.2 million.

## Software Piracy: A Global Disaster

Finally, there is the question of illegal copying of computer software. The International Planning & Research Corporation (IPR) estimates that worldwide losses to software companies amounts to US$11.75 billion a year. The illegal copying of software is considered by some international business experts to provide an interesting glimpse into the overall maturity of the business ethics of a region.

In the Asia Pacific region, losses through software piracy are now well over US$6 billion per year, with the worst piracy rates reported in Vietnam (98 percent of all software is pirated), China (91 percent) and Indonesia (85 percent). Asia-Pacific was the only region with an increasing software piracy rate with its regional average rising to 51 percent.

In the US, one in four business software applications is illegally copied or pirated, resulting in US$3.2 billion in lost revenue for software manufacturers.

The report cited Eastern Europe as the region with the highest piracy rate—63 percent. Latin America was second at 58 percent, the Middle East third at 57 percent and Africa fourth at 52 percent, followed by Asia at 51 percent. North America had the lowest rate at 25 percent, followed by Europe at 34 percent.

## How Companies Are Responding

The question corporations now face is what, if anything, they should do about these abuses of technology. Judging by the increase in sales of sophisticated monitoring software, the answer would seem to be plenty. Sales of such software has a growth rate of more than 50 percent a year.

In efforts to control employee misuse or personal use of company telecommunications equipment, most corporations have written policies for employee use of e-mail and the Internet and copying of software. A large number of firms use "blocking" software to prevent both telephone connections to unauthorized numbers and Internet connections to unauthorized Web sites. Many companies try to limit abuse by blocking outgoing e-mails for several hours in the morning and afternoon.

A survey conducted by the American Management Association in conjunction with the ePolicy Institute and US News and World Report magazine found that 82 percent of corporations monitored employees electronic communications in the workplace, 82 percent had a formal written policy on e-mail use and 77 percent had a written policy on Internet use.

Companies cited these reasons (in descending order) as to why they monitored employees:

1. Legal Liability.
2. Security Concerns.
3. Productivity Measurement.
4. Legal Compliance.
5. Performance Review.

Companies recognize, however, that any attempt to completely ban personal Web surfing at work is probably not practical and they are prepared to tolerate some if the employee does not abuse the process. The same goes for personal use of e-mail.

---

NOTE: Many firms negotiate the personal use of the Internet as an employee "benefit" when hiring or promoting staff.

---

The same AMA survey found that only one-in-five employers totally banned personal use of office Internet connections while 65 percent of employers allowed some personal use but restricted the type of Web sites that could be visited. Only 12 percent of companies allowed for full, unrestricted personal use of Internet connections.

When it comes to e-mail, 39 percent of companies allowed full and unrestricted personal use of a corporate e-mail system and 24 percent banned personal use completely.

## A Matter of Degree

A survey by the Society of Financial Service Professionals found that despite enormous potential costs to companies, only a slight majority of both employees and employers viewed Web surfing on the job as a violation of ethics (perhaps, a little Web surfing is considered OK, but it becomes an ethical violation when it has a serious impact on productivity). Web surfing on the job is an ethical violation according to 58 percent of employees and 56 percent of employers. Just half of the employers and 45 percent of employees polled indicated that personal e-mail correspondence at work was a violation of business ethics.

The survey strongly indicates that there is much confusion—and some difference in opinion—as to what is ethical or unethical behavior in the workplace. Interestingly enough, employers are not likely to encounter much resistance to the practice of limiting employee access to specific types of Internet sites; only 16 percent of employees and 19 percent of employers viewed limiting employee access to specific Web sites as a serious ethical violation.

But spending resources on monitoring software and adopting strict written policies on e-mail and Internet use carry some risk for corporations. Potential consequences of spying on employees in the workplace is the demoralization of the workforce and an erosion of employer-employee trust, which is essential in building a productive corporate culture that will in the long-run contribute to a company's reputation and ultimately its bottom line.

### EMPLOYEE INTERNET BEHAVIORS

Employee Internet-related behavior rated as extremely serious or very serious business ethics violations:

| | Employee Opinion | Employer Opinion |
|---|---|---|
| E-mail Harassment of Another Employee | 91% | 94% |
| Circulating Pornography Through Company E-mail | 85% | 93% |
| Using Company Resources for Personal Web surfing | 58% | 56% |
| Using Company Resources and Time for Personal E-mail | 45% | 50% |

### EMPLOYER INTERNET PRACTICES

Employer Internet-related practices rated as extremely serious or very serious business ethics violations:

| | Employee Opinion | Employer Opinion |
|---|---|---|
| Monitoring Employee E-mail | 44% | 33% |
| Monitoring Employee Web-surfing Content | 32% | 28% |
| Limiting Employee Access to Specific Types of Internet Sites | 16% | 19% |

## What An Effective Personal Use Policy Should Contain

The ePolicy Institute recommends that these elements are vital to establishing an effective corporate policy on Internet and e-mail use within the workplace:

- The policy should notify employees that the systems are primarily for business use and that the company reserves the absolute right to review, audit and disclose all matters sent over the system or placed into its storage. In addition to the written notification in the handbook or other written materials, ongoing notice to employees can be provided by programming a message that would appear on the employee's monitor each time the employee accesses the system. The policy should also specify that the employer reserves the right to access any messages or information entered into the system.
- The policy should specify that the system should not be used to communicate any improper communications, e.g., messages which are derogatory, defamatory, obscene or inappropriate.
- In order to reduce any reasonable expectation of privacy, the policy should not limit the employer's reasons for monitoring the system as any such limitation could be argued to restrict the scope of the employee's consent to the monitoring. Make clear to employees that using private passwords/codes or making e-mail confidential/private will not limit the employer's ability to monitor its system. A more cautious, but more limiting, approach would be to establish a business purpose that would be articulated in connection with any monitoring so as to defeat any possible expectation of privacy.

## Five Ways to Keep Employees in Line While They're Online

1. Establish a written Internet Policy that prohibits employees from using company computer assets to visit inappropriate Web sites or upload or download objectionable material from the Internet.
2. Clearly communicate the fact that the organization's computer resources are not to be wasted, but are to be used strictly for approved business purposes.
3. Enforce cyber language and content guidelines designed to keep Net copy clean and clear.
4. Don't leave compliance to chance. Back up your Internet policy with monitoring and filtering software.
5. Don't expect your employees to train themselves. Reinforce your Internet policy with ongoing employee education.

SAMPLE ONLINE LANGUAGE STATEMENT

Employees are prohibited from posting or transmitting material that is obscene, hateful, harmful, malicious, threatening, hostile, abusive, vulgar, defamatory, profane, or racially, sexually or ethnically objectionable.

(Source: The ePolicy Handbook © 2001, Nancy Flynn, executive director, The ePolicy Institute, www.ePolicyInstitute.com.)

- Consistent with the limitation on non-business use of the system, the policy should be subject to the employer's no-solicitation rule as should all other means of intra-company communication. Such a rule would encompass any solicitation, whether for charitable, personal, business or union organizing purposes.
- In order to further diminish the reasonable expectation of privacy, the policy should contain a warning that the mere deletion of a message or file may not fully eliminate the message from the system.
- As further protection, the employer could include a form which employees should be required to sign acknowledging that they have read the policy and acknowledging the employer's absolute right to access the system's information. This could also be accomplished by notice upon login. These will further minimize any expectation of privacy in the information transmitted and should prevent an employee from claiming that he/she was unaware of the policy.
- The policy should make clear that a violation of the policy may result in disciplinary action up to and including discharge from employment.
- Monitoring of electronic communications should be limited to situations where such monitoring is necessary to protect the employer's business purposes. The least intrusive method of monitoring the communications should be utilized and excessive intrusion into personal communications should be avoided.
- In order to reduce the potential for defamation and/or invasion of privacy claims, disclosure of the information obtained from the system should be limited to those who have a legitimate need to know.

Source: The ePolicy Handbook © 2001, Nancy Flynn, Executive Director, The ePolicy Institute, www.ePolicyInstitute.com.

## Employee Signoff

Finally, the ePolicy handbook recommends that employers ensure that all employees sign a statement of confirmation regarding a company's e-mail and Internet usage policies. The Institute provides an excellent example of what an appropriate employee sign-off document should contain.

### Acknowledgement of E-mail and Internet Access Policy

As an employee of Employer, I understand that the confidentiality and protection of Employer's information is of the utmost importance. I have read and understand Employer's Policy on acceptable use of e-mail and Internet access.

If I receive a password for access to e-mail, the Internet or any other system of electronically-stored computer information, I will use it only for authorized purposes. I agree not to use a code, access a file or retrieve any stored communication other than where explicitly authorized unless there has been prior clearance by an authorized representative of Employer. I will notify Information Systems immediately if I believe that another person may have unauthorized access to my password

I understand that all information stored in, transmitted or received through Employer's systems of printed or computer information is the property of Employer, and is to be used primarily for job-related purposes. I further understand that authorized representatives of Employer may monitor the use of Employer's systems of printed or computer information from time to time to ensure that such use is consistent with Employer's policies and interests. Further, I am aware that use of an Employer-provided password or code does not in any way restrict Employer's right or ability to access electronic communications.

I am aware that any violation of Employer's e-mail or Internet Access Policy may subject me to disciplinary action, up to and including discharge from employment.

(Name)____________________________

(Signature)________________________

(Date)_____________________________

Source: The ePolicy Institute, www.ePolicyInstitute.com.

## Beyond Ethics: Global Concerns On Data Protection

The protection of privacy is one of the most important issues on the Internet and the global debate over the "right" policy threatens a "Web War" between nations. Internet users regardless of their country of origin routinely report that privacy protection is one of their greatest concerns. Many Internet sites collect personal information from users through online registrations, surveys, and forms. Information is also collected from users with "cookies." Web users—and governments—are understandably concerned about the potential loss of privacy.

Cookies are a general mechanism which server-side connections (CGI—originally pronounced "coogy"—stands for Common Gateway Interface) use to store and retrieve information on the client side of the connection. The addition of a simple, persistent, client-side "marker" significantly extends the capabilities of Web-based client/server applications. To put it plainly, a cookie is a mechanism that allows a Web site to record your comings and goings, usually without your knowledge or consent.

---

NOTE: The CGI marker has benefits for the average person surfing the Net as it allows the storage of page information for easier downloads and referrals. Most Web browsers can be set to notify users of the CGI or even to "deny" cookies, but this process greatly limits access to Web sites.

---

But how much protection is enough? There is a growing trend towards the enactment of comprehensive privacy and data protection acts around the world. Currently, over 40 countries have or are in the process of enacting such laws. The self-regulatory approach that has been offered as an alternative to strong legal and technical protections is not working. Because of ethical lapses on the part of marketing companies, especially in the United States, public support for privacy legislation has grown during the time that self-regulatory policies have been pursued.

Double Click, a New York-based Internet advertising company planned to merge off-line and online information about consumers without their permission and sell the data to other marketers. Because of public and government outcry, the plan was scrapped. Then there was the case of Toysmart, which planned to raffle off customer data to the highest bidder—again without permission from customers. The dubious ethics of many Internet companies has led some to conclude (Plato would probably be pleased) that government regulation is indeed necessary to protect Internet users.

## Europe Takes The Lead

A European Union paper on "Illegal and harmful content on the Internet" probably best sums up the fears of governments about the Internet:

- National security (instructions on bomb-making, illegal drug production, terrorist activities).
- Protection of minors (abusive forms of marketing, violence, pornography).
- Protection of human dignity (incitement to racial hatred or racial discrimination).
- Economic security (fraud, instructions on pirating credit cards).
- Information security (malicious hacking).
- Protection of privacy (unauthorized communication of personal data, electronic harassment).
- Protection of reputation (libel, unlawful comparative advertising).
- Intellectual property (unauthorized distribution of copyrighted works, software or music).

In October 1998, the European Union passed its Directive on Data Protection that limited to a far greater extent than any other region of the world, the secondary use of personal information collected from consumers or employees. The Directive requires that all those processing personal data must guarantee data subjects access to their personal data, the opportunity to correct it, to be informed of how the data is to be used and to have the right to opt out before the data is disclosed to someone else.

While this echoes many of the self-regulating but voluntary codes in place in many nations, it takes things one step further. The Directive prohibits the transfer of all personal data about EU citizens to countries that do not satisfy the EU's adequacy test on data protection. In essence, the Directive sets up the EU as judge and jury over the adequacy of privacy protections of other countries. The EU has set up a series of commissions to investigate the data privacy policies in place in other regions throughout the world and will base its decisions on these commissions' findings. Its ability to enforce any decisions is, however, questionable.

While other countries are following the European approach and adopting new laws and new technical measures to protect privacy, the United States is becoming increasingly isolated in the global debate over privacy protection by leaning towards industry self-regulation.

Because Europe is fully committed to the enforcement of the Directive, failure by other nations to adequately address the data privacy issue, either by government or industry regulation, will have specific economic consequences for international firms and trans-border data flows. For example:

- Airlines and hotel chains doing business in Europe could find themselves unable to transfer data about travelers' eating, seating and other preferences to reservations systems in their home countries.
- Pharmaceutical companies could find themselves unable to share data from European research trials with researchers in other countries.
- The global insurance and reinsurance industries would be hampered because not having access to relevant data would make it impossible to properly assess risk on European clients.
- Investment bankers wanting to execute deals in Europe could find themselves unable to collect and transfer data about the personnel of European companies their clients may want to purchase.
- International accounting firms could be prohibited from conducting audits of transactions involving European residents.

---

WARNING: Ultimately, Europe may pay a very heavy price for its obsession with privacy. Already severely behind in technology, further restrictions on the growth of Internet services may see technological companies bypass European venues.

---

## Culture and The Law: Copyright On The Web

While some hold out hope for a truly global set of Internet privacy laws and codification of the protection of intellectual property on the Web, the likelihood of such harmony is poor. Why? Because different cultural traditions result in different laws to protect the same type of property. Take, for example, the notion of a universal copyright law for the Web. Different traditions make it virtually impossible:

- The European tradition emphasizes the moral rights of authors. These are related to the person of the author and concern the integrity and authorship of her/his work as well as her/his reputation.

- The Anglo-American tradition emphasizes property or economic rights. These rights can be transferred. According to this tradition, "original works of authorship in any tangible means of expression" should be protected.
- The Asian tradition considers copying as a matter of emulation of the master.

## Privacy in Japan

Japan has found a "third way" to ensure Internet privacy for users, combining government oversight with industry self-regulation. The committee of the Electronic Network Consortium has investigated appropriate ways to protect and control personal data collected by Japanese online service providers and it has prepared guidelines for protecting personal data in the Internet age. The committee is a trade organization run by the New Media Development Association, an auxiliary organization of the Ministry of International Trade and Industry. A total of 92 organizations are members of the ENC, including most of the major online service providers in Japan. The guidelines echo those contained in the European Union's Directive:

**The Electronic Network Consortium's Key Guidelines:**

1. The guidelines clearly state that personal data may only be collected with the consent of the individuals concerned. For example, they apply to the use of cookies because using cookies to gather historical information on personal Web access patterns is "possibly without the consent of the individuals concerned."
2. The guidelines clarify the right to veto the use of personal data; personal data already available to an online service provider cannot be used or transferred to a third party without the consent of the individual concerned.
3. To ensure the proper management of personal data, a manager within the organization who understands the objectives of the guidelines and who is capable of implementing them should be appointed to manage personal data.
4. The privacy information management system P3P is now available on the Internet to provide assistance and guidelines for e-commerce.

In another effort to keep pace with Europe, the Japanese Information Processing Development Center (JIPDEC) has developed a privacy mark following the Guidelines Concerning the Protection of Personal Data in Electronic Commerce in the Private Sector prepared by the Ministry of International Trade and Industry (MITI). The private enterprises that follow the guidelines gain permission to use the privacy mark.

## The Chief Privacy Officer: Big Brother with a Heart

The position of Chief Privacy Officer—unheard of in any corporation in the mid 1990s—is now considered a key management and compliance office in large and small corporations alike. Hundreds of CPOs have been created in such multinational corporations as IBM, American Express, General Motors and AT&T.

The job requires familiarity with both technology and the law, and generally gives the individual a role in a wide range of corporate operations, from product development to human resources. A CPO oversees a company's privacy policies and practices, monitoring how the corporation handles confidential information about consumers and employees.

The first loyalty of the CPO should be to the company's customers and business partners. The CPO needs to ensure the right processes are in place to prevent data from getting into the hands of anyone that's not supposed to see it. After that, they can keep a company on the right side of the law, improve security and help grow the business. Below is a sample job description of the position of Chief Privacy Officer:

## Chief Privacy Officer
## Job Description

IMMEDIATE SUPERVISOR: CHIEF EXECUTIVE OFFICER, SENIOR EXECUTIVE

General Purpose: The privacy officer oversees all ongoing activities related to the development, implementation, maintenance of, and adherence to the organization's policies and procedures covering the privacy of, and access to, patient health information in compliance with federal and state laws and the healthcare organization's information privacy practices.

RESPONSIBILITIES

- Provides development guidance and assists in the identification, implementation, and maintenance of organization information privacy policies and procedures in coordination with organization management and administration, the Privacy Oversight Committee, and legal counsel.
- Works with organization senior management and corporate compliance officer to establish an organization-wide Privacy Oversight Committee.
- Serves in a leadership role for the Privacy Oversight Committee's activities.
- Performs initial and periodic information privacy risk assessments and conducts related ongoing compliance monitoring activities in coordination with the entity's other compliance and operational assessment functions.
- Works with legal counsel and management, key departments, and committees to ensure the organization has and maintains appropriate privacy and confidentiality consent, authorization forms, and information notices and materials reflecting current organization and legal practices and requirements.
- Oversees, directs, delivers, or ensures delivery of initial and privacy training and orientation to all employees, volunteers, medical and professional staff, contractors, alliances, business associates, and other appropriate third parties.
- Participates in the development, implementation, and ongoing compliance monitoring of all trading partner and business associate agreements, to ensure all privacy concerns, requirements, and responsibilities are addressed.
- Establishes with management and operations a mechanism to track access to protected information, within the purview of the organization and as required by law and to allow qualified individuals to review or receive a report on such activity.

- Establishes and administers a process for receiving, documenting, tracking, investigating, and taking action on all complaints concerning the organization's privacy policies and procedures in coordination and collaboration with other similar functions and, when necessary, legal counsel.
- Ensures compliance with privacy practices and consistent application of sanctions for failure to comply with privacy policies for all individuals in the organization's workforce, extended workforce, and for all business associates, in cooperation with Human Resources, the information security officer, administration, and legal counsel as applicable.
- Initiates, facilitates and promotes activities to foster information privacy awareness within the organization and related entities.
- Reviews all system-related information security plans throughout the organization's network to ensure alignment between security and privacy practices, and acts as a liaison to the information systems department.
- Maintains current knowledge of applicable privacy laws and accreditation standards, and monitors advancements in information privacy technologies to ensure organizational adaptation and compliance.
- Serves as information privacy consultant to the organization for all departments and appropriate entities.
- Works with organization administration, legal counsel, and other related parties to represent the organization's information privacy interests with external parties (national, provincial/state or local government bodies) who undertake to adopt or amend privacy legislation, regulation, or standards.

## The Ten Commandments of Personal Computer Ethics

The Computer Ethics Institute has devised what it terms the Ten Commandments of Computing based on a mix of common sense and basic ethical behavior:

1. Thou shalt not use a computer to harm other people.
2. Thou shalt not interfere with other people's computer work.
3. Thou shalt not snoop around in other people's computer files.
4. Thou shalt not use a computer to steal.
5. Thou shalt not use a computer to bear false witness.
6. Thou shalt not copy or use proprietary software for which you have not paid.
7. Thou shalt not use other people's computer resources without authorization or proper compensation.
8. Thou shalt not appropriate other people's intellectual output.
9. Though shalt think about the social consequences of the program you are writing or the system you are designing.
10. Thou shalt always use a computer in ways that show consideration and respect for your fellow humans.

## Internet Marketing Codes

Many international organizations have devised guidelines for Internet advertising and marketing designed for global use. Most are based on national privacy laws as well as codes of conduct in related, non-Internet marketing fields. Most codes cover a range of ethical issues, including protection of users' personal data as well as messages directed at children. They advise adherence to all applicable laws and regulations with no use of Internet marketing that would be illegal, if conducted by mail, telephone, fax or other media. The aims of these codes are to:

- Enhance the confidence of the public in advertising and marketing provided over the Internet
- Prevent the abuse of freedom of expression by advertisers and marketers, while safeguarding that same freedom
- Avoid governmental legislation of the medium
- Adhere to consumer rights and privacy expectations

These codes agree that information collected from customers should be confidential and used only for expressed purposes. All data, especially confidential customer data, should be safeguarded against unauthorized access. Also, the expressed wishes of others should be respected with regard to the receipt of unsolicited e-mail messages.

## International Chamber of Commerce

The Paris-based International Chamber of Commerce (ICC) has devised a set of guidelines for Internet advertising and marketing designed for global use and as the basis for national codes of conduct. Scores of leading international companies have endorsed the guidelines, including: Dun & Bradstreet, Eastman Chemical, Leo Burnett, Nestlé UK, Readers Digest and Shell International. Endorsements for the guidelines have also come in from advertising and other business associations in Belgium, the Netherlands, Sweden, Switzerland and the United States.

The ICC code can be summarized as follows:

1. All advertising and marketing should be legal, decent, honest and truthful and adhere to accepted principles of ethical marketing.
2. Messages should not be designed or transmitted in such a way as to impair overall public confidence in the Internet as a medium and marketplace.
3. Marketers should always disclose their identity.
4. Marketers should clearly inform users of the cost, if any, of accessing messages.
5. Marketers should not abuse public forums and post advertisements on sites and forums that are not of a commercial nature.
6. Privacy policies must be clearly posted.

7. Users' rights should be protected and marketers should disclose the purposes and potential further uses of personal data that is collected. They should also take reasonable precautions to safeguard the security of their data files.

8. Marketers should not send unsolicited messages to users and users should be given an easy and reliable way to opt out of solicitations.

9. Special care needs to be taken when marketing or advertising to children, including encouragement of children to obtain parental permission to respond to any message and provide parents with information on ways to protect their children's privacy and identity online.

## OECD (Organization for Economic Cooperation and Development)

The following are the OECD's "Guidelines for Consumer Protection in the Context of Electronic Commerce."

These guidelines are designed to ensure that consumers receive the same, or certainly no less, protection when shopping on the Internet as when they buy from their local store or order from a catalog. By setting out the core characteristics of effective consumer protection for online business-to-consumer transactions, the Guidelines are intended to help eliminate the uncertainties that both consumers and businesses encounter when buying and selling online. The aims of the Guidelines are to encourage fair business and advertising and marketing practices; provide clear information about an online business's identity, the goods or services it offers and the terms and conditions of any transaction; a transparent process for the confirmation of transactions; secure payment mechanisms; fair, timely and affordable dispute resolution and redress; privacy protection and consumer and business education. The Guidelines can be summarized as follows:

1. Consumers who participate in electronic commerce should be afforded transparent and effective consumer protection that is not less than the level afforded in other forms of commerce.

2. Businesses engaged in electronic commerce should pay due regard to the interests of consumers and act in accordance with fair business, advertising and marketing practices. Business should not make any representation or omission or engage in any practice that is likely to be deceptive, misleading, fraudulent or unfair.

3. Businesses engaged in electronic commerce with consumers should provide accurate, clear and easily accessible information about themselves sufficient to allow at a minimum:

- Identification of the business—including the legal name of the business and the name of the business under which it trades
- Prompt, easy and effective consumer communication with the business
- Appropriate and effective resolutions of disputes
- Service of legal process
- Location of the business and its principals

4. Businesses engaged in electronic commerce with consumers should provide accurate and easily accessible information describing the goods and services offered; sufficient to enable consumers to make an informed decision about

whether to enter into the transaction and in a manner that makes it possible for consumers to maintain an adequate record of such information.

5. Businesses engaged in electronic commerce should provide sufficient information about the terms, conditions and costs associated with a transaction to enable consumers to make an informed decision about whether to enter into the transaction. This information should include:

- Total costs
- Terms of delivery or performance
- Terms, conditions and methods of payment
- Restrictions, limitations or conditions of purchase
- Instructions for proper use including safety and health care warnings
- Information on after sales service
- Conditions related to withdrawal, termination, exchange or returns
- Warranties and guarantees

6. To avoid ambiguity concerning the consumer's intent to make a purchase, the consumer should be able, before concluding the purchase, to identify precisely the goods or services he or she wishes to purchase, identify and correct any errors or modify the order; express an informed and deliberate consent to the purchase and retain a complete and accurate record of the transaction.

7. Consumers should be provided with easy-to-use, secure payment mechanisms and information on the level of security such mechanisms afford.

8. Consumers should be provided meaningful access to fair and timely alternative dispute resolutions and redress without undue cost or burden.

9. Business-to-consumer electronic commerce should be conducted in accordance with the recognized privacy principles set out in the OECD Guidelines Governing the Protection of Privacy and Transborder Flow of Personal Data as well as the OECD's Ministerial Declaration on the Protection of Privacy on Global Networks.

10. Governments, business and consumer representatives should work together to educate consumers about electronic commerce, to foster informed decision-making by consumers participating in electronic commerce, and to increase business and consumer awareness of the consumer protection framework that applies to their online activities.

## The Pros and Cons of Regulating Privacy on the Internet

The debate—whether or not governments should regulate Internet marketing and privacy policies—still rages in many countries throughout the world. The European Union has already settled its debate, coming down in favor of a relatively strict policy aimed at ensuring consumer privacy rights and forcing a code of practice and ethics on Internet marketers. In brief, here are the pros and cons of government versus industry/private regulation:

### THE ARGUMENT FOR INDUSTRY REGULATION

The basic argument is that freedom works. Technology can only flourish in a self-regulated environment that can adapt to rapid changes absent the high costs often imposed by government regulations and restrictions. Those who favor self-regulation argue that restrictions on targeted marketing and the cost of regulation could fundamentally alter the medium itself, transforming it from a largely "free" marketplace to a "pay as you go" service, stifling growth and innovation. Finally, there is concern that government simply has not demonstrated the expertise to regulate—and keep pace with—the complex, fast-moving medium.

### THE ARGUMENT FOR GOVERNMENT REGULATION

The main argument centers around the lack of will of the industry to regulate itself and to often take the path of least resistance. For them, regulation and government are impediments to progress, not guarantors of success. So far, self-regulation has not worked adequately in any country. Those who favor more government intervention argue that the current system not only fails to adequately address privacy concerns, it actually penalizes those who attempt to do so. For example, under its current authority the US Federal Trade Commission can sanction a company for "deceptive trade practices" if the company fails to adhere to a posted privacy policy; a company that has no policy at all escapes any scrutiny or punishment. In addition, they argue that self-regulation will not provide the uniformity needed for meaningful privacy protection, forcing users to learn a new privacy policy and "read the small print" every time they log onto a site. Consumers will not feel confident in privacy protection online unless they know they have a right protected by law with meaningful enforcement and a place to go for redress.

---

NOTE: Like many international legal quandaries, no one has figured out how to enforce global cyber-policies. Even when the French courts won a ruling to restrain Yahoo's auction sites, it was overruled by US courts who said that France has no right or ability to control American firms operating within US boundaries.

---

CHAPTER 14

# Global Bribery And Corruption – How Much For Your Ethics?

*FEW MEN HAVE THE VIRTUE TO WITHSTAND THE HIGHEST BIDDER.* – GEORGE WASHINGTON

THE WEALTHY ECONOMIES OF THE WORLD have long ago grown tired of having their firms solicited for bribes when conducting international negotiations. It is a highly inefficient means of planning and operating a company. Corporations recognize, however, that there are ethical failures on both sides. The demand side (officials who accept or demand bribes) and the supply side (businesses, small and large) share the blame, though not equally. To eliminate corruption both the demand and supply sides must be addressed.

## Bribery and Corruption: It's Everywhere

The attack on international business bribery is two-fold. First, countries and corporations have come to the conclusion that fighting bribery and corruption is no longer simply a moral and ethical imperative, but also a question of bottom line economics. Second, governments of wealthy economies realize that their demands for ending bribery fall on deaf ears in poor economies where corruption is often the standard means of getting things done.

## The International Corruption Index

Transparency International (TI), a non-governmental organization dedicated to increasing government accountability and curbing international and national corruption, is the best-known non-governmental agency tracking corruption in the world today. Based in Berlin, Germany, Transparency International has chapters in 77 countries. Its vision is of a world in which government, politics, business, civil society and the daily lives of people are free of corruption.

Transparency International has produced its much-watched Corruption Perceptions Index (CPI) for over a decade. Perceptions of corruption, which are measured in the CPI, are precisely what their name suggests—perceptions—but they are a tremendously important indicator, telling government leaders how country analysts and business people around the world view their country. CPI's methodology is based on a series of surveys specific to each nation.

The index ranks 102 countries. Some of the richest countries in the world—Finland, Denmark, New Zealand, Canada, Iceland, Singapore and Sweden—scored 9 or higher out of a clean score of 10 in the CPI, indicating very low levels of perceived corruption. But 70 countries—many of which are among the world's poorest—scored less than 5, suggesting high levels of perceived corruption in government and public administration. Scores of less than 5 were registered by countries on every continent—including members of the Organization of American States and the European Union. The countries with a score of 2 or less are Angola, Azerbaijan, Kenya, Indonesia, Madagascar, Nigeria, Paraguay and Bangladesh.

---

NOTE: For all of its good intentions, TI will have to add patience to its long list of virtues. Its modus of "name and shame" has little effect in "kleptocracies," like Russia or Nigeria. It has even less effect in places like China where access to data, such as that compiled by TI, is restricted.

---

## Who's Corrupt and Who's Not?

According to the recent Transparency International CPI, here are the nations with the least and most corruption:

| THE TOP TWENTY LEAST CORRUPT (Number 1 as least corrupt) | THE BOTTOM TWENTY MOST CORRUPT (Number 1 as most corrupt) |
|---|---|
| 1. Denmark | 1. Somalia |
| (tie) Finland | 2. Myanmar |
| (tie) New Zealand | 3. Iraq |
| 4. Singapore | 4. Haiti |
| (tie) Sweden | 5. Uzbekistan |
| 6. Iceland | (tie) Tonga |
| 7. Switzerland | 6. Sudan |
| (tie) Netherlands | (tie) Chad |
| 9. Canada | (tie) Afghanistan |
| (tie) Norway | 7. Laos |
| 11. Australia | (tie) Guinea |
| 12. Luxembourg | (tie) Equatorial Guinea |
| (tie) U.K. | (tie) D.R. Congo |
| 14. Hong Kong | 8. Venezuela |
| 15. Austria | (tie) Turkmenistan |
| 16. Germany | (tie) Papua New Guinea |
| 17. Ireland | (tie) Central African Rep. |
| (tie) Japan | (tie) Cambodia |
| 19. France | (tie) Bangladesh |
| 20. U.S.A. | 9. Zimbabwe |
| | (tie) Tajikistan |

## Through The Looking Glass: Corruption Barometer

Keeping with the spirit that bribery and corruption is indeed a two-headed ethical coin. Transparency International commissioned Gallup International Association to conduct in-depth interviews with private sector leaders in 14 emerging market economies; these combine to account for over 60 percent of imports of all emerging market economies, namely India, Indonesia, Philippines, South Korea, Thailand, Argentina, Brazil, Colombia, Hungary, Poland, Russia, Morocco, Nigeria and South Africa.

The scale of bribe paying by international corporations in the developing countries of the world is massive. Actions by the majority of governments of the leading industrial countries to curb international corruption are modest. Business executives and business professionals in leading emerging market countries view international bribe-paying to be greatest in the public works and construction sectors, followed by the arms industry.

TI's Corruption Barometer is a pioneering effort to measure the supply side of bribery: the relative propensity to pay bribes by companies from leading exporting states in emerging economies. The questions in this survey, including those on business sectors, focused on large-scale business transactions. A score of 10 represents a perceived level of negligible bribery while 0 represents responses indicating very high levels of bribery. Below is a sampling. More details can be found at www.transparency.org

### THE CORRUPTION RANKINGS

| | | | |
|---|---|---|---|
| 1. | Australia | 8.5 | Less Bribery |
| 2. | (tie) Sweden | 8.4 | ↑ |
| | Switzerland | | |
| 4. | Austria | 8.2 | |
| 5. | Canada | 8.1 | |
| 6. | (tie) Netherlands | 7.8 | |
| | Belgium | | |
| 8. | UK | 6.9 | |
| 9. | (tie) Germany | 6.3 | |
| | Singapore | | |
| 11. | Spain | 5.8 | |
| 12. | France | 5.5 | |
| 13. | (tie) Japan | 5.3 | |
| | United States | | |
| 15. | (tie) Malaysia | 4.3 | |
| | Hong Kong | | |
| 17. | Italy | 4.1 | |
| 18. | South Korea | 3.9 | |
| 19. | Taiwan | 3.8 | ↓ |
| 20. | People's Republic of China | 3.1 | More Bribery |

## What Causes Bribe Taking?

A third of the business leaders in emerging market countries surveyed by TI also said they perceived corruption as worsening; they rated the low salaries of public-sector officials as the main cause. Evidently, many officials in the public sector believe that they not only can secure immunity for themselves against prosecution, but that the chances of their criminal activities being discovered are low. One way to effectively battle corruption from the demand side would be to raise public service salaries, which in turn would improve government revenue collection (tax money goes into government coffers rather than civil servant pockets) and allow for better services to be provided to the public.

### WHY DO OFFICIALS TAKE BRIBES?

- Low Public Sector Salaries.
- Immunity of Public Officials.
- Secrecy in Government.
- Greed.
- Worsening Public Procurement Practices.
- Increased Foreign Investment and Trade.
- Restrictions on the Media.

## Unfair Practices or Commercial Savvy

What some countries, cultures and governments perceive as good and ethical business practices meant to boost the competitive advantage of their home country corporations are often seen as just the opposite—bordering on the unethical and providing an unfair advantage over competitors.

The respondents to Transparency International's Corruption Barometer saw diplomatic or political pressure as the leading unfair practice in international business apart from bribery. The reality today is that almost all countries use their foreign embassies, notably their commercial departments, to build and secure business opportunities for home country corporations. Some diplomatic services do this more effectively than others and some, notably from large industrial countries, have greater political access and influence, which may well strengthen the competitive positioning of their companies.

Competing corporations from smaller nations have turned that argument on its head, saying they must use bribery to overcome the use of diplomatic or political pressure by companies from other countries. Ethically, it is an argument that is hard to justify. Perceived unfair practices cannot excuse bribery, whatever the circumstances.

By an overwhelming margin, the business leaders from developing nations singled out the United States as the country that most frequently and effectively uses tools like diplomatic and political pressure to secure "unfair" advantage for its home country companies. France and Japan tied for second. The irony is, of course, the relationship between big business and government in the US is often seen as antagonistic while the French and Japanese governments have a much closer relationship with businesses at home.

The countries cited by developing nations for using economic and political pressure:

|  | | |
|---|---|---|
| 1. United States | 61% | Uses More Economic and Political Pressure |
| 2. France | | 34% |
| 3. Japan | | 34% |
| 4. China/Hong Kong | | 32% |
| 5. Germany | | 27% |
| 6. Italy | | 24% |
| 7. South Korea | | 23% |
| 8. United Kingdom | | 23% |
| 9. Spain | | 17% |
| 10. Malaysia | | 16% |
| 11. Taiwan | | 16% |
| 12. Singapore | | 13% |
| 13. Belgium | | 9% |
| 14. Australia | | 8% |
| 15. Canada | | 8% |
| 16. Sweden | | 8% |
| 17. Netherlands | | 8% |
| 18. Austria | | 7% |
| 19. Switzerland | 6% | Uses Less Economic and Political Pressure |

NOTE: Developing countries face their own ethical dilemmas. While they may resent the economic or political pressure placed upon them by the wealthy economies, they are more than willing to accept aid to prop up their regimes. Sadly, much of this aid never reaches the proposed recipients, but is instead siphoned off into their secret bank accounts of political leaders and bureaucrats.

## Business, Money and Politics

Big businesses are often the largest contributors to political campaigns, either legally or illegally, in such bastions of democracy as the United States, United Kingdom, France, Germany and Japan. The object is to win influence upon the decision-making process of lawmakers. It is not always just business making these "quid pro quo" contributions either. The Chinese government itself made substantial contributions to the Democratic party in the US in hopes of working with a more pliant White House.

While there are international conventions banning payoffs to government officials, there is no such convention prohibiting corporate donations to foreign political parties. There is a moderate effort underway to formulate a set of global standards dealing with corporate donations to foreign political parties, but the obstacles are enormous. Many countries would view such attempts as interference in their internal affairs and in the political and election systems of other countries. This may be the case even if the countries practice the same form of government. Finding a set of ethical guidelines that would work on a global stage is a huge challenge.

## Leading the Fight Against Bribery and Corruption

The OECD and the United Nations are generally seen as the leading multinational organizations in the fight against corruption. The United States was the first nation to make foreign bribery illegal for home country companies through the introduction of the Foreign Corrupt Practices Act of 1977. It has since been emulated by the OECD.

The OECD Anti-Bribery Convention is considered the key international convention in the fight against bribery and corruption in international business affairs. While all countries have some law against the bribing of their own officials, the Convention obliges signatories to adopt national legislation that makes it a crime to bribe foreign public officials. All 30 members of the OECD have signed the convention as well as four non-members (Argentina, Brazil, Bulgaria and Chile).

The convention is having an impact—at least on the supply side of the bribery equation. Until the OECD Convention came into force in 1999, French, Japanese and German companies could make bribes paid abroad tax deductible at home. In the regulatory and legislative spheres, that era has thankfully ended. Another key multinational inter-governmental initiative is the 31-member Financial Action Task Force, which is focusing on the laundering of money, especially from the illegal drug trade; this is seen as one of the root causes of corruption in many countries. How big is the problem? The International Monetary Fund has stated that the aggregate size of money laundering in the world could be somewhere between two and five percent of the global gross domestic product. These percentages would indicate that money laundering ranged between US$590 billion and US$1.5 trillion. The lower figure is roughly equivalent to the value of the total output of an economy the size of Spain. The retail revenue alone in the illegal drug trade is estimated by the UN at US$400 billion, nearly double the revenue of the legitimate pharmaceutical industry.

CHAPTER 15

# Regional Ethics: Japan, Russia and Islamic Banking Ethics

*HE WHO SEEKS FAME AND FORTUNE THROUGH IMMORALITY, MISCONDUCT, AND DECEPTION WILL NEVER ACHIEVE IT. EVEN IF HE ACHIEVES TEMPORARY FAME AND FORTUNE THROUGH SOME STROKE OF LUCK, IT WILL BE ONLY AS A FLOATING CLOUD IN THE HEAVENS, SOON TO BE DISPERSED BY A GUST OF WIND.*

– SHIBUSAWA EIICHI (1841-1931) CONSIDERED BY MANY TO BE THE FATHER OF JAPANESE CAPITALISM.

THE VALUES THAT PEOPLE HOLD, either consciously or unconsciously, guide human behavior and ultimately determine their ethics. Today, an international business-person must have a clear understanding of the ethical value system he or she is working in. Often a clue can be found in religious traditions and philosophies.

For example, the ethical system of many of the Western industrialized democracies is based on Christian teachings and Biblical themes. Hong Kong, China, Korea, Singapore, Taiwan, Vietnam and Japan are all a part of a common cultural universe based on the teachings (many would says it is really a civil religion) of the ancient philosophers Confucius and Buddha.

## Ethics In Japan: Confucianism At Work

During the 1990s, Japan has been in the midst of ethics angst. Political and corporate scandals have grabbed headline after headline. Four senior officials at Mitsubishi Motors were charged with hiding defects in autos. Other major corporations, such as Bridgestone, Mitsubishi Electric and Sanyo Electric, have been accused of covering up defects in tires, television sets and solar cell systems. There have been payoffs to *sokaiya* (corporate racketeers) by Ajinomoto, Takashimaya and Nomura Securities, huge loans to *sokaiya* without adequate collateral by Daiichi Kangyo Bank and the disclosure of unfair trade in copper by Sumitomo Corporation. Japan's major political parties also have been tainted by kickback scandals and payoffs to gangsters.

What does all this mean? Could it be that the Japanese are witnessing a collapse of ethical behavior? Sure, there are individuals that have no qualms about behaving unethically in Japanese society just as there are unethical individuals in all societies. But are the Japanese with their generous business gifts, lavish business entertainment and cross-shareholding of corporations less ethical than any other culture?

Remembering there is no ethical absolute in business, the answer would have to be a resounding "NO." But if you asked if the Japanese (like many other Asian cultures) follow a different drummer when it comes to business ethics, the answer would have to be "Yes." What is becoming clear is that as the globalization of business takes place, Japan's bedrock principle of preserving group harmony and saving face (which were efficient social and political systems when the country was isolated from the rest of the world) is now, at best, a mixed blessing on the international business scene.

## THE ETHICS OF RECIPROCITY

As mentioned earlier, the dominant religious philosophy within a culture can have a much greater impact on an individual's approach to business ethics than most expect—even if that individual is not a devout follower of a particular religion. This is particularly true in the case of Japan, a country whose culture is deeply ingrained with the teachings of Confucianism.

Confucianism is concerned with establishing well-ordered families and a harmonious society organized along clearly defined lines of power. The Japanese believe that long-term, give-and-take relationships are the hallmark of a harmonious society.

According to Confucius, when things and people function in accordance with the "Mean," they exist in a relationship of mutual reciprocity or cooperation. When the principle of the Mean is followed, things and people flourish, nourishing one another without conflict or injury. Thus, a person who acts in accordance with the Mean thinks and acts in a socially correct manner.

Traditionally, Japanese managers often questioned the basic European and North American business practices of downsizing, mergers and acquisitions and broad shareholder ownership; these were seen as a violation of the Mean, and thus, bordering on unethical behavior. To a Japanese businessperson, employees and companies are tightly linked by the ethic of reciprocity.

Link adherence to the Mean with the demands of group harmony and clearly defined hierarchies of power and there is little wonder why whistle-blowing on one's boss for an ethical violation in a Japanese corporation is unlikely. In fact, it is not only unlikely, but the act of whistle-blowing can be viewed as an unethical act in itself—violating the Mean.

Consequently, the "collectivist" Japanese cannot easily distance themselves from the organizations they work for and are more likely to be influenced by the norms of these organizations than more "individualistic" North Americans or Europeans.

---

NOTE: The rough economic justice of the 1990s brought the once mighty "Japan Inc." to its knees and exposed its underlying fiscal weakness. Layoffs, once thought unthinkable, are now commonplace.

---

## PRACTICAL APPLICATIONS

With the globalization of business, pressure from foreign shareholders and movement towards a universal business ethics code, Japanese corporations and the government are now struggling to interweave these codes with traditional culture. There is a growing consensus that traditional relationships of ethics and law in Japan are no longer serving the society well.

Part of the reason that it took Japanese companies longer to adjust their business ethics was that they are not scrutinized as closely by Japanese consumers as North American and European companies are scrutinized by consumers in those countries. Also, the cultural notions of lifetime employment and the strict seniority system contributed to a reluctance to adapt to the global movement. Businesses didn't have to think for themselves, but rather followed rules laid down by powerful government ministries.

One of the problems is that the codes of ethics now utilized by most Japanese corporations are too vague and abstract, relying on tacit understanding of employees rather than spelling out in detail what is required, as most North American and European businesses do. Indeed, a survey by the Japan Federation of Economic Organization found that 60 percent of 700 responding companies plan to introduce or revise ethics and conduct codes.

Because of the collective nature of the society, and the fact that company policy—not personal ethics principles—is the key factor that influences ethical decision-making in Japanese corporations, it is essential that Japanese corporations institutionalize ideas of social responsibility and business ethics. For strong ethical patterns to take root, Japanese companies must incorporate ethical standards into their corporate culture.

## Ethics in Russia: Business in a Moral Vacuum

It was only slightly more than a decade ago that the central Russian government was the locus business. It owned and ran everything from the smallest retail store to the largest armaments factory. The Communist Party and its ideology of Marxism-Leninism were the source of collective moral authority. Once that ideology had been rejected, its subjects were set adrift from any moral mooring. Virtually overnight in 1991, the social order of the past 70 years in Russia vanished. What were previously crimes (economic speculation and private enterprise) suddenly became virtues. The ability to think and act independently, traits that even ancient Russians shunned, are now the essence of not only success but survival. For 70 years, managers in Russia had operated in a centrally planned economy and had little need or desire to make ethical decisions. That came crashing down with the Soviet empire.

While it is difficult to find a foreign businessperson who has not experienced difficulty and questioned local ethical standards in doing business in Russia, the confusion and chaos of basic cultural transformation that dominates Russia today may not necessarily mean the Russians are inherently unethical when it comes to private enterprise; it just means they are new to it.

Because Russians have been living under authoritarian and autocratic rule for more than a millennium, they have no institutional memory of free markets, unlike other recently "freed" Communist nations, such as Poland, Hungary and East Germany. (Even the Russian Orthodox Church, which imbued Russians with Christian values, did not value commerce as virtuous. People in business were suspected of being selfish.) Communism crushed private initiative and incentive. The value of hard work (or more accurately the reward) was relatively unknown. Because the system was so corrupt and dishonest, dishonesty and deception were necessary "street" virtues that the average Russian needed to beat the system—and to survive.

Because of the dramatic shift in cultural values, there is no clear moral compass to guide leaders through complex dilemmas about what is right or wrong. In a poll of Russian children at the end of the 1990s, they were asked what would prevent them from stealing. Out of 100 questioned, 99 answered they would be afraid of getting caught. One said he would not steal because it is wrong. Recent estimates put the value of corruption at over US$10 billion in lost revenue for the Russian Government.

"What is happening in Russia is well beyond a change in economic or market systems. It is a change in the very fabric of what defined the Russian character and Russian culture," says an Italian businesswoman who has resided in Moscow for more than three decades. "This is an all out assault on the culture, even on the language, on perceptions of such basic concepts as good and evil," she says.

## STARTING FROM SCRATCH

In Russia, business is deeply personal and highly idiosyncratic. The basic ethics of Russians seem to change, depending on the relationship. Moral and ethical requirements are different for friends versus business associates. Russians place a high value on personal friendships and extended family. During the Soviet era friends and family often were the only people you could trust when it came to business transactions. Friendships were based on trust. Business relationships were not.

In the early days after the fall of communism, the robber-baron era of business that overtook the country left many Russians highly suspicious of businessmen, and with good reason. It was an "eat what you kill" mentality, which has soften somewhat as the country's business acumen matures.

The importance of the institutionalization of corporate or business ethics (as well as individual business ethics) cannot be underestimated in Russia. The importance of introducing and enforcing ethics codes on the corporate level are magnified because the country has no system of enforceable commercial or business law or clear government policies. Evaluating the ethics of Russian business should be viewed from the perspective of Russians trying to build a business culture from scratch.

## RUSSIANS AND SOFTWARE: IS PIRACY ETHICAL?

One of the most interesting examples of where the old and new mentality clash in Russia has to do with piracy of computer software. The country has one of the world's worst records when it comes to piracy of computer programs. One possible explanation is that, as mentioned earlier, Russians seem to play by a different set of rules with friends as opposed to businesses. Russians are used to communal living, and in the Soviet era, any material good fortune—a banned book, a Western rock cassette—were quickly copied and shared among friends and neighbors. Since many Russians now feel that businesspeople, like the former government, are conniving and deceptive, they feel justified in exercising their own forms of trickery and deception—and that includes piracy of software.

## THE NEW ETHICS CODE FOR RUSSIAN BUSINESS

The following excerpts from the Basic Guidelines for Codes of Business Conduct, developed by the Russian Chamber of Commerce and Industry in cooperation with the US-Russia Business Development Committee, are a primer in basic business do's and don'ts. Their purpose is to articulate general principles and standards that have been accepted in international business transactions. While some may find their simplicity almost quaint, they are a clear indication of just how undeveloped the concept of business ethics is in the new Russia.

### Basic Guidelines for Codes of Business Conduct

#### PRINCIPLES IN PERSONAL AND PROFESSIONAL RELATIONS

No laws or contracts can anticipate the possible vicissitudes of life. Very often an entrepreneur must make a decision based on the prompting of common sense and conscience. The key is to embody ethical and moral principles into personal and professional relations, and remember to:

- Always do business within one's means.
- Have respect for the partners and participants in a shared business venture.
- Refrain from violence or the threat of violence as methods of achieving business success.
- Resist crime and corruption, and do one's part to see that crime and corruption become unprofitable for everyone.
- Live up to the trust placed in you; trust is the foundation of entrepreneurship and a key to success. Endeavor to earn a reputation for integrity, competency and excellence.

#### RELATIONSHIP WITH EMPLOYEES

Enterprises have an important responsibility towards their employees. A number of basic principles typically guide the attitudes of successful enterprises towards their employees:

- Due regard for labor laws.
- Commitment to adequate standards of worker health and safety.
- Non-discrimination in the recruitment, compensation and promotion of employees.
- Respect for the rights of workers to engage in union activity.
- Effective systems for consultation with employees on employment conditions and other issues that affect the employees.
- Clearly stated and transparent policies relating to compensation, benefits, promotions and other employment conditions.
- Commitments by the enterprise for contributions to pension plans and strict protection of the integrity of company-sponsored pension plans.

These principles do not limit the right of an enterprise to enforce discipline on its labor force or to terminate workers in accordance with applicable law.

## RELATIONSHIP WITH OTHER ENTERPRISES

A relationship of mutual trust in which all parties benefit is the most significant aspect of relations between partners in joint ventures and contractual arrangements or business relations with other enterprises. The reputation of a company is its most valuable asset. Once the reputation of an enterprise is tarnished, it is very difficult to gain trust with the same or other business relations. A number of basic principles that typically promote mutual trust in business relations include:

- Commitment to excellence in products and services.
- Commitment to gain respect and trust in all business relations.
- Respect for the sanctity of contracts and business relations.
- In case of a commercial dispute, a willingness to negotiate and compromise in order to reach an amicable solution.
- Respect for the sanctity of rule of law, including abiding in a timely manner with decisions of any court, arbitration panels or other administrative bodies.

## RELATIONSHIP WITH THE GLOBAL COMMUNITY

As a company is an integral part of the community in which it operates, a sound relationship with the community is essential. Caring for the environment is a responsibility of the enterprise towards the immediate community, but it also extends to all communities and areas whose environment may be affected by the enterprise's activities. Enterprises must:

- Be sensitive to concerns of the local population.
- Communicate with the local population.
- Abide by all applicable environmental laws and regulations.
- Show tolerance for people of other cultures, races, beliefs and countries.

## RELATIONSHIP WITH GOVERNMENT AUTHORITIES

Well-managed enterprises are law abiding enterprises. To maintain a sound relationship with governmental authorities, enterprises must:

- Pay all taxes that are owed and due.
- Abide by all mandatory government and local regulations.
- Obtain all governmental permits, licenses and approvals required to do business.
- Deal with government authorities on an arm's length basis, and make no attempts to improperly influence governmental decisions.
- Establish transparent procedures regarding transactions engaged in by enterprises with any government agency or official or in dealings with any enterprise owned or controlled by a government agency or official.
- In transactions with any government agency or officials or with any enterprise owned or controlled by government or government officials, include appropriate provisions to ensure compliance with international or national codes against extortion and bribery.

## PROPER CHECKS AND BALANCES

A proper system of checks and balances is necessary to ensure the ongoing integrity of the enterprise and of its relationship with its constituencies. Such a system must be based on the general principles of full disclosure, management accountability, separation of responsibility and sound internal controls.

An enterprise should have a full disclosure policy concerning:

- Statements of the enterprise's strategic aims and policies, including how these have been achieved in the past reporting period and how the enterprise will act in the future.
- Prompt reports to the enterprise's constituencies on events that could have a material effect on the enterprise.
- Prompt disclosure of all important relationships between officials of the enterprise and other parties.

The key element of a system of checks and balances is that the shareholders are able to monitor management's performance and to condemn poor performance, including the removal of management.

## PREVENTION OF EXTORTION AND BRIBERY

Principles concerning prevention of extortion and bribery are intended as a method of self-regulation by businesses. The voluntary acceptance of these principles by enterprises will not only promote high standards of integrity in business transactions, whether between enterprises and public bodies or between enterprises themselves, but will also protect enterprises that are subject to attempts at extortion.

The business community objects to all forms of extortion and bribery. The highest priority should be directed to ending extortion and bribery involving politicians and senior officials. Bribery and extortion threaten democratic institutions and cause grave economic distortions.

All enterprises should observe both the letter and spirit of the following rules:

- No one may, directly or indirectly, demand or accept a bribe.
- No enterprise may, directly or indirectly, offer or give a bribe, and any demands for such a bribe must be rejected.
- Enterprises should take measures reasonably within their power to ensure that any payment made to any agent represents no more than an appropriate remuneration for legitimate services rendered by the agent; that no part of any such payment is passed on by the agent as a bribe or otherwise in contravention of these principles.
- All financial transactions must be properly, accurately and fairly recorded in appropriate books of account available for inspection by the board of directors as well as by auditors. Enterprises must take all necessary measures to establish independent systems of auditing in order to bring to light any transactions that contravene these principles. The enterprise must then take appropriate corrective action.
- The board of directors of the enterprise should periodically review compliance with these principles and take appropriate action against any director or employee who acts in a manner inconsistent with these principles.
- Contributions to political parties or to individual politicians may be made only in accordance with applicable law and in accordance with all applicable requirements for public disclosure of such contributions.

## When Religion is The Guiding Principle: Islamic Banking

After centuries of hibernation, Islamic banking has re-emerged in recent years and has gained increasing acceptance in the Middle East and parts of Asia. It is one of the few areas of international commerce where a religious philosophy wholly dictates the terms and ethics of the business relationship. Islamic banks now handle more than US$100 billion in assets worldwide and asset growth at Islamic banking institutions has been between 10-15 percent per year. Even some large Western banks, such as US-based Citibank, now have Islamic branches.

Islamic financial products and services are based on profit-sharing principles so as not to break the Islamic prohibition on *RIBA*, or usury. The essential feature of Islamic banking is that the payment of interest is forbidden by the Koran, Islam's holy book. In general, Islamic law requires that risks should be shared between the financier and the entrepreneur. Islamic scholars argue that the concept of Islamic banking contributes to a more equitable distribution of income and wealth and increases participation in the economy by common people. Islamic banks do not pay regular pre-determined interest to depositors, nor do they charge pre-determined interest rates to borrowers. Rather, the banks take a share of the profits (or losses), which are again shared with depositors. What makes profit-sharing permissible in Islam, while interest is not, is that in the case of the former it is only the profit-sharing ratio, not the rate of return itself that is predetermined.

### ISLAMIC ECONOMIC ORDER

The concept of Islamic banking is part of what Middle Eastern scholars call the Islamic Economic Order, which is based solely on the teachings of the Koran. It strives to build a society based on an Islamic sense of social justice, equity and moderation. All activities must conform to *Shariah*—the Islamic legal code. Under *Shariah*, all resources available to humans must be put to optimum use; no one—not even the government—has the right to hoard them, waste them or to let them lay idle.

Islamic banking relies on four basic techniques to keep economies and commerce moving: *MURABAHA*, *MUSHARAQA*, *IJARA* and *MUDARABA*. The most common is *MURABAHA*.

- *MURABAHA* is basic cost-plus financing. It involves a three-party contract between the bank, its client and a purchaser for the sale of goods with a profit margin agreed by all parties. Most Islamic banking operations are based on *MURABAHA*.
- *MUSHARAKA* is simply a partnership deal in which all parties contribute towards the financing; profits and losses are shared according to equity input.
- *IJARA* is a leasing agreement in which the bank buys or leases equipment or other assets to the business owner for a fee.
- *MUDARABA* is an agreement between two parties in which one party provides 100 percent of the capital and the other party manages the venture. Profits are distributed according to a pre-agreed ratio. Losses are borne only by the lender.

## BASIC RULES OF ISLAMIC FINANCE

The rules regarding Islamic finance are quite simple and can be summarized as follows:

1. Any predetermined payment over and above the actual amount of principal is prohibited.
2. The lender must share in the profits or losses arising out of the enterprise for which the money was lent. Islam encourages Muslims to invest their money and to become partners in order to share profits and risks in the business instead of becoming creditors. Translated into banking terms, the depositor, the bank and the borrower should all share the risks and the rewards of financing business ventures. This is unlike the interest-based commercial banking system where all the pressure is on the borrower.
3. Making money from money is not acceptable in Islam. Money is only a medium of exchange—it has no value in itself, and therefore, should not be allowed to give rise to more money via fixed interest payments The human effort, initiative, and risk involved in a productive venture are more important than the money used to finance it.
4. *GHARAR*, which means speculation or uncertainty, is prohibited. Under this prohibition, any transaction entered into should be free from uncertainty, risk and speculation. Contracting parties should have perfect knowledge of the counter values intended to be exchanged as a result of their transactions.
5. Investments should only support practices or products that are not forbidden by the Koran. Thus, no Islamic bank would finance a brewery or a casino.

CHAPTER 16

# Case Studies: Personal Decisions

*THE MEASURE OF A MAN'S CHARACTER IS WHAT HE WOULD DO IF HE KNEW HE NEVER WOULD BE FOUND OUT.*

– BARON THOMAS BABINGTON MACAULEY, EARLY 19TH-CENTURY ENGLISH HISTORIAN

THE HEART AND SOUL OF ETHICS TRAINING is the case study. They are used to illustrate how individuals should analyze situations they are likely to meet on a regular basis in the performance of their duties—especially those tricky "gray areas." As in real-life situations, the cases presented in this chapter do not always have a "right" or "wrong" answer. The key point to many of these cases is that when dealing in an international environment, a manager or businessperson must consider many different factors before deciding on a course of action. Culture can, and often does, play an important role in formulating what an individual may view as the best ethical course of action. And not all cultures, nor individuals within a single culture, will agree what that course is.

## Case One: The Super Salesman

You are the marketing director in the Eastern European region for a large British-based multinational manufacturer of consumer retail products. Competition from other multinationals, as well as from locally branded products, is particularly intense in home cleaners. You have a salesman in Romania who not only meets his monthly sales targets of cleaners, but also exceeds them by a wide margin. It comes to your attention (from a competitor, no less) that this super salesman may be involved in some practices that are against your company's basic ethics code. You know that these practices, like promising a small "rebate" to the customer against the salesman's commission, are common practice in Romania. What course of action would you take?

A. Fire the salesman. He is in clear violation of the company ethics code and should be dismissed.

B. Look the other way. After all, you know that his practices are acceptable in Romania, and besides, he is producing.

C. Explain to the salesman that your corporate ethics code and the company's global ethical standards supersede those often followed locally and he needs to bring his practices in line with company standards, even if it will cost him and the company sales.

EXPLANATION

Alternative A (firing the salesman) may be an appropriate answer if he worked for the company in its home country. In this case, it shows cultural insensitivity and no understanding of how the real world operates in "ethical gray areas." The punishment appears to be too harsh. Alternative B (looking the other way) is morally a dead end. If allowed to continue it could make managing the operation in Romania impossible. It could also have a negative impact on morale, both at home and in the local country. Why have an ethics policy at all?

Alternative C is probably the best answer. For a corporate ethics code to be effective (and payoff on the bottom line), it must be enforced, and employees must be trained and encouraged to follow it. If this company is serious about its international ethics policy, it will take the time to educate and train foreign staff in its importance and how to use it. It must be made clear that high ethics standards are more important than the value of incremental sales made unethically. It is the company's task to show how the global ethics policy is connected to the big picture.

## Case Two: The Borrower

You find that your company's local agent in Moscow (ownership of the local enterprise is split 50-50) has been using office equipment to help run some of the other businesses he owns in the country. He has "borrowed" software to run his payroll for the other businesses and even used a dump truck to remove rubble from a renovation project for offices in his own businesses. This seems to overstep the ethical line. This is a smart and fairly sophisticated guy and you can't believe his explanation that he didn't really see what you were so upset about. "I didn't do anything wrong," he says. You feel he is playing you for a sucker.

EXPLANATION

To your Russian partner, it is certainly reasonable to use the equipment since he has ownership rights in both companies. The arrangement is efficient and does not appear to be unethical. The ethics of private property ownership are new to Russia. He is the owner of two companies, hence, the equipment is his to use as he sees fit. No, he is not playing you for a sucker; he simply may not fully understand that the capital belongs to the joint venture, not to him personally.

## Case Three: The Reluctant Whistle-Blower

Your North American company has a thriving accounting and auditing business in Japan. A junior employee learns through after-hours conversations that her boss has been engaged in some less than ethical behavior with a client that constitutes a clear conflict of interest; yet, she says nothing, choosing to ignore your company's "international ethics hotline" meant for just such an occasion. What is your reaction when the scandal comes to light?

A. Fire them both. Knowing and failing to report a violation is the same as actually committing the violation.

B. Send a memo out to all Japanese employees about the importance of using the hotline to report violations.

C. Fire the boss and keep the junior employee—with a warning put in her personal file for failing to report the violation

EXPLANATION

None of these alternatives seem completely appropriate in this case. First, whistle-blowing in any Asian culture may be viewed as an unethical act in itself; any employee that does not take advantage of a corporate hotline should not be held to blame. Silence, even about illegal conduct, is considered a method of mutual protection from arbitrary accusation and punishment.

Also, respect for elders and the strict hierarchy of power (in Asian cultures) would prevent any junior employee from informing on a superior. The thought of upsetting group harmony (a key to the teachings of Confucius is maintenance of group harmony) by informing on a boss is probably unthinkable to most Asian workers. The notion that a junior employee would cause a boss to lose face is far-fetched, even today.

## Case Four: The Personnel Manager in China

You have what you consider to be a first rate local director of human resources for your company's joint manufacturing venture in China. She is young (36 years old), enthusiastic and highly competent. However, after more than two years in the job, you begin to notice a pattern emerging. She refuses to hire anyone older than herself, despite the great qualifications and experience of some candidates. You tell her that failure to consider older qualified candidates is hurting the company. She promises to do better, yet the pattern persists. What is happening here?

EXPLANATION

Confucian norms dictate that among the five relationships that should always be observed is the deference youth pays to maturity. Chinese culture, age and experience are highly valued and Chinese business leaders look down on young negotiators. They cannot take them seriously. The Chinese human resources director is subconsciously avoiding a situation that would abrogate the norm—one in which she would appear to be superior to an elder.

## Case Five: A Factory's Safety Standards

Intermake is a European-based clothing manufacturing corporation with plants in several sub-Saharan African countries. The company pays above average wages and provides better than average working conditions for the region. It also pays its expatriate foreman on a European scale. The local media has been critical of Intermake because it has a two-tiered approach to injuries on the job. If an expatriate worker is injured, he/she is taken to the region's private hospital. If a locally hired worker receives the same type of injury, he/she is taken to the local, poorly-staffed hospital or simply sees the company nurse.

Intermake says its treatment of local staff is comparable, if not better, than other manufacturers in the country. Most don't even have a plant nurse on staff. Also, the company's medical policy has not deterred locals from applying for work. In fact, it has a huge backlog of potential hires. Besides, in order to recruit expatriates to work at the plant it has to provide exceptional medical care.

### EXPLANATION

While there appears to be only one answer to this question in theory—it isn't fair to discriminate under any circumstances—in reality you have to determine if Intermake's two-tiered policy is discriminatory in the classic sense of the word. Is Intermake really discriminating based on race or ethnicity in this case? Perhaps not. There are two different ethical considerations. First, there is hard core ethics. Can you treat employees on a discriminatory basis for a similar illness? The answer is obviously no. The second part deals with what kind of facility a person is entitled to—and there the standard should be similar to the perks and status that they enjoy in relation to other working conditions. Bosses get perks—and the perks may include superior medical care.

The key is whether the medical care offered local workers is sufficient to ensure the same likely outcome of an injury. Some would argue that it is only Intermake's ethical responsibility to ensure that the care it gives its local workers is adequate to ensure a good chance of recovery. It doesn't have to provide them with the best care (as the expatriates may demand in order to relocate there). It just has to provide them with adequate care. Others would argue that if the medical care was so poor that employees were put at extraordinary risk compared to other local factories, then no one would work there, despite the higher wages.

## Case Six: Layoffs In Saudi Arabia

You're a British consultant sent to Saudi Arabia to have a look at a new joint venture your company has just taken a stake in—a family-run, light manufacturing firm with 400 employees. You look at the books and mention that you think the workforce is terribly bloated. Output and revenue per employee is below average. You suggest laying off up to 20 percent of the workforce. The Saudi owners look at you horrified, saying layoffs are downright unethical and there is more to business than maximizing profits. You are equally horrified.

### EXPLANATION

Most business in Arab societies—where the collectivist culture is dominant—place far greater value on the loyalty of employees than on the efficiency of employees, and are right to view layoffs as unethical. This notion is reinforced by the tenets of Islamic law, which are designed to stress the social obligations of a company, making profit maximization secondary. Indeed, to fire a loyal worker to maximize profits is indeed unethical behavior.

When faced with this situation in real life, the British consultant and the Saudi owners came to an interesting solution: cut pay across the board and reduce worker's hours. The workers understood. No one complained and many even thanked the owners for saving their jobs. The lesson learned: when dealing in a highly collectivized culture it may be wiser to trim the pay of all workers in a downturn rather than lay off individuals. The workers themselves may actually want it that way. The case is an excellent example of how a different cultural mindset can bring forth creative solutions to universal business problems. Multinational corporations and expatriate managers should take notice.

## Case Seven: The Female Work Colleague In a "Man's World"

June Smith is traveling on an international sales trip with her colleague, Nigel, one of the company's most experienced salesmen. The trip is successful, but when they get back, June complains about an incident that occurred on the trip. At the end of the final day, with the contract in hand, the customer proposed that Nigel join him at his men's club to celebrate.

If you were Nigel's boss you would have advised him to:

A. Accept the invitation; don't rock the boat.

B. Propose an alternative venue so June could join them.

C. Refuse the invitation.

D. Take a male partner next time.

### EXPLANATION

This is the type of incident that can and does occur with some regularity in certain venues, particularly in Japan and the Middle East, though the age of globalization has sensitized virtually all cultures to such an incident. Answer A (accept the invitation) is clearly not fair to your work colleague and may be against, if not the letter of company policy, most likely the spirit of it. In a world of globalization of business, her complaint is probably justified.

However by choosing B or C, would June and Nigel be guilty of "cultural imperialism?" Some would argue that both the company and June should have been prepared for this kind of incident. "Preparation" might mean coping with the situation sensitively and diplomatically so that she and Nigel could shape events before an embarrassing situation arose. Answer C is simply rude in any culture—and risks alienating future business for no good reason.

Others would argue that "preparation" entailed not sending June to countries where she would not be included—answer D. The culture of those countries is not "wrong," just different, and it is important for companies to minimize those differences. Companies need to be sensitive to the local culture. In fact, the very notion of a male-female sales team traveling together can be offensive in some cultures.

Probably the best answer to this quandary would be B (propose an alternative venue where June could attend). Today, few customers would be offended by such a compromise.

There is yet another view—namely, of how the incident may affect June's career. Some experts would believe that it is unfair to exclude her from participation in social events if it impairs her business effectiveness and may cause her to lose future opportunities. Another view is that June should not complain if missing the celebration did not hurt her long-term career prospects. After all, wasn't the real reason for the trip "to get the deal?"

## Case Eight: Sexual Harassment

You are a middle manager in a large North American corporation. You are sitting in a tavern and strike up a conversation with a woman sitting next to you whom you recognize as an employee of the same company you work for. She mentions that her boss at work is sexually harassing her. You know who she works for and you are friends with her boss. What action do you take?

A. Tell her you know her boss and she must be mistaken.

B. Stay out of it.

C. Begin your own investigation to determine the facts and perhaps clear her boss.

D. Advise her to report the allegations to the human resources department and offer to go with her.

E. Call human resources and the ethics office the next business day to report your conversation.

### EXPLANATION

The first two answers A and B are, of course, while the easy way out of the dilemma, a betrayal of your ethical responsibilities to your organization. Still, they are appealing and it is easy to see how they could be rationalized—after all, the conversation took place out of work hours and out of the office environment; so it really isn't your duty to report it. In fact the first three answers (A, B, and C) could all lead to more serious trouble down the road, for you and your company. While failing to report your suspicions could allow the situation to grow even worse than it is, conducting an unprofessional and botched investigation could increase your company's potential liability exponentially.

While D seems like a reasonable solution, it still probably does not go far enough. Only E covers all the ethical bases by fulfilling the manager's ethical duty to the organization and its employees.

## Case Nine: Competitive Intelligence

Your company is in a highly competitive bidding process (for a multi-million dollar contract) with your major rival. Your customer sends the final specifications in the mail and you discover the papers include the final offer sheet of your competitor. You are not sure if it was an accident or on purpose. What do you do?

A. Throw it away without a glance.

B. Review the document and adjust your company's offer to beat it.

C. Decide that it went out to all the other bidders as well, so everyone has the same information and will adjust their bids appropriately.

D. Call your boss and the legal department and report the incident.

EXPLANATION

In this case, there is only one correct answer—D. While A sounds very much like the right thing to do, the discovery of the information must be reported to superiors and the corporate legal department. Failure to do so might lead to serious consequences for your corporation. Obviously B is just downright unethical. There is no way to rationalize the action with any known ethical standard. C is simply an attempt to rationalize bad behavior.

## Case Ten: The Computer Hardware Vendor

You run a small Internet business and need to purchase computer hardware for an upgrade and expansion. You know that your next venture is highly risky, will involve hiring expensive staff and runs the risk, if unsuccessful, of severely limiting your cash flow. Although the terms of the contract are 45 days payment, you don't expect to be able to pay the vendor bill for at least six months, until the expansion is complete and the new project is up and running—and hopefully, making money. The vendor has done his due diligence and runs the usual credit checks. However none of the checks would reveal your secret and risky expansion plan. You decide to:

A. Inform the vendor of your plans; there are other suppliers after all.

B. Keep silent.

C. Postpone the expansion until you can afford it out of current cash flow.

EXPLANATION

In fact, all three answers to this question seem reasonable. Even though a "lie of omission" is still a lie, in this case, the vendor might find it hard to criticize the entrepreneur's silence. There has been a change in business, particularly in the West, away from the old *CAVEAT EMPTOR* (let the buyer beware) towards a *CAVEAT VENDITOR* (let the seller beware) attitude. The vendor is assumed to have a good degree of marketplace acumen and should realize that many firms "age their payables" beyond the normal 30-60-90 day process to protect their own cash flows. Answer B assumes such acumen as well as assuming that the buyer will eventually pay the bill—maybe even with interest penalties.

While both A and C cover the ethical ground of not misleading the vendor, C is a very conservative (and potentially, a poor business decision) path to take in the highly competitive Internet business world. Answer A would seem to cover both the ethical and business issues effectively. Negotiating payment terms is part of business. The reputation for honesty is likely to mean more to the company's bottom line in the long run than more favorable payment terms in the short run.

CHAPTER 17

# Glossary

ADVERTISING A form of public notice that seeks to inform, persuade and otherwise modify consumer attitudes toward a product, with the objective of triggering an eventual purchase.

ANONYMYZER An Internet site that disguises the user's e-mail address and identity.

BARRIERS TO ENTRY Conditions that make it difficulty for competitors to enter a market. For example, copyrights, trademarks, patents, exclusive distribution channels and high initial investment requirements.

BARRIERS TO TRADE Policies that make it difficulty for enter a foreign market. For example, high rates of import duty, special requirements for imported products and subsidies to domestic producers.

BIG PICTURE The overall, long-term view of a business deal, transaction or policy. To be a Big Picture thinker means you have the ability to get past the minutia and details or individual transaction to think ahead to see how it fits into a company's overall strategy.

BONA FIDE Latin for "good faith." Refers to documents, materials and promises that show commitment by a company or individual to a particular line of business, transaction or outcome. It is generally taken to mean that a company or individual is serious and are who they say they are.

BOTTOM LINE The last line in a financial statement, indicating a company's profit or loss.

BRIBE PAYERS INDEX is a pioneering effort by Transparency International to measure the supply side of bribery: the relative propensity to pay bribes by companies from leading exporting states in emerging economies.

BRIBERY Payments or concessions made to an individual holding a position of power and trust to influence the outcome of a business transaction. Morality aside, bribery is an entrenched part of doing international business, though some uniformity in the fight against it as bad economic policy is beginning to take shape among the world's more powerful economies.

BUSINESS INTELLIGENCE The process of monitoring the competitive environment. It enables senior managers in companies of all sizes to make informed decisions. Effective Business intelligence is a continuous process involving the legal and ethical collection of information, analysis that doesn't avoid unwelcome conclusions and controlled dissemination of actionable intelligence to decision makers. Also referred to as Competitive Intelligence.

CAUSE RELATED MARKETING (CRM) Marketing that connects a business' products to a particular cause or set of values in the hope that consumers who hold those values will be more likely to purchase the products as a way of supporting that cause.

CAUX ROUND TABLE A group of business leaders from Europe, Japan and the US committed to energizing the role of business and industry as a vital force for innovative global change. (www.cauxroundtable.org)

CHIEF PRIVACY OFFICER A business executive that oversees a company's privacy policies and practices, monitoring how the corporation handles confidential information about consumers and employees. Unheard of in any corporation in the mid 1990s, the position is now considered a key management and compliance office in large and small corporations alike.

CHILD LABOR Children working in businesses. A broad ethical problem that includes such issues as children working in family businesses (and on farms), education of children, forced labor, and the minimum age at which hazardous or any work should be performed by a young person.

The United Nations says the minimum age for admission to employment or work should, in principle, not be less than the age for completing compulsory schooling and in no event less than the age of 15; hazardous work should be prohibited for those under 18.

CODE OF HAMMURABI An 18th century set of commercial and societal rules named for the famous ancient chief of Babylon. The code was the first to set basic ethical guidelines for organized commerce.

CULTURAL RELATIVISM The view that there are no absolute moral values. It holds that one should not view another country's beliefs or behaviors as wrong, but simply as different.

COLLECTIVISM A cultural value that places great emphasis on the harmony of the group and appreciates individuals who subordinate their needs and wants to that of the group. A person thinks of the group first and follows the orders of those in charge.

CONFIDENTIALITY AGREEMENT An obligation to protect the confidentiality of proprietary information exchanged between parties exploring a commercial relationship. Also referred to as a nondisclosure agreement (NDA). Use of a confidentiality agreement is generally a condition to the availability of trade secret protection in most countries.

CONFUCIANISM The moral and religious system of China based on the teachings of the philosopher Confucius, who died in 479 BC. His teachings are based on ethical precepts—benevolent love, righteousness, decorum, wise leadership, sincerity—designed to inspire and preserve the good management of family and society. Its precepts are practiced in many Asian societies outside of China and form the basis of social organization and administration in these societies.

COOKIE (CGI) A mechanism that allows a Web site to record your comings and goings, usually without your knowledge or consent.

CORPORATE CITIZENSHIP The responsibility a corporation has to employees, shareholders, customers, suppliers and the community where it conducts business and serves markets. At minimum, it entails observance of laws, regulations and accepted business practices where it operates. It goes beyond the traditional economic view of a corporation's responsibilities that included only the increasing a corporation's profitability and productivity. The failing of this view was that it did not take into account the relationship between the firm's actions and the social setting in which it exists.

CORPORATE CULTURE The bond that holds an organization together. It incorporates an organization's values, norms of behavior, policies and procedures and is heavily influenced by national cultural values, ownership structure and the nature of the industry in which the corporation operates.

CORPORATE ESPIONAGE The use of illegal means to gather competitive intelligence on a business. It differs from Business Intelligence or Corporate Intelligence in its use of illegal rather than legal means to obtain information.

CORPORATE GOVERNANCE The exercise of direction and control over a business entity. The term implies both profit-making and stewardship responsibilities.

CORPORATE INTELLIGENCE The collection, analysis and use of information regarding any aspect of countries, industries, companies, institutions and individuals to help make informed business decisions.

CORRUPTION PERCEPTION INDEX A much-watched report produced by Transparency International every year since 1995. It measures perceptions of corruption, which are an important indicator telling government leaders how country analysts and businesspeople around the world view their country. Its methodology is based on a series of surveys specific to each nation.

CROSS-CULTURAL A comparison of beliefs and attitudes of different cultures or nationalities with another set of beliefs and attitudes. In management, it is a concept that deals with the challenge of managing a team of workers from different cultures.

CULTURE A set of learned core values, beliefs, standards, knowledge, morals, laws and behaviors shared by individuals and societies that determines how an individual acts, feels and views himself/herself and others.

DIRECTIVE ON DATA PROTECTION A directive instituted by the European Union in October of 1998, limiting (to a far greater extent than any other region of the world) the secondary use of personal information collected from consumers or employees. It requires that those processing personal data must guarantee data subjects access to their personal data, the opportunity to correct it, to be informed of how the data is to be used and to have the right to opt out before the data is disclosed to third parties.

DISCRIMINATION The essence of discrimination in respect of employment and occupation is any distinction, exclusion or preference which has the effect of nullifying or impairing equality of opportunity or treatment in employment or occupation and is made on the basis of race, color, sex, religion, political opinion, national extraction or social origin.

DOMINI 400 SOCIAL INDEX The best-known stock index that tracks the performance of global stocks that meet specific requirements for socially responsible investors. The index monitors the performance of 400 US corporations that pass multiple, broad-based social screens.

DOW JONES SUSTAINABILITY INDEX A group of indices launched in 1999 that track the performance of the top 10 percent of the leading sustainability-driven companies in the Dow Jones Global Index of 2,000 firms.

DUE DILIGENCE INVESTIGATION Preliminary research and exchange of data between parties contemplating a commercial transaction, such as a joint venture. The data covers each party's business and affairs and specific matters relating to the proposed business plan.

ECONOMIC ESPIONAGE ACT Enacted by the United States Congress in 1996, it provides stiff jail terms and fines for individuals and companies guilty of stealing trade secrets. The act also broadened the definition of a trade secret to include an idea of process that has potential to make substantial profits for a company.

ENVIRONMENTAL RESPONSIBILITY The responsible and ethical management of products and processes from the point of view of health, safety and environmental aspects.

ENVIRONMENTALLY SOUND TECHNOLOGIES (ESTS) A broad term describing technological processes that protect the environment, are less polluting, use resources in a more sustainable manner, recycle more of their wastes and products and handle residual wastes in a more acceptable manner than the technologies for which they were substitutes.

ETHICAL DECISION-MAKING The process of evaluating and choosing among alternatives in a manner consistent with ethical principles.

ETHICS Moral principles and values of an individual or company in personal and business relationships. The word is derived from the Greek word for "character," and describes an attitude having to do with moral obligations and responsibilities. Cultural influences and attitudes usually have a great impact on ethics.

FACE A deeply-held value, especially in Asian and Middle Eastern cultures, related to dignity, respect from others as well as self-respect and self-esteem. While in the West, losing face—being embarrassed by an error or bad behavior—is associated with personal failure, in Asian and Middle Eastern cultures it is a group concept. Shame is brought not only to individuals, but to the group or organization they represent.

FEMININE CULTURE Societies with so-called feminine values such as the appreciation of inter-personal relationships, putting quality of life before material acquisition and applauding concern for individuals and less-fortunates. A feminine culture contrasts with a masculine culture.

FORCED LABOR OR COMPULSORY LABOR All work or service that is exacted from any person under the menace of a penalty and for which the person has not offered himself voluntarily. Providing wages or other compensation to a worker does not necessarily indicate the labor is not forced or compulsory.

FOREIGN CORRUPT PRACTICES ACT A US law that makes it a federal crime for US companies, citizens or their agents to bribe foreign officials to gain commercial advantage. In certain circumstances, the act allows for 'facilitation' payments; those made to an individual to do something quickly that they would have done anyway. The act is sometimes seen as an impediment to US businesses whose competition may not face similar restrictions.

*GIRI NINJO* One of the most powerful and fundamental principles governing personal and business interactions in Japan. It is a sense of honor, loyalty and empathy that makes business operations sometimes seem like an extended family.

GLOBAL COMPACT A set of global business principles introduced at the World Economic Forum in Davos, Switzerland in January 1999 covering topics in human rights, labor and the environment. These principles challenge world business leaders to "embrace and enact" the Global Compact, both in their individual corporate practices and by supporting appropriate public policies.

GLOBALIZATION The growing economic and social interdependence of countries worldwide through increasing volume and variety of cross-border transactions in goods and services and of international capital flows, and also through the more rapid and widespread diffusion of technology and communication.

HERMES The ancient Greek god of commerce and the market. While the official patron of traders and merchants, he was also the official patron of thieves. Not to be confused with the giant British pension fund investor.

HIGH CONTEXT CULTURE A culture that places great value in the intangible aspects of a negotiation or business deal. Individuals from such cultures look beyond the facts and figures and take into consideration such factors as personal relationships, atmosphere and attitudes toward respect, religion and trust. In a high context culture, business can never be conducted without a face-to-face meeting.

HOTLINE/HELPLINE A special telephone number employees or other interested parties can call to report problems or have questions answered by trained personnel concerning corporate ethics and related issues. (Hotlines are used for many other purposes in other fields as well.) Hotlines are often used to manage a global corporate ethics program and can be a major component of success—or a cultural faux pas—depending on how and where they are used. While some view such hotlines as "snitch lines" for anonymous accusations, they can be successfully used as a communications tool to help employees with questions concerning ethics policies.

HUMAN DIGNITY The sacredness or value of each human individual as an end, not simply as a means to the fulfillment of others' purposes.

*IJARA* A term used in Islamic banking and finance which describes a leasing agreement in which the bank buys or leases equipment or other assets to the business owner for a fee.

INDIVIDUALISM A cultural value that places great emphasis on the independent thinker and appreciates and honors personal success over that of the group.

INSTITUTIONAL INVESTOR An organization rather than an individual investor. Includes pension funds, trusts, mutual funds and endowments that manage assets on behalf of someone else.

INTERNATIONAL CHAMBER OF COMMERCE (ICC) A non-governmental organization serving as a policy advocate for world business. The ICC aims to facilitate world trade, investment and an international free market economy through consultation with inter-government organizations. This Paris-based organization is also an international leader in issues related to arbitration and dispute resolution, business self-regulation, fighting corruption and combating commercial crime.

INTERNET The public network of computer networks which enables the transmission of information between users, or between users and a place on the network, as well as to all interactive media and electronic networks, such as the World Wide Web and online services.

*KYOSEI* A Japanese concept which means living and working together for the common good, enabling cooperation and mutual prosperity to coexist with healthy and fair competition.

LEVEL PLAYING FIELD A business environment where everyone is subjected to the same set of rules and regulations.

LOW CONTEXT CULTURE A culture that assumes a high degree of shared knowledge on the behalf of a transaction partner and thus deals only in such tangible aspects of the deal as facts, figures and performance. The atmosphere and the personal relationship with the business partners means little. In a low context culture, business can be conducted without ever meeting face-to-face.

MASCULINE CULTURE Societies with so-called masculine values where, for example, aggressiveness, assertiveness and the goal of material acquisition is respected. A masculine culture contrasts with a feminine culture.

MEAN A social structure of mutual reciprocity and cooperation in relationships. A leading principle of the Chinese philosopher Confucius. When the principle of the Mean is followed, things and people flourish, nourishing one another without conflict or injury. A person who acts in accordance with the Mean thinks and acts in a socially correct manner.

*MUDARABA* An agreement used in Islamic business and finance between two parties in which one party provides 100 percent of the capital and the other party manages the venture. Profits are distributed according to a pre-agreed ratio. Losses are borne only by the lender.

*MURABAHA* In Islamic banking and finance, a term which refers to basic cost-plus financing. It involves a three-party contract between a bank, its client and a purchaser for the sale of goods, with a profit margin agreed by all parties. Most Islamic banking operations are based on *MURABAHA*.

*MUSHARAKA* In Islamic banking and finance, a term which describes a partnership deal in which all parties contribute toward the financing, and profits and losses are shared according to equity input.

NON-GOVERNMENTAL ORGANIZATION (NGO) An organization not affiliated with government or private business devoted to a specific cause.

**ORGANIZATION OF ECONOMIC CO-OPERATION AND DEVELOPMENT (OECD)** Headquartered in Paris, France, the group of 30 countries that includes the major industrialized democracies of Asia, Europe and North America was established in 1961 to promote economic and social welfare in member countries and to stimulate and harmonize relations with developing nations. The OECD is considered the leading global organization when it comes to fighting bribery and corruption in business; it is a leading force in developing a global ethics standard for business.

**OUTSIDE DIRECTOR** A member of a corporation's board of directors who is not an employee of the company and has no operational responsibilities within the company.

**POWER DISTANCE** A cultural dimension that describes how individuals within a society view power and in turn how they view their roles in the decision-making process. In high-power distance cultures, people see themselves far removed from the boss and seek no decision-making role. In low power distance cultures, workers are more empowered and hence will demand some say in the decision or implementation process. Because of respect for authority, high power distance cultures tend to be more formal than low power distance cultures.

**PROXY** A power of attorney authorizing a specified person to vote corporate stock on behalf of a shareholder or group of shareholders.

**REGULATION FAIR DISCLOSURE** Regulations adopted by the US Securities and Exchange Commission in 2000 that bar companies from disclosing non-public information to a select group and requires certain information to be issued to the public through a press release or an SEC filing. The regulation is designed to protect small investors from insider trading and level the playing field for all stock market investors.

**RELATIONSHIP DRIVEN CULTURE** A culture that relies on personal friendships and personal chemistry to do business. Personal trust must be built in such a culture before any business can be conducted. The opposite of a task-driven culture.

**SA 8000** A standard created by the Council on Economic Priorities Accreditation Agency (CEPAA) to promote socially responsible production in facilities worldwide. SA 8000 stands for "Social Accountability 8000." To qualify for certification, organizations must meet verifiable standards for child labor, forced labor, health and safety, freedom of association, discrimination, disciplinary practices, working hours, compensation and management systems.

**SHAREHOLDER ACTIVISM** A growing global and often confrontational movement through which both large and small shareholders are challenging corporations to be more ethically and financially responsible. The movement represents a fundamental change in the relationships between management and corporate boards and investors. The movement took root in the United States in the 1980s.

***SHARI'AH*** The Islamic legal code. Under *SHARIAH*, all resources available to humans must be put to optimum use; no one—not even the government—has the right to hoard them, waste them or to let them lay idle.

**SOCIALLY RESPONSIBLE INVESTING** Investment in businesses based on social or moral criteria. Generally, socially responsible investing is investment in enterprises that promote socially, ethically and environmentally responsible business practices that in turn contribute to improvements in the quality of life throughout society.

**STAKEHOLDER** Any individual or group that is affected by the actions and fortunes of a business or organizational entity. The term includes owners, consumer advocates, customers, competitors, media, employees, environmentalists, suppliers, governments and local community organizations. These all have legitimate stakes in the business and all can affect business outcomes.

STRATEGY The art or science of creating a plan using all the social, economic, political, legal, cultural and other forces available to achieve a goal.

SUBJECTIVISM The notion that it is the decision of the individual, not the society that determines which moral principles are valid. While considered a valid theory in philosophy, its practice in the business world can cause problems if a company is simply a reflection of what the boss "thinks" is proper behavior.

SUSTAINABILITY A business approach to create long-term shareholder value by embracing opportunities and managing risks deriving from economic, environmental and social developments.

*TAKAFUL* A kind of mutual-aid society that serves as an alternative to conventional insurance for Muslims.

TASK-DRIVEN CULTURE A culture were completion of a narrow and specific task—like signing a contract—is the main objective of doing business. Individuals in a task-driven culture separate business from personal relationships. You don't have to be friends to do business. It is the opposite of a relationship-driven culture.

TIME HORIZON The length of time a company or individual is willing to wait before a business deal begins to make sense or a profit. Because of a less obsessive view about time, Asian executives usually adopt a longer time horizon—often years—than Americans or Europeans, who view time as a commodity to be spent. Shorter time horizons are linked to task-driven cultures.

TRANSPARENCY (a) he clear understanding by all parties of a uniform set of rules, standards and laws governing a transaction. (b) The extent to which laws, regulations, agreements and practices affecting international trade are open, clear, measurable and verifiable. The concept is especially important in corporate governance as companies seek to list shares on markets where the rules of accounting and disclosure are more rigid than in their home country.

TRANSPARENCY INTERNATIONAL A non-governmental organization dedicated to increasing government accountability and curbing international and national corruption. Publishers of the Corruption Perceptions Index. Headquartered in Berlin, Germany, the organization has offices in 77 countries.

UNCERTAINTY AVOIDANCE A cultural value that dictates how individuals and societies feel about and react to stability, ambiguity and risk. This value is often seen in business organizations and views on employment. It is in Japan, a high uncertainty avoidance culture, where workers still cling to the idea of a job for life in exchange for ceding personal mobility.

VALUES Concepts that are important to a culture and influence social interactions and individual outlooks. The most basic value difference found in cultures is whether a society emphasizes individualism or collectivism.

WASTE ARCHEOLOGY A slang term used in the Business Intelligence or Corporate Espionage industry to describe carefully looking through a competitor's trash for product or marketing secrets.

WORLD BANK (Technically, the International Bank fot Reconstruction and Development.) An intergovernmental financial institution located in Washington, DC. Its objectives are to help raise productivity and incomes and reduce poverty in developing countries.

*YAKUZA* Individual members of, or collectively, criminal gangs in Japan.

*ZAKAT* Money or charitable works which a Muslim of means must distribute among the poor every year.

CHAPTER 18

# Researching Business Ethics Resources

A good starting point for researching resources about business ethics is the Internet. There are literally hundreds of Web sites providing a range of information from philosophical arguments about ethics to how to construct a corporate conduct code. Of course, more traditional sources can also provide a wealth of information. The local library is obvious, but also local trade missions, embassies and consulates of countries in your target region are usually cooperative, if not flattered, by your interest. Also, many governments sponsor cultural institutes in foreign countries to promote both the business and culture of their home country. Among the largest:

THE GOETHE-INSTITUTE Funded by the German government, it promotes German business and culture abroad. The Institute maintains about 150 locations in more than 70 countries. Among these are large Institutes with up to 70 employees in New York, London, Paris, Tokyo, Moscow, Cairo, Jakarta and Rome. The Institute has a total of about 3,600 German and foreign employees worldwide.

THE ALLIANCE FRANCAISE The largest network of French language and cultural centers in the world. There are 1,300 Alliance chapters established in 112 countries—including 150 chapters in the US—serving more than 400,000 students.

THE JAPAN FOUNDATION maintains two Japan Cultural Institutes, five Japan Cultural Centers and 11 Offices in 17 countries. The Japan Foundation was established in 1972 under the auspices of Japan's Ministry of Foreign Affairs for the purpose of promoting mutual understanding and friendship on the international scene. Its activities are financed by operation profits on government endowments, aid from the Japanese government and funding and donations from the private sector.

US INFORMATION AGENCY An agency of the US federal government it operates cultural centers, including libraries and multi-media resources, in over 90 countries. Its aim is to promote US business and US culture (what the French term an oxymoron) throughout the world.

## Internet Resources

This is by no means meant to be an exhaustive list of international-related business ethics links. Most of the Web sites have their own set of additional Web links, and many were used as resources for this book.

AUSTRALIAN BUSINESS ETHICS NETWORK http://www.bf.rmit.edu.au/Aben/
Includes educational programs, a calendar of conferences and events, an extensive list of suggested Web sites and The Ethics Forum that contains discussion papers on a variety of management and ethical topics.

BUSINESS FOR SOCIAL RESPONSIBILITY http://www.bsr.org/
Business for Social Responsibility (BSR) is an organization that helps companies achieve "long-term commercial success by implementing policies and practices that honor high ethical standards." With more than 1,500 members, BSR sponsors conferences and

programs on ethics and codes of conduct, in addition to more global corporate social responsibility issues.

THE CAUX ROUND TABLE http://www.cauxroundtable.org/
Includes the first international code of business ethics. The Round Table serves as a stimulus for implementation of its Principles for Business, conducts Global, Regional and National Dialogues and publishes Position Papers on key global issues.

COUNCIL FOR ETHICS IN ECONOMICS http://www.businessethics.org
The Council for Ethics in Economics includes some good publications as well as "Conversations on Ethics," which are presentations and discussions of business ethics issues. There are also interactive case studies.

ETHICS OFFICER ASSOCIATION http://www.eoa.org
The EOA is a non-profit organization which promotes ethical business practices and serves as a forum for the exchange of information and strategies among individuals responsible for ethics, compliance and business conduct programs.

ETHICS RESOURCE CENTER http://www.ethics.org
The Ethics Resource Center is a nonprofit, educational organization that provides consulting services and training to help companies establish and implement effective business ethics policies.

INSTITUTE FOR BUSINESS AND PROFESSIONAL ETHICS http://www.depaul.edu/ethics
The Institute is maintained by DePaul University in the United States and includes the "Online Journal of Ethics" as well as other newsletters and a global calendar of ethics-related events.

INSTITUTE FOR GLOBAL ETHICS http://www.globalethics.org
The US-based Institute for Global Ethics provides a number of services designed to elevate public awareness and discussion of ethics in a global context. The Institute maintains offices in London and Toronto.

INTERNATIONAL BUSINESS ETHICS INSTITUTE http://www.business-ethics.org
The Washington D.C.-based International Business Ethics Institute's goal is to help companies establish and implement standards that further "economic progress through global citizenship and ethical conduct." The Institute has offices in Brazil and the United Kingdom. The Web site is in three languages: English, French and Portuguese.

TRANSPARENCY INTERNATIONAL http://www.transparency.org
An excellent multi-language site (information is given in more than a dozen languages) that provides all you need to know about fighting corruption in business and government. Transparency International is a not-for-profit, non-governmental organization, whose mission includes: curing corruption through international and national coalitions encouraging governments to establish and implement effective laws, policies and anti-corruption programs; and encouraging all parties to international business transactions to operate at the highest levels of integrity. The site contains excellent links as well.

INTERNATIONAL CHAMBER OF COMMERCE http://www.iccwbo.org
Information about world business and investment in the free market system. This Paris-based organization also provides a set of international ethics codes.

CSR EUROPEAN DATABANK http://www.csreurope.org/CSR_europe/Databank/databankindex.htm
"The Reference Point on Corporate Social Responsibility in Europe" provides an abundant

amount of information on various companies and their current practices and plans relating to Corporate Social Responsibility.

JOSEPHSON INSTITUTE http://www.josephsoninstitute.org

The US-based Josephson Institute is a non-profit membership organization focused on improving the ethical quality of society. Probably best known for their Character Counts! program for school age children. This Web site has extensive links to other ethics Web sites.

BUSINESS ETHICS IN JEWISH LAW http://www.jlaw.com/Articles/

Provides several articles dealing with the subject of business ethics from the perspective of Jewish Law. Includes the articles "Jewish Business Ethics—An Introductory Perspective," "Value Conflicts In Jewish Business Ethics: Social Versus Fiduciary Responsibility" and "The Good Samaritan: Monetary Aspects."

ISLAMIC PATHS http://www.islamic-paths.org

A very comprehensive site featuring information about Islamic business ethics and principles.

ISLAMIC CHAMBER OF COMMERCE AND INDUSTRY http://www.islamic-commerce.org/

This site is dedicated to encourage Muslims to network and assist advancement of Muslims in corporate and professional careers. It also educates those unfamiliar with Islamic business practices. Good links to other Islamic business Web sites.

CANADIAN BUSINESS FOR SOCIAL RESPONSIBILITY http://www.cbsr.bc.ca/ index.html

Includes facts about corporate social responsibility, ten steps to CSR, "Good Company," the organization's online newsletter and CBSR Guidelines. There is also a "self-audit" section which businesses may use to evaluate their CSR programs.

COMPUTER PROFESSIONALS FOR SOCIAL RESPONSIBILITY http://www.cpsr.org/program/ethics/ethics.html

The CPSR Ethics Working Group "strives to stimulate and heighten awareness of the social and ethical implications of all aspects of computers and information technology, including design, manufacture, disposal, and applications derived for any purpose." Includes helpful articles and useful links to other Net resources.

EUROPEAN BUSINESS ETHICS NETWORK http://www.eben.org/

Its role is to stimulate and facilitate meetings of minds, discussion and debate on common ethical problems and dilemmas. Network members include businesspeople, public sector managers and academics.

SOCIAL FUNDS www.socialfunds.com

Run by SRI World Group, this site specializes in information about socially responsible mutual funds. It offers performance statistics plus fund descriptions.

INTERNATIONAL SOCIETY OF BUSINESS, ECONOMICS AND ETHICS

Société internationale d'éthique, d'économie et de gestion

http://www.nd.edu/~isbee/

The aim of the Society is to facilitate the dissemination of information and to foster interaction among businesses, academics, professional societies and others interested in the ethical dimensions of business and economics on the international level.

THE CENTER FOR CREATIVE LEADERSHIP http://www.ccl.org

The center is an international, non-profit educational institution that, through research, develops models of global and international managerial practice.

## Books

*COUNTRY BUSINESS GUIDE SERIES*
World Trade Press, Novato, California 1994-2002. 12 country-specific comprehensive texts on doing business in major emerging markets.

Curry, Jeffrey Edmund, *A SHORT COURSE IN INTERNATIONAL NEGOTIATING*
World Trade Press, Petaluma, CA 2008.

Flynn, Nancy. *THE E-POLICY HANDBOOK: DESIGNING AND IMPLEMENTING EFFECTIVE E-MAIL, INTERNET, AND SOFTWARE POLICIES*
AMACOM, New York 2001.

Hofstede, Gert, *CULTURES CONSEQUENCES: INTERNATIONAL DIFFERENCES IN WORK-RELATED VALUES*
Sage Publications 1984.

Lewis, Richard D., *WHEN CULTURES COLLIDE: MANAGING SUCCESSFULLY ACROSS CULTURES*
Nicholas Brealey Publishing, London, England 1996.

Mitchell, Charles, *A SHORT COURSE IN INTERNATIONAL BUSINESS CULTURE*
World Trade Press, Novato, California 2000.

Morgan, Eileen, *NAVIGATING CROSS-CULTURAL ETHICS: WHAT GLOBAL MANAGERS DO RIGHT TO KEEP FROM GOING WRONG*
Butterworth-Heinemann (Trd), Newton MA, 1998.

*PASSPORT TO THE WORLD SERIES*
25 country-specific books on the business culture of countries.
World Trade Press, Novato, California 1996-2003.

Schell, Michael S. and Solomon, Charlene Marmer, *CAPITALIZING ON THE GLOBAL WORKFORCE: A STRATEGIC GUIDE FOR EXPATRIATE MANAGEMENT*
Irwin Professional Pub, New York, New York 1996.

Zadeck, Simon, *THE CIVIL CORPORATION: THE NEW ECONOMY OF CORPORATE CITIZENSHIP*
Earthscan Publications Ltd., London 2001.

## Studies and Reports

Alexander, Lucy. *THE GLOBAL INVESTOR AND CORPORATE GOVERNANCE: WHAT DO INSTITUTIONAL INVESTORS WANT?*
The Conference Board, New York 2001.

Berenbeim, Ronald. *COMPANY PROGRAMS FOR RESISTING CORRUPT PRACTICES: A GLOBAL STUDY*
The Conference Board, New York 2000

Berenbeim, Ronald. *GLOBAL CORPORATE ETHICS PRACTICES: A DEVELOPING CONSENSUS*
The Conference Board, New York 1999.

Hodess, Robin, Banfield, Jessie, Wolfe, Toby. *GLOBAL CORRUPTION REPORT 2001*
Transparency International, Berlin 2001.

Zadeck, Simon. *DOING GOOD AND DOING WELL: MAKING THE BUSINESS CASE FOR CORPORATE CITIZENSHIP*
The Conference Board, New York 2000.

## Corporate Governance

### AUSTRALIA

Australian Investment Managers' Association (AIMA), "Corporate Governance: A Guide for Investment Managers and Corporations" (Blue Book), Second Edition, AIMA: Sydney, July 1997. Working Group representing Australian Institute of Company Directors, Australian Society of Public Accountants, Business Council of Australia, Law Council of Australia, The Institute of Chartered Accountants in Australia and Securities Institute of Australia, "Corporate Practices and Conduct" (Bosch Report), Third Edition, Information Australia: Melbourne, 1995.

### BELGIUM

Brussels Stock Exchange (BSE), "Report of the Belgium Commission on Corporate Governance" (Cardon Report), BSE: Brussels, 1998.

### BRAZIL

Brazilian Institute of Corporate Governance, "Code of Best Practice," Brazilian Institute of Corporate Governance, São Paulo, June 1999.

### CANADA

Pension Investment Association of Canada (PIAC), "Corporate Governance Standards," Fourth Publication, PIAC: Toronto, June 1998.

Toronto Stock Exchange Committee on Corporate Governance in Canada, "Where were the Directors?" (Dey Report), Toronto Stock Exchange: Toronto, December 1994.

### FRANCE

Hellebuyck Commission on Corporate Governance, "Recommendations on Corporate Governance" (AFG), Association Francaise de la Gestion Franciare: Paris, June 1998.

Marini, Philippe, "Marini Report," Conseil National du Partonat Français (CNPF) and Association Francaise des Enterprises Privés (AFEP): Paris, 1996.

Vienot, M. Marc, et al, "The Boards of Listed Companies in France," Conseil National du Partonat Français (CNPF) and Association Francaise des Enterprises Privés (AFEP): Paris, 1995.

### GERMANY

Deutsche Bundestag, "Gestez zur Kontrolle und Tranzparenz im Unternehmensbereich" (Law on Control and Transparency in the Corporate Sector) (KonTraG), Deutsche Bundestag: Bonn, March 1998.

### HONG KONG

Hong Kong Society of Accountants (HKSA), "A Guide for the Formation of an Audit Committee," HKSA: Hong Kong, December 1997.

Stock Exchange of Hong Kong (SEHK), "Guide for Directors of Listed Companies," SEHK: Hong Kong: September 1997.

SEHK, "The Listings Rules, Listing Agreements (Appendices 7a, b and i to the Listings Rules)," SEHK: Hong Kong, 1999.

### INDIA

Confederation of Indian Industry (CII), "Desirable Corporate Governance: A Code," CII: New Delhi, April 1998.

### IRELAND

Irish Association of Investment Managers (IAIM), "Corporate Governance, Share Option and other Incentive Scheme Guidelines," IAIM: Dublin, March 1999.

### ITALY

Draghi, Mario, "Le Proposte della Commissione Draghi," (The Proposals of the Draghi Commission), II Sole 24 Ore On Line: Rome, July 1998.

### JAPAN

Pension Fund Corporate Governance Research Committee, "Action Guidelines for Exercising Voting Rights," Kosei Nenkin Kikin Rengokai: Tokyo, June 1998.

Corporate Governance Committee, "Corporate Governance Principles," Corporate Governance Forum of Japan: Tokyo, May 1998.

### KYRGYSTAN

Kenenbaev, Temirbek, et al, "Civil Code for the Public Company," formerly "Handbook on Best Practice," Civil Code of Kyrgyzstan: Bishbek, 1996-97.

### MALAYSIA

High Level Finance Committee on Corporate Governance, Chapter 5, "The Malaysian Code on Corporate Governance," High Level Finance Committee Report on Corporate Governance: Kuala Lumpur, February 1999.

### THE NETHERLANDS

Vereniging van Effectenbezitters (VEB), "Ten Recommendations on Corporate Governance in the Netherlands," VEB: The Hague, 1997.

Peters Committee, "Corporate Governance in The Netherlands-Forty Recommendations," Secretariat Committee on Corporate Governance: Amsterdam, June 1997.

### ORGANIZATION FOR ECONOMIC CO-OPERATION AND DEVELOPMENT

Organization for Economic Co-Operation and Development (OECD), "Principles of Corporate Governance," OECD: May 1999.

### RUSSIAN FEDERATION

Yeltsin, Boris, President of the Russian Federation, "Decree on Measures to Ensure the Rights of Shareholders" (formerly "Declaration of Shareholder Rights"), Parker School of Foreign and Comparative Law, Legal Matters, Columbia University, Release No. 28, Transnational Juris: New York, 1996.

### SINGAPORE

Stock Exchange of Singapore, "Listing Manual (as amended) and Best Practices Guide," Stock Exchange of Singapore: Singapore, 1999.

SOUTH AFRICA

King, Mervyn E., et al, "The King Report on Corporate Governance," Institute of Directors of Southern Africa: Johannesburg, November 1994.

SPAIN

Olivencia Ruiz, Dr. Manuel, et al, "Tendencias en los Mercados de Valores," Special Commission to Consider a Code of Ethics for Companies' Boards of Directors: Madrid, February 1998.

SWEDEN

Swedish Academy of Directors, "Good Boardroom Practice," Swedish Academy of Directors: Stockholm, March 1994.

THAILAND

Stock Exchange of Thailand (SET), "The SET Code of Best Practice for Directors of Listed Companies," SET: Bangkok, 1998.

UNITED KINGDOM

London Stock Exchange (LSE), "Hampel: The Combined Code," London Stock Exchange: London, June 1998.

Committee on Corporate Governance (Hampel Report), "Final Report," London Stock Exchange: London, January 1998.

Study Group on Directors' Remuneration (Greenbury Report), "Final Report," London Stock Exchange: London, July 1995.

Cadbury, Adrian, et al, "The Financial Aspects of Corporate Governance," London Stock Exchange: London, December 1992.

UNITED STATES

California Public Employees' Retirement System, "Corporate Governance Market Principles," CalPERS: Sacramento, April 1998.

New York Stock Exchange and National Association of Corporate Directors (NACD), "Report of the NACD Blue Ribbon Commission on Improving the Effectiveness of Corporate Audit Committees," New York Stock Exchange: New York, December 1998.

National Association of Corporate Directors (NACD), "Report of the NACD Blue Ribbon Commission on CEO Succession," NACD: Washington, D.C., July 1998.

Council of Institutional Investors (CII), "Core Policies," CII: Washington, D.C., March 1998.

Business Roundtable, "Statement on Corporate Governance," The Business Roundtable: Washington, D.C., September 1997.

General Motors Board of Directors, "GM Board of Directors Corporate Governance Guidelines on Significant Governance Issues," Second Edition, General Motors: Detroit, June 1997, Revised March 1999.

National Association of Corporate Directors (NACD), "Report of the NACD Blue Ribbon Commission on Director Professionalism," NACD: Washington, D.C., November 1996.

Teachers Insurance and Annuity Association—College Retirement Equities Fund (TIAA-CREF), "TIAA-CREF Policy Statement on Corporate Governance," New York, October 1997.

## The Author

### CHARLES MITCHELL

Charles (Chuck) Mitchell has spent more than half of his working life in foreign lands, providing him ample opportunity to commit numerous cultural faux pas and witness the day-to-day workings of business, social and political life on several continents. Chuck began his journalism career as a reporter for the Rand Daily Mail in South Africa before joining United Press International as southern Africa correspondent, covering wars and independence struggles in Rhodesia, Angola and Mozambique.

As UPI bureau chief based in Nairobi, Kenya, Chuck traveled to more than 20 African and Middle Eastern nations reporting on famine, conflict and economic development for UPI as well as several British newspapers. Moving to Moscow in 1986 with UPI, Chuck reported on the transformation of the Soviet Union under Mikhail Gorbachev's "terrible twins", glasnost and perestroika, covering the Chernobyl nuclear disaster as well as three U.S.-Soviet summits and Gorbachev's historic visit to China.

Chuck later served as Foreign Editor of the Detroit Free Press newspaper and as Senior European Editor for WorldBusiness magazine, traveling and reporting extensively in Europe.

A graduate of the University of Pennsylvania, he is currently the Publishing Director for The Conference Board, a not-for-profit business and economic research organization based in New York City. He coaches Little League and resides in Bedford Hills, New York with his wife, Fiona, and their three children